# Studs and Spikes

# Studs and Spikes
## Denis Cussen
## Ireland's Fastest Man

By

Des A Ryan
with
John Cussen

Copyright © 2026

All rights reserved. No parts of this book can be reproduced in any manner whatsoever without written permission, except in the case of brief quotations embodied in critical articles and reviews.

First printing 2026

Published by TTT Press

ISBN 9781068672842

For the proud people of Limerick

Luimneach Abú

# Acknowledgements

This project was only possible because of the incredible record keeping of Mary Moylan Cussen (1879-1969). Mary kept scrapbooks of the adventures of her sons. Thankfully, the Cussen family have preserved these precious records, much of which should be in a museum.

Thank you to John Cussen for trusting me with the family records and the family legacy. You are a remarkable man from a remarkable family. It has been a pleasure to work with you on this project and an honour to uncover your uncle's story with you.

Carol, Dearbhla and Cormac. My father, Des Snr for sharing his love of history, Eadaoin and the Griffith family.

Deirdre Cussen Snr, Kate, Deirdre, John and Michael Cussen.

Bernard Jackson - A great rugby man and greatly appreciated for his support on this project.

Stephen Ruschitzko. One of Limerick's finest and a long-time friend. Thank you for encouragement, insight and proof reading.

The crew at 'All Things Rugby' – Eoin Grant, Ciaran Doran, Ian Fitzgerald, James O'Dwyer, Ronan Furlong, Andrew Valder, Arthur Riordan, Brendan O'Brien, Declan Burke, Declan Keane, Des Fortune, Kev O'Shea, Sean Devaney, Tim Clifford, Conor Norris and Brendan Grant

Nicholas Trainor at Blackrock College Archives, Kevin Keane at the Olympic Federation of Ireland, The one-eyed Garda Siochana, Kevin Brown at Imperial College Healthcare NHS Trust, Chiará Morgan at the Royal College of Physicians of Ireland, Caroline at Trinity College Dublin, Paul Dudman at University of East London, Adam Staunton at GAA Museum, Clare Wilkins at Harrow School Archives, Selina at UCD Archives and Dan Murphy.

# Sources

The majority of the information I relied on in putting Denis Cussen's remarkable career together, came from the family scrapbooks kept by his mother. In them (there were many) were cuttings from Irish Independent, Irish Times, Evening Herald, Irish Field and other newspapers and periodicals.

I also consulted the following books for reference:

The Politics of Irish Athletics by Padraig Griffin
Wearing the Shamrock by Catherine and Colm Murphy
The Irish Championships by Colm Murphy
The International Rugby Championship 1883-1983 by Terry Goodwin
St Mary's by EA Heaman
Blackrock College 1860-1995 by Sean Farragher
The Barbarians: The Official History by Nigel Starmer-Smith
Dublin University Football Club 1866-1972
The Eight Olympiad Paris 1924 – Official Report
The Ninth Olympiad Amsterdam 1928 – Official Report
The Blackrock College Archives
IRFU and Leinster Archives
Athletics Ireland Archives

| | |
|---|---|
| Foreword | 1 |
| Introduction | 5 |
| Honours | 7 |
| Early Life | 11 |
| Blackrock College | 17 |
| Trinity | 49 |
| Hospitals Rugby | 85 |
| Leinster Provincial Team | 101 |
| English Clubs | 121 |
| Rugby Sevens | 135 |
| Ireland International | 139 |
| Rugby Centenary Match 1923 | 203 |
| Barbarians | 211 |
| National Athletics | 219 |
| 1924 Tailteann Games, Dublin | 229 |
| 1928 Ireland's Fastest Man | 243 |
| International Athletics | 253 |
| 1928 Amsterdam Olympics | 265 |

1928 Tailteann Games, Dublin .......................................................... 287

Post Retirement Athletics ................................................................. 291

Professional Life ............................................................................... 305

The Cussen Family ........................................................................... 323

# Foreword

It is a genuine privilege to pen the foreword for Studs and Spikes, the story of Denis Cussen, an athlete whose achievements span a golden era of Irish sport, both on the rugby pitch and the running track. I am honoured to have been involved in the support of this project.

Author Des Ryan became intrigued by Denis Cussen while researching Limerick rugby history for his previous book "Limerick Lions: Limerick and the British and Irish Lions 1888-1988". He quickly concluded that Cussen's story needed to be told, not merely as one of Limerick's sporting greats, but as one of Ireland's greatest ever sportsmen.

Cussen hailed from Newcastle West, County Limerick where he was born in 1901. His family's deep roots in the game began with his father, Robert (Bob) Cussen, who captained Blackrock College's first ever rugby XV in 1881. This book chronicles how Denis followed this path, becoming a truly unique figure in Irish sports history. In a time when specialisation was rare, Cussen excelled in multiple domains: he was an international rugby player who was also a world-class sprinter and an Olympian. His legacy was further cemented by his illustrious medical career and his pioneering work in the emerging area of sports science after his playing days ended.

The foundation of this incredible biography lies in the meticulous records kept by his mother, Mary Moylan Cussen, who religiously preserved scrapbooks documenting her sons' burgeoning achievements in sport and academia. Without these precious family records, much of Cussen's extraordinary story might have been lost. Ryan, working with Cussen's nephew John Cussen, has pieced together Cussen's career, adding further insights and building the historical context that surrounds his achievements.

An interesting aspect of this book, alongside the meticulous research into Cussen's career, is that Ryan sets it against what was happening in Ireland at the time. Cussen was in his prime when Ireland was fighting the War of Independence and then the Civil War. The author has taken the time to document the major events in Irish history that dotted through Cussen's career. For example, he outlines the events of the

Easter Rising that took place outside the gates of Blackrock College while Cussen was a student there, using diary entries kept by the students inside the gates of the school to show what Cussen himself experienced.

Denis Cussen's rugby career was astonishing by any metric. As a schoolboy at Blackrock College, he was part of a remarkable dynasty, securing three Leinster Schools' Senior Cup titles (1917, 1918, and 1919), captaining the victorious team in his final two years. He then moved on to Trinity College Dublin (DUFC), the oldest rugby club in Ireland. Despite initially playing for the second XV, his explosive performances soon propelled him into the first team. He secured two Leinster Senior Cup titles with DUFC (1920 and 1925) and added the Bateman Cup in the spring of 1926. That success led him to representative level rugby. As I did by playing initially for Connacht, Cussen played for a province other than his native one and was a regular in the Leinster team for most of the 1920s.

It was on the international stage, however, that Cussen truly shone. He earned 15 caps for Ireland between 1921 and 1927, contributing five tries. His pinnacle on the rugby field came during the 1926 Five Nations Championship, a landmark season for Ireland. Having not won the championship since 1912, Ireland desperately sought a victory to bolster pride in the fledgeling Irish Free State. Cussen was instrumental in securing Ireland's victory that year (shared with Scotland). He was considered the 'Man of the Tournament', notably scoring two tries in the crucial 19-15 win over England at Lansdowne Road, marking Ireland's first defeat of our great rival in fifteen years. He also scored what was deemed a controversial disallowed try against Wales, which cost Ireland a first-ever Grand Slam.

Beyond the domestic and international scenes, Cussen's status was recognised through his inclusion in historic fixtures. He played in the 1923 Rugby Centenary Match at Rugby School, celebrating the game's origins, and earned three caps for the prestigious Barbarians (1926 & 1927). He also competed in the first ever Middlesex Rugby Sevens event at Twickenham in 1926.

What elevates Cussen beyond just being a great rugby player is his sheer parallel dominance in athletics. While studying medicine at Trinity, he achieved the distinction of being an Irish triple champion in 1921, winning the national titles for the 100-yards, 220-yards, and the long jump. He retained the 100-yards and long jump titles the following year.

An ankle injury, suffered in 1923, cost him eighteen months, at least five Ireland rugby caps and possibly a place on Ireland's first ever Olympic team in 1924. Having suffered a broken leg during my own career, the frustration of getting back to full fitness must have been acute for him, as it was for me. Cussen did return to full fitness, and he hadn't lost his pace when he returned to action. In fact, he got faster.

Cussen's track and field ambition culminated in 1928, an Olympic year. That year he won the 100-yards Irish National Championship for the fourth time, setting a sensational new national record of 9.8 seconds, the first Irish man to break the 10 second barrier. This record time was achieved on grass and, as well as setting the Irish national record, equalled the world record for 100-yards on that surface at the time. This performance secured his place at the 1928 Amsterdam Olympic Games, where he competed in the 100m. In the lead-up to Amsterdam, Cussen twice defeated Arthur Porritt of New Zealand, the 1924 Olympic 100m bronze medallist. At the Olympics, Cussen successfully navigated the first round of the 100m, finishing second in his heat in 11 seconds, and qualifying for the semi-final round. Alas, he didn't make the final.

Cussen's sporting brilliance brought him into contact with some legends of history. While at Blackrock College he played against Irish republican Kevin Barry who was playing for Belvedere College at the time. Later he played against, and defended brilliantly against, the future 400m Olympic champion Eric Liddell (of Chariots of Fire fame) while playing for Trinity against Edinburgh University and then again when playing for Ireland against Scotland in 1923. In fact, Cussen eluded Liddell's grasp and scored a try against the man who set the world record for 400m the following year. Arthur Porritt, whom he defeated on the track on two occasions in 1928, went on to become Sir Arthur Porritt the Governor General of New Zealand. While at St Mary's Hospital he rubbed shoulders with Alexander Fleming at the time he was discovering the power of penicillin and later he watched the emergence of Roger Bannister, the first four-minute miler.

Cussen's ability to juggle top-level international rugby alongside national athletic dominance and a demanding medical career highlights the sheer dedication required of the amateur sportsman of that generation. To do so when Dublin was in turmoil makes it even more impressive.

The final chapter of Denis Cussen's contribution to sport demonstrates his commitment to scientific excellence. Having graduated from Trinity Medical School in December 1925, he began working at St Mary's Hospital in London and, like myself, played with English clubs for a few seasons before retiring. He quickly transitioned his competitive drive into medical innovation and administration in the emerging field of sports medicine.

Cussen was appointed as the Honorary Chief Medical Officer to the British Olympic Team for both the 1956 Melbourne Games and the 1960 Rome Games. This role saw him trackside in Melbourne to congratulate his fellow countryman, Ronnie Delany, immediately after Delany won Olympic gold in the 1500m. For the 1960 Rome Olympics, Cussen brought a revolutionary approach, pioneering the use of science to improve performance. He introduced acclimatisation protocols by conditioning athletes in a 'sweat box' to prepare them for the summer heat of Rome.

His vision extended to the institutional level: he was a founding member of the British Association of Sports Medicine (BASM) in 1952, serving as secretary and treasurer. He then led and co-founded the British Institute of Sports Medicine in 1963. These organisations provided a vital professional and academic structure for the field of sports science and undoubtedly helped thousands of athletes achieve their personal goals.

This brilliant book, painstakingly brought to life using the family records kept by his mother, honours a man who was an outstanding international rugby player, Ireland's fastest man, an Olympian, and a medical pioneer. Denis Cussen's story is a profound reminder of the breadth of athletic and professional achievement possible in one lifetime, connecting the golden age of Irish amateur sport with the dawn of modern scientific sports medicine. I commend this book entirely, it is a great addition to the library of Irish sporting history, and it restores Denis Cussen to the prominence his, almost forgotten, career deserves.

Bernard Jackman
December 2025

# Introduction

In the spring of 2025, I co-authored a book entitled 'Limerick Lions – Limerick and the British and Irish Lions 1888-1988' with Stephen Ruschitzko. As we were researching that book, I came across the name Denis Cussen but as he hadn't played for the Lions, didn't dwell on him or his career. Soon after the book was published, I was contacted by John Cussen. We discussed rugby history and his uncle Denis. Over a series of meetings, during which it was clear we shared a passion for Limerick rugby and history, I became more and more intrigued by his uncle. Quickly it became clear that there was a story to be told about not only one of Limerick's great sporting men, but one of Ireland's greatest ever sports men.

Spring 2026 marks the 100th anniversary of a landmark Five Nations Championship for Ireland. In 1926, it had been fourteen years since Ireland had last won the championship. It had been fifteen years since Ireland had last defeated her great rival England. Ireland had recently become an independent state and a win would strengthen pride in the fledgeling nation. Ireland beat France in Belfast (11-0), England in Dublin (19-15) and Scotland in Edinburgh (0-3). Ireland went to Cardiff in search of a first ever grand slam. Alas, a controversial disallowed try snatched that dream away. Ireland did win the Five Nations and Denis Cussen was the man of the tournament. He scored twice against England and he scored the disallowed try in Wales.

Cussen had an incredible rugby career. Three Leinster Schools Senior Cup wins with Blackrock College. Two Leinster Senior Cup wins and a Bateman Cup win with Trinity. Leinster caps. Ireland caps. Barbarians caps. He played in some historic games, such as the first rugby sevens game played at Twickenham and the 1923 Rugby Centenary Match at Rugby School. But rugby was only part of his story.

Denis Cussen was also an Olympian. He was the national champion in the 100-yards sprint on four occasions. He was the long jump national champion. He was the first Irish man to break ten seconds for 100-yards and he equalled the world record for 100-yards on grass in 1928. His list of achievements seems endless.

His contribution to sport didn't end when he retired from rugby and athletics. Denis Cussen was a doctor and an innovative one. He was the Chief Medical Officer to the British Olympic team in 1956 and again in 1960. In Melbourne in 1956, he was one of the first to congratulate Ronnie Delany on the track after his Olympic gold medal performance. In 1960, Cussen introduced acclimatisation to the British Olympic team preparations, using science to improve performance. Denis also co-founded both the British Association of Sports Medicine and the British Institute of Sports Medicine.

There is so much to this man, that with the help of John and the scrap books kept by Denis' mother, his story had to be told. One hundred years after one of the high points of his career, his two tries against England in the Five Nations, let me re-introduce you to a great sportsman and a great Limerickman, Denis Cussen.

Des Ryan

December 2025

# Honours

The following is an overview of some of the more significant honours won by Denis Cussen. It is not exhaustive but it is impressive.

## Rugby

Represented Blackrock College, Leinster Schools, Trinity College (DUFC), Baggot Street Hospital, Dublin Unified Hospitals, Leinster, Ireland, the Barbarians, Blackheath, Middlesex, St Mary's Hospital and London Unified Hospitals.

- 3 x Leinster Senior Schools' Cup winner (1917, 1918 & 1919) with Blackrock College. Captain in 1918 and 1919
- 2 x Leinster Senior Cup winner (1920 and 1925) with DUFC
- Bateman Cup winner (1925) with DUFC
- 6 x Leinster Schools Caps & 2 Tries. Captain in 1919
- 12 x Leinster Senior Caps & 8 Tries
- 15 x Ireland International Caps & 5 Tries (1921-1927)
- 2 x Five Nations Championship Wins (1926 and 1927)
- 3 x Barbarians Caps (1926 & 1927)
- 2 x Middlesex County Caps (1926)
- Played in Rugby 100 Year Centenary Game – 1923
- Played in first ever Middlesex Rugby Sevens event - 1926

## Boxing

- Trinity College Heavy Weight Boxing Champion - 1921

## Athletics

- Leinster Junior Schools 100-yards Champion 1916
- National Senior Schools Championships 1917
    – 120 yards Hurdles Champion
    – 4x400-yards Relay Champion
- National Senior Schools Championships 1918

- High Jump Champion
- Shot Put Champion
- Long Jump Silver Medal
- 120 yards Hurdles Silver Medal
- 4x400-yards Relay Silver Medal
- 100-yards Bronze Medal
- Trinity College Athletics Championships 1920
  - 100-yards for Freshmen Champion
  - 100-yards Champion
  - Long Jump Champion
  - 4x100-yards relay Champion
  - High Jump Silver Medal
  - Vice Chancellors Cup Winner
- Tri-Nations International Championship 1920
  - 100-yards Bronze Medal
  - Long Jump Silver Medal
- Trinity College Athletics Championships 1921
  - 100-yards Champion
  - Long Jump Champion
  - 220-yards Silver Medal
- Irish Amateur Athletic Association Championships 1921
  - 100-yards (President's Cup) Champion
  - 220-yards Champion
  - Long Jump Champion
- Tri-Nations International Championship 1921
  - Long Jump Silver Medal
  - 100-yards fourth place
- Trinity College Athletics Championships 1922
  - 100-yards Champion
  - Long Jump Champion
- Irish Amateur Athletic Association Championships 1922
  - 100-yards (President's Cup) Champion
  - Long Jump Champion
- Tri-Nations International Championship 1922
  - Long Jump Silver Medal
  - 100-yards fourth place
- Trinity College Athletics Championships 1924
  - 100-yards Champion
  - Long Jump Silver Medal
- National Athletic & Cycling Association Championships 1924
  - Long Jump Bronze Medal
- Inter-University Athletics Championships 1924
  - 100-yards Bronze Medal

- – Shotput Silver Medal
- Trinity College Athletics Championships 1925
    - – 100-yards Champion
    - – Discus Champion
    - – Shot put Champion
    - – 220-yards Bronze Medal
- National Athletic & Cycling Association Championships 1925
    - – 100-yards (President's Cup) Champion *Tied national record
- Tri-Nations International Championship 1925
    - – 100-yards Bronze Medal
- National Athletic & Cycling Association Championships 1928
    - – 100-yards (President's Cup) Champion
    - *Set National Record
    - *Equalled World Record

Olympian – 100m in 1928 Amsterdam Olympic Games
Tailteann Games – 1924 & 1928

## Medical

Founding member of British Association of Sports Medicine (BASM) 1952

Hon Chief Medical Officer - British Olympic Team Melbourne 1956

Hon Chief Medical Officer - English Empire Games Team Cardiff 1958

Hon Chief Medical Officer - British Olympic Team Rome 1960

Founding member of the British Institute of Sports Medicine 1963

# Early Life

Denis Cussen's father, Robert Cussen (known as Bob), was born in 1865 in Kilcolman, Rathkeale, County Limerick, one of seventeen children of John Cussen and his wife Kate (née Donovan). Though the Cussen family had begun with modest means, by the late nineteenth century they had established themselves as prosperous farmers with a four-hundred-acre tenant farm and prominent butter merchants in the region. This success enabled them to invest substantially in their children's education, including that of Bob.

Bob's formative years coincided with the rapid spread of rugby football across Ireland. The sport's introduction to the province of Munster can be traced to Sir Charles Burton Barrington, 5th Baronet (1848–1943), a native of Limerick who had attended Rugby School in England from 1864 to 1866. There, Barrington mastered the game that had originated at the school in 1823. Upon returning to Ireland, he matriculated at Trinity College Dublin and joined Dublin University Football Club, the first rugby club in Ireland, founded in 1854. Elected captain in 1867, Barrington served until 1870. He later recalled encountering only *"a rugby of sorts"* with few formal rules; in 1868, together with R. M. Wall, he codified a set of regulations that provided the foundation for organised rugby throughout Ireland. Over the following two decades, clubs proliferated nationwide, including several in County Limerick, ensuring that a young man of Bob Cussen's social standing would undoubtedly have been exposed to the game.

In November 1874, when Bob was nine, the first documented rugby match in County Limerick took place in Rathkeale itself. Rathkeale Football Club faced a fifteen selected by the local landlord, Mr Massey. The following season saw two further fixtures: one against a side organised by Mr Harkness, and another against a combined team of military and constabulary players. At this early stage, rugby remained largely the preserve of the gentry and professional classes. Given the Cussen family's commercial prominence, it is highly probable that they socialised with the Massey and Harkness families and that members of the family, possibly including Bob's older siblings, participated in these pioneering rugby encounters. Bob's brother Dr Michael Cussen also

# Early Life

had interest in the GAA and was a founding member of Knockaderry GAA Club in 1910.

A pivotal figure in the democratisation of Limerick rugby was William Lamb Stokes. Originally from Galway, Stokes had settled in Limerick by the mid-1870s and emerged as a leading butter merchant and civic notable in Limerick. Although Rathkeale Football Club proved short-lived, its existence inspired Stokes and Barrington to co-found Limerick County Cricket and Football Club in 1876. Stokes not only played for the new club but also served successively as captain, secretary, and honorary president. He is widely credited with broadening participation in the sport beyond the traditional elite, making it accessible to the city's mercantile and working classes. Operating in the same butter-trade networks, Bob Cussen and Stokes almost certainly moved in overlapping circles and may well have played alongside one another.

For his secondary education, Bob was sent to Blackrock College, Dublin, one of Ireland's leading Catholic institutions. In 1881 he captained the college's inaugural rugby XV, marking the beginning of a distinguished sporting career that would later influence his sons' path in the game.

> **FOOTBALL.**
> BLACKROCK FRENCH COLLEGE F C 1st XV v DECTIVE FC 2nd XV.—The above match, which was the opening one of the season for the first-named club, took place yesterday on the Nine Acres, Phœnix Park, and, after a most enjoyable game, ended in a victory for the visitors by one goal and three tries to two tries. The College tries were obtained by T Dennehy (2), O'Donnell, and P Fitzgerald, the first-named gentleman making a splendid run for each of his contributions, one of which R Cussen (captain) converted into a goal. For Bective (who played short) the first try was secured by A Brown after a brilliant and plucky run, whilst R A Daniel cleverly gained the second by a splendid dribble from the half way post. Besides those mentioned, Piers, Alexander, W Daniel (backs), and May (forwards) played excellently. The following comprised the French College team:—T Dennehy (full back), Cussen (captain) and C Dennehy (half backs), O'Donnell and O'Dwyer (quarter backs), Fitzgerald, Sheehy, O'Neill, O'Gorman, Langan, Brennan, Nunan, J O'Meara, P O'Meara, Hayes (forwards).

*Bob Cussen listed as Blackrock College captain in December 1881*

# Early Life

> DUNDRUM F C v FRENCH COLLEGE, BLACK-
> ROCK.—Played at Blackrock and resulted in an unsatisfactory draw. Those who showed best form were Dennehy, Cussen, O'Donnell, and O'Neill for home team; Johnston, Lewis and James for Dundrum.

*Bob Cussen mentioned in the Blackrock College team in February 1882*

The Leinster Schools Senior Challenge Cup was not inaugurated until 1887, by which time Bob had already progressed to study law at the Four Courts in Dublin. Consequently, he never competed in the competition that would later bring distinction to all four of his sons.

Upon qualification in 1889, Bob returned to County Limerick and established a legal practice on North Quay, Newcastle West. The firm, Robert Cussen & Son, remains in operation today under the stewardship of the fourth generation of the family, a testament to its enduring prominence.

Newcastle West was then, as now, the second-largest urban centre in County Limerick after Limerick City itself. With a population of approximately three thousand at the turn of the century, it functioned as the commercial, administrative, and market hub for west Limerick's predominantly rural and Catholic hinterland. Agricultural labour sustained most households, yet the professional classes, solicitors, doctors, and merchants, occupied a distinct social stratum. As a university-educated Catholic solicitor, Bob enjoyed considerable local influence. His wider family in nearby Rathkeale, still prosperous butter merchants and landowners, further reinforced the Cussens' standing across the region.

In 1899 Bob married Mary Moylan, daughter of Newcastle West's postmaster, DJ Moylan. DJ who is reputed to have jumped the length of the mall in Newcastle West square is perhaps the source of some of the incredible athletic ability that runs in the family. The couple made their home in the town and raised six children: John (Jack) in 1900, Denis in 1901, Robert (Bertie) in 1903, Catherine (Kitty) in 1904, Margaret (Maura) in 1907, and Michael in 1909. Each of their four sons would excel in rugby at a senior level while forging distinguished careers in law or medicine, ensuring that the Cussen name became synonymous with both sporting and professional achievement in twentieth-century Ireland.

# Early Life

Denis John Cussen was born in Newcastle West, County Limerick, on 1st July 1901, the second child of Robert (Bob) and Mary Cussen. He was named Denis John in honour of his two grandfathers, John Cussen and John Denis Moylan.

*Denis Cussen's birth record 1901*

*Catherine, Denis, Bertie, Jack, Maura and their mother Mary Cussen*

Tragedy marked Denis's earliest months. In January 1902, when he was only six months old, his paternal grandfather John Cussen died at the age of eighty-five. The elder John's lifetime of enterprise as a farmer and butter merchant left a substantial estate of £2,523, an impressive sum for the era, which was divided among his seventeen children and their families. Six years later, in April 1908, Denis's maternal grandfather, John Denis Moylan, died suddenly from a cerebral haemorrhage. Neither grandfather lived to see the extraordinary sporting career their grandson would forge.

## Early Life

In 1907, at the age of six, Denis followed his elder brother John (Jack) to the local Courtenay School, named after the local landlords, the Courtenays, Earls of Devon of Powderham Castle in Exeter, County Devon. A capable and engaged pupil, Denis showed no early signs of the exceptional athletic talent that would later define him.

*Denis Cussen at Courtney School (Back row, 4th from left)*

**PROFOUND PEACE.**

**JUDGES' STRIKING TRIBUTES.**

A state of profound peace reigns in West Limerick, as well as in East Limerick, according to the address of Judge Adams to the Grand Jury at Newcastle West Quarter Sessions.

That happy state of things, he added, was attributable to many causes, but above all to the growing belief amongst all decent Irishmen that under present circumstances he was a deadly enemy to Ireland who committed a breach of the law, however small.

Judge Craig, who was presented with white gloves at the Castleblayney Quarter Sessions, complimented the county on its crimeless condition.

White gloves were presented to Judge Bird at Macroom Quarter Sessions yesterday. The civil business of the Sessions has declined considerably within the past three years, and there has been no criminal business for a lengthened period.

After completing primary education at Courtenay in 1913, he spent two further years at St Catherine's Convent preparatory school in Newcastle West, a local, elite fee-paying establishment that prepared boys for secondary boarding schools.

The opening decade of Denis's life unfolded against a backdrop of remarkable tranquillity in west Limerick, despite gathering storm clouds elsewhere. The First World War loomed on the horizon, and the Irish War of Independence was only a few years away, yet local court records testify to an almost idyllic calm. In 1905, Mr Justice

Ross, presiding at the Limerick Assizes, publicly commended the *"state of profound peace"* prevailing in the region, attributing it to *"the growing belief amongst all decent Irishmen that, under present circumstances, he was a deadly enemy to Ireland who committed a breach of the law, however small"*.

The Cussen brothers' secondary education began in earnest at Blackrock College, Dublin. Jack departed for the prestigious Catholic boarding school in 1914; Denis joined him in September 1915; Bertie arrived in 1917; and the youngest, Michael, followed in 1923, by which time his three elder brothers were already undergraduates at Trinity College Dublin.

Sending four sons to such an elite institution was a significant financial commitment that underscored the family's comfortable circumstances. In 1910, sixty per cent of the Irish workforce was engaged in agriculture or low-skilled labour, with average annual earnings around £50 (one guinea per week). Blackrock College, by contrast, charged forty guineas per annum, roughly £42, making it accessible only to the professional and mercantile classes to which the Cussens firmly belonged.

Boarding in Dublin meant that Denis returned to Newcastle West only for brief Christmas holidays and the long summer break which the family often spent in Ballybunion, County Kerry. Separation from home fostered a prolific correspondence with his mother, Mary, who meticulously preserved his letters alongside newspaper clippings chronicling his burgeoning achievements in sport and academia over the coming years. Those scrapbooks are the foundation for this book.

*Denis' mother Mary Moylan Cussen who religiously kept scrapbooks of her sons' achievements*

# Blackrock College

Blackrock College was founded in 1860 by Père Jules Leman CSSp, a French priest of the Congregation of the Holy Ghost. Ordained in 1851, Leman had been dispatched to Ireland in 1859 with the primary mission of recruiting educated young Irishmen for the Spiritans' African apostolate. Finding suitable candidates scarce, he concluded that the most effective strategy was to establish a secondary school where boys could be formed intellectually, morally, and spiritually from an early age, with a view to future missionary vocation.

After evaluating several locations, Leman selected Dublin for its large Catholic population and educational infrastructure. Although the southside suburbs contained a Protestant majority and a working-class Catholic population unlikely to afford substantial fees, a three-acre site at Williamstown, Blackrock, formerly occupied by a Protestant boys' school, became available in 1860. Leman acquired the property, and Blackrock College, initially known as "The French College," opened its doors that autumn.

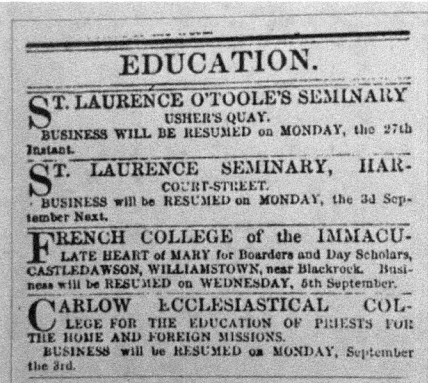

*Press notice for Blackrock College opening day 1860*

The curriculum was modelled on the rigorous French lycée system, and the entire teaching staff in the early years was French. In the absence of a national Irish syllabus, the college offered a broad classical and scientific programme designed to prepare students for university entrance or the higher civil service. Subjects included Mathematics, English, Latin, Greek, French, History, Geography, Natural Sciences, Music, and Art. Discipline emphasised positive reinforcement rather than corporal punishment; miscreants forfeited holidays or extracurricular privileges. Pupils enjoyed seven weeks' annual leave, five in summer and a fortnight at Christmas.

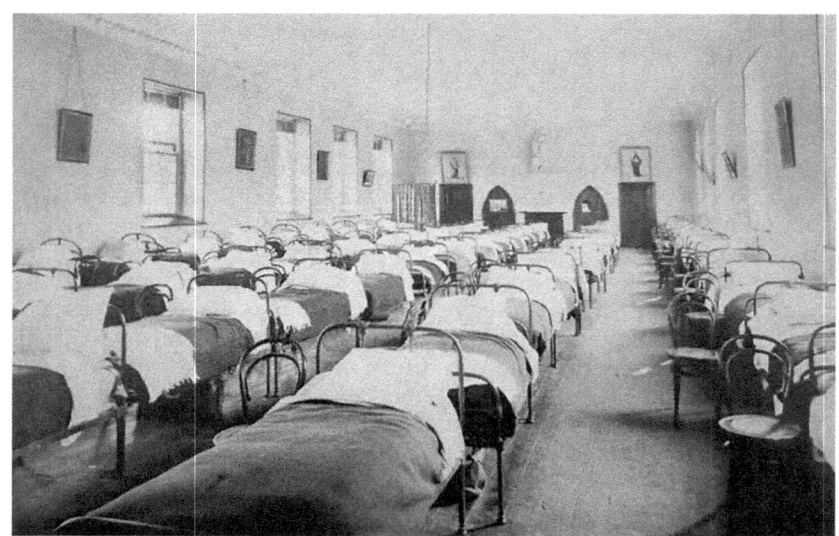

*Immaculate Heart dormitory in 1906*
*Photo Courtesy of Blackrock College Archives*

*Students in the science laboratory*
*Photo Courtesy of Blackrock College Archives*

Blackrock College

In its inaugural year the college enrolled only two boarders and six day-boys. Clad in distinctive quasi-military uniforms of dark blue with red piping, the students quickly earned the local nickname *"Boney Boys"* in playful reference to Napoleon. Yet rapid growth followed. High-profile early alumni, academic excellence, and the striking appearance of the boys in public combined to attract notice. By 1870 enrolment had reached two hundred, necessitating significant expansion of buildings and grounds.

*Dining Hall 1901*
*Photo Courtesy of Blackrock College Archives*

Physical education and competitive sport were integral to the French pedagogical tradition and thus central to Blackrock's identity from the outset. The college fielded its first representative cricket XI in 1865. Michael Cusack, later co-founder of the Gaelic Athletic Association, taught at Blackrock during the 1870s and helped shape an energetic sporting culture. Athletics became a permanent fixture, and Cusack is credited with introducing an early form of hurling on the college grounds.

***Blackrock College First Ever Rugby Team 1882***
*Back row: T Brennan (Louth), J Sheehy (Kildimo), F O'Callaghan (Killarney), A Conan (Dublin)*
*Middle row: J O'Donnell (Dingle), H O'Neill (Tyrone), D Bolger (Kilrush), Fred Dennehy (Dundalk), Charles Dennehy (Dundalk), F O'Meara (Waterford)*
*Front row: T O'Dwyer (Co Clare), Robert Cussen (Rathkeale) (Captain), J Langan (Drogheda), M Boyle (Dublin)*

Photo Courtesy of Blackrock College Archives

Rugby football arrived soon afterwards, reportedly through brothers Fred and Charles Dennehy. The inaugural Blackrock College XV took the field in the 1881–82 season under the captaincy of Robert (Bob) Cussen, father of the future Denis Cussen. Among his teammates was Dan Bolger, an Irish international, whose younger brother Larry would tour South Africa with the British and Irish Lions in 1896. Rugby swiftly eclipsed all rivals in popularity. Blackrock entered the newly established Leinster Schools Senior Challenge Cup in 1887, winning the inaugural title and retaining it the following year. Since then, the college has claimed the cup on seventy occasions, more than all other schools combined, establishing an unrivalled dynasty in Irish schools' rugby.

Père Leman died suddenly in June 1880 at the age of fifty-four, by which time Blackrock was firmly established among Ireland's elite secondary institutions. Continuous investment followed: new dormitories, classrooms, science laboratories, a chapel, and extensive recreational facilities transformed the original modest estate into a thirty-five-acre campus. By the time Denis Cussen arrived as a boarder in September 1915, Blackrock College stood as one of the finest educational establishments in the country, its amenities and reputation the envy of contemporaries and a benchmark for generations to come.

*Newspaper article showing Michael Cusack as English and Maths teacher at Blackrock in 1875*

## 1915/1916

With World War One entering its second year, the Cussen family was rocked by a family war casualty in August 1915. Denis' cousin Robert who had enlisted at the outbreak of the war, died of dysentery and fever on board a hospital ship at Suvla Bay, Gallipoli. He was in the 7th Royal Munster Fusiliers who were sent to Gallipoli to take part in the August Offensive, an attempt to break out of the stalemate that had taken hold there since the April 25th ANZAC Gallipoli landings. Most of the 7th RMF troops had no combat experience and thousands were killed during their landing and in the first few days after they had landed. It is thought Robert survived the chaos of the landings but was injured, most likely during the landing itself. He was removed from the battlefield and sent to a military hospital in Alexandria, Egypt where he succumbed to his wounds on 12th August. He is buried in Alexandria.

Two weeks after the death of his cousin, Denis Cussen set off to boarding school at Blackrock College, Dublin. His first day was 1st September 1915 which was when the boarders all reported for term.

The Scholastics (students who were studying for the priesthood) kept a daily journal of what was happening in the school and it gives a wonderful insight into the day-to-day life of the students. The entries for the first few days of Denis' time read,

> "Thursday 2nd: Unpacking as our trunks come in. Mass of Holy Ghost at 8.30 followed by reading of classes in large study. Classes of 15 minutes are held from 12 until 1. Recreation afterwards. Correspondence from 6-7pm. Night prayer in oratory, confessions and bed at 9".

> "Friday 3rd: First Friday mass in the oratory. Half days' classes commencing at 8.30, Swim at 5.30. Study at 6. Benediction at 7.45 followed by study until 9pm. Then rosary, night prayer and bed."

> "Saturday 4th: Same as yesterday. Swim, study etc. No visit at 7.45. Study until 9pm. Rosery, night prayer and bed"

> "Sunday 5th: Rising at 6.45. Mass and morning prayer in the oratory. High mass at 0.30. Mr Kenna, Mr Mansfield and Master Maguire have since returned. Study at 11am. Congratulations from Fr Superior on the results of the examinations at 11.30am. Sleep at 9pm"

> "Monday 6th: Rising at 6.30am. Morning prayer and mass in the oratory. Study till 8.10. Rest as usual. Full days' class. Weather dull and showery but warm. Master O'Dwyer surprises dormitory by a sudden reappearance at 10pm".

The journal illustrates why rugby is so important to Blackrock. With the exception of an occasional walk to the nearby pier, or a trip to Kingstown library, the daily routine was study, prayer, lessons and evening debates or lectures on subjects such as *"Was Pitt a great leader"* or *"Did England do most to beat Napoleon?"*. Sport and rugby in particular, gave the pupils the opportunity to enjoy a half day, go out of the school and get a short break from their routine.

## Athletics

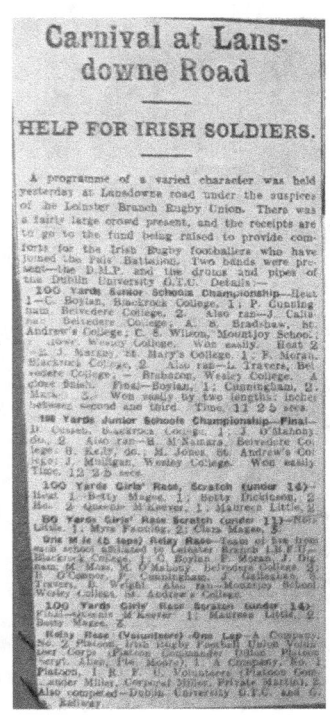

Just a month after arriving at Blackrock, Denis took part in the IRFU (Leinster Branch) Sports day. Held at Lansdowne Road which would become a second home for him in the coming years, Denis won the Leinster Junior 100-yards Championship. In the final be won by two yards in a time of 12.4 seconds.

## Rugby

Going into the 1915/1916 season, Denis was already fifteen years old and so was too old to play for the Blackrock College Junior (U15) Rugby team. He turned out instead for the Under 17 team. The first game they played was on November 20th against St Mary's. Blackrock won easily by a score of 27-6. While Denis didn't get on the scoreboard, he is mentioned in the match report. The first of many mentions of him in the news for his rugby exploits.

While Denis Cussen wasn't involved, in the Cup competitions 1915/1916 was a mixed year for Blackrock. The Junior team were given a bye in the first round and came up against Masonic in the second round of the Junior Cup. Blackrock registered a massive 57-0 win in the game which was played at Williamstown on 9th March 1916. In the semi-final Blackrock were drawn against Castleknock and lost the game 3-0 at Lansdowne Road. Castleknock went on to win the cup by beating Kings Hospital School.

In the Senior Cup, Blackrock beat Castleknock in the final 14-3. It was their second win on the trot and their twenty-first win in the competition. The final was played at Lansdowne Road on 15th April, two weeks before the Easter Rising.

Blackrock College

> part of the...
> beat all opposition, and scored a capital try, thus equalising
> the scores.
>
> **Blackrock (under 17) (27) v. St. Mary's (under 17) (6).**
>
> Blackrock visited Rathmines on Saturday with a strong combination, having five of their senior schools' cup team, and won a good game by three goals and four tries to a penalty goal and a try. The visitors were first to get going, and pressed for a while, but were up against a sound defence. From a scrum in the home 25 O'Carroll gave to Ross, and after a good passing movement Power got in at the corner. Mary's forwards began to make things lively, and a good rush headed by Cussen, led up to a try by Tierney, which was not converted. The visitors were soon again attacking, and Finn, receiving from Courtney, ran through for an easy score. A few minutes afterwards Blackrock were penalised in their own 25, and Kilduff dropped a good goal.
>
> In the second half the 'Rock forwards did well with a heavy ball. Masterson and O'Connor were conspicuous for good footwork. Scores were quickly registered by O'Carroll (2), Masterson (2), and O'Connor. Just before the end Tierney got away for a capital run for Mary's, and when within inches of the line was well tackled by Courtney. For the winners O'Carroll, Ross, Finn, and O'Connor were best. The pick of the losers were Tierney, Kilduff, Brady, and Cussen.

*Blackrock U17 Match Report – November 1915*

*Easter Rising – April 1916*

Between 23rd and 29th April 1916, the Easter Rising took place, primarily in Dublin. While none of the fighting took place in or around

Blackrock itself, there were a number of battle sites on the south side of Dublin where fighting took place. Boland's Mills, Jacob's Factory, and the College of Surgeons were all within a few miles of the College. The students wouldn't have known it at the time, the rising was being orchestrated by a Blackrock alumnus, Eamon De Valera, who had been a student between 1898 and 1902, and who also taught at the school for a couple of years subsequently. He led the 3rd Battalion of the rebel forces who had taken over Boland's Mills.

The scholastics' journal recorded what was happening within the gates at Blackrock at the time. It shows how, in the absence of official news, rumours spread. It also shows how, with the city in revolt, the students continued on their routine inside the gates of Blackrock.

*"Sunday: Easter Day. Republican troops (Sinn Fein) have driven the British from the capital. Gen MacNeill defeated the British Cavalry in College Green and has captured Dublin Castle. For the first time in eight centuries the Republican flag is gloating over Dublin Castle. Long live our Republic!"*

*"Monday: The princes are mobilising. Defeat of British attack on Dublin Castle by the Republican General McDonagh. British losses 70 killed, wounded not known"*

*"Tuesday: Fighting all night in the city. Nothing very definite, as newspapers are not appearing"*

*"Wednesday: Cricket match, no library. Two British defeats this evening near Lansdowne. In the second their losses included a machine gun, and 150 dead, amongst them a Major. Desperate fighting all night, generally to the advantage of the republicans."*

*"Thursday: More British troops arrive with a large naval gun. An engagement was fought close to here at about 1pm with what result we do not know. The long expected German assistance is said to have arrived in Galway and Admiral Von Leapelle is said to be sweeping the channel with his submarines. Yarmouth lad in ashes by German destroyer".*

*"Friday: Parts of the city have been set on fire by the artillery of the belligerents. Another desperate night of fighting. The republican rifle fire and bayonet fighting is completely demoralising the British, who*

have brought up heavy artillery, but without much appreciable effect. Today reinforcements from Connaught are enroute for the capital, the Germans will probably affect a junction with them".

"8,000 troops pass the Blackrock Lodge gate about 12 o'clock to Dublin. At present heavy fighting. 12.35pm. Noise of canon quite distinct. The study hall is perfectly quit so as to hear the roar of the canon. It feels like the trenches. All loyal citizens of Dublin have been asked to leave the city (reported). Blackrock still unshaken. General excitement among the lads. No trams or trains."

"Saturday: The British have occupied St Mary's College, driving our fathers over here. The British casualties yesterday, according to Fr Baldwin CSSP who was acting chaplain where 1,000. Republican marksmanship again! Fighting all night".

"Sunday: Cricket match. Victory of triple alliance. No peace yet. Fires again! Republic proclaimed. British driven from Ringsend by a rear attack".

"Monday: There begins to be talk of peace. Some of our troops after a most heroic resistance have been compelled to surrender to overwhelming numbers and artillery. British are still losing heavily to snipers."

"Tuesday: Last day's fighting. Peace terms today. Temporary cessation of Republican war. British say that conscription is not to be enforced here and that a reduction in taxation is to be made. On these conditions the section of the Republicans now in arms have consented to surrender. Master Sinnott returning after 8 days had brought this news".

"Wednesday: Victory of Munster over the other three provinces in cricket match this afternoon".

## Athletics

The inaugural IAAA Schools Championships were scheduled to take place at Lansdowne Road on 20th May. In the aftermath of the Easter Rising, they were postponed and the leaders of the 1916 Easter Rising were executed at Kilmainham between 3rd and 12th May.

# 1916/1917

In the aftermath of the Easter Rising, Blackrock old boy, Eamon De Valera was, like the other leaders of the rebellion, sentenced to death. Unlike the others, his sentence was immediately commuted to life. Over the summer of 1916, while Denis was home in Newcastle West, there was uproar about the executions and concern for Limerick raised De Valera. De Valera was held at Dartmoor prison in England and was eventually released in June.

Denis and his fellow students returned for term on 4th September 1917. The war in Europe was still ongoing but Dublin a little more peaceful than when Denis left two months earlier.

## Rugby

When the 1916/1917 rugby season kicked off in November 1916, Denis Cussen had progressed and was now playing on the Blackrock College Senior team. He was one of the youngest on the team. Also on the team were John Bermingham from Offaly who would be capped by Ireland four times, Daniel Liston from Foynes who went on to be the bishop of Mauritius, Albert Odbert the son of a civil servant whose brother Reginald Odbert played for Ireland. Another team mate was Walter Finn. He had been orphaned at six and his uncle sent him to the priesthood at Blackrock College.

Four members of the team would win national athletics medals during the year. Bermingham, prop on the rugby team, won the shot-put national schoolboy title; Michael J Ross won the 100-yards, long jump and high jump at the schoolboy championships. Bermingham, Ross, O'Mahoney and Cussen were 4x100 yard relay champions that year. The Blackrock senior rugby team clearly had speed.

Their first game of the season was in the Schools' League against High School. Blackrock won the game 23-nil and Denis was, as he would so often be in the future, on the scoresheet. Later that month he also played in the league fixtures against Belvedere (11-8 win) and Mountjoy (24-3 win).

In December 1916, Denis played his first game in Belfast when Blackrock played a friendly against Royal Academical Institution at Ormeau (11-nil win). After the game in Belfast, Denis returned home to Newcastle West for the Christmas break. The students returned to Dublin, in heavy snow, on 16th January 1917.

In the lead up to the Leinster Senior School Cup, Blackrock played against High School at Lansdowne Road in January (34-0 win) and Mountjoy (3-3 draw).

Blackrock were drawn against Wesley in the first round of the cup. The game was played on 24th February 1917 at Lansdowne Road and Blackrock were easy winners, scoring four goals and eleven tries. Denis Cussen had no difficulty competing at the higher-level despite being one of the youngest on the field. The match report in the Sunday Independent stated *"Throughout the entire game the Wesleyians were kept busy defending and not on one occasion did they get any way close to the 'Rock line. Seven tries came in each half, while Clavin also dropped a clever goal in the second period. The try getters in the first half were Ross, Finn, Glynn, O'Carroll, Cussen, O'Donoghue and Odbert, and with Finn adding the extra points on three occasions, Blackrock crossed over leading 27 points to nil. The second half was equally as one-sided as the first. Clavin and O'Connor each scored twice in this moiety, while Ross, Finn and Cussen added further tries."*

Cussen's performance was so strong that he was called up a week later to play in the Leinster Schools Inter-provincial trial and was selected to play on the probables side. That game was played at Lansdowne Road on Saturday 10th March. His team mates, Ross, O'Carroll, Cleary, O'Connor, Finn, Clavin, Odbert and Condron were also called for the trial.

> Power and Murphy added two more ners will meet Belvedere in the semi-final.
> **INTER-PROVINCIAL TRIAL MATCH.**
> The following teams have been picked for next Saturday's Leinster trial game:—
> Probables—M'Elligott (Castleknock), Joyce (Belvedere), Harris (High Sch.), Cussen, Ross, O'Carroll (Blackrock), Cunningham (Belvedere), O'Cleary, O'Connor, Finn (Blackrock), Small, Lett (Andrew's), Renny, Lees (Mountjoy), Moloney (Benedict's).
> Possibles—O'Brien (Belvedere), W. Jackson (Benedict's), Russell (Mountjoy), Clavin (Blackrock), Greene (Wesley), Redline (Andrew's), Odbert, Condron (Blackrock), Bracken, T. Crean (Belvedere), Mayne, West (Mountjoy), Bell (High Sch.), Browne (Andrews), Carroll (Benedict's).
> Subs.—Cleary (Blackrock), Hurst (Columba's), O'Donoghue (Blackrock), Davitt (Belvedere), Nunan (Mountjoy), Cullen (Castleknock), Speedy (Andrew's), Bermingham (Blackrock), Sutton (Mountjoy).

*Probables team at Leinster Schools Trial – March 1917*
*Denis Cussen standing second from the right*

In the second round (semi-final) of the senior cup, Blackrock were drawn to play Mountjoy School. Again, they ran out easy winners. Blackrock scored four goals and three tries (23) to Mountjoy's goal (5). Cussen was again very prominent. He scored a first half try and followed it up with two more in the second half.

# Blackrock College

*Denis Cussen seated on the right with the Blackrock team in 1917*

## RUGBY FINAL

### Another Cup for Blackrock

#### BELVEDERE'S FINE FIGHT.

**Blackrock 21 pts  Belvedere nil.**

The 1916/17 Leinster Schools Cup Final was played at Lansdowne Road on 24th March. Blackrock's opponents were Belvedere who were going for a cup double. They were also in the Junior final which was played the following week.

The scholastics diary shows the students *'started for Lansdowne Road at 2.30pm'*. Blackrock were going for a third senior cup in a row and had the best of the opening half. Cussen *"picked up and ran right through"* for one of the tries in the first half. Blackrock were 8-nil up at half time. Cussen was prominent in the second half too but didn't add to his first half try. Blackrock won the game 21-nil.

## Blackrock College

*One of Denis' three Leinster Schools Senior Cup Medals*

Playing against Cussen for Belvedere were some future team mates for Leinster and Ireland. Bill Cunningham would play for Ireland eight times and play for the British and Irish Lions in 1924. Eugene Davy would play for Ireland on thirty-four occasions and went on to set up Davy Stockbrokers.

The 1916/17 Cup win was the first of a remarkable three senior cup titles won by Denis Cussen. To celebrate the boarders at Blackrock had *'no study'* that evening.

**Blackrock College Senior Cup Winners 1917**
A Condron – E Mooney – J Dorr – W Finn – J Bermingham – T Glynn
K Cleary – D Cussen – M Ross – T O'Carroll (Capt) – J Clavin – M O'Mahoney – D Liston
E O'Donoghoe    A Odbert

*Photo Courtesy of Blackrock College Archives*

## Schools Inter Provincial Rugby

Having been selected on the Leinster schools' team, Denis Cussen made his Leinster debut against his home province, Munster, on St Patricks Day at the Mardyke in Cork. Denis Cussen's first Leinster match was a successful one. Leinster were up 6-3 at half time. In the second half Cussen had a great chance after a pass from Bill Cunningham but, perhaps due to nerves, he knocked the ball on and the opportunity was lost. Leinster did dominate the second half and won the game 23-6. The match report said, *"Harris, in the centre, stood out as the best three-quarter on the field. Cussen, his co-centre, was fair, but is bound to improve with experience, as he is very young"*.

### RUGBY INTERPROVINCIAL.
#### Leinster v. Munster.

Played at Cork. Teams:—

Leinster—Full-back, M'Elligott (Castleknock); centre, Harris (High Sch.), Cussen (Blackrock); wings, Ross (Blackrock), Joyce (Belvedere); halves, O'Carroll (Blackrock), Cunningham (Belvedere) (capt.); forwards, O'Cleary, O'Connor, Finn, Condrin (Blackrock), Small (St. Andrew's), Lees and Kenny (Mountjoy) Bell (High Sch.).

Munster—Full, O'Reilly (Rockwell); three-quarters, Breen and M'Claude (Rockwell), Walsh and Shamahan (Christian Bros.); halves, Nolan (Presentation), Walsh (Rockwell); forwards, Casey and Ryan (Presentation), Reynolds and Mahony (Christian Coll.), Burke, Lyons, Harrington and Breen (Rockwell).

Half-time score:—
LEINSTER—2 tries (6 points).
MUNSTER—1 try (3 points).

*Cussen – Seated 2nd right - with the Leinster Schools team that beat Ulster in 1917*

# Blackrock College

A week after he was on the Cup winning team for Blackrock, Denis Cussen played his second Leinster Interprovincial game; this time against Ulster. Played at Lansdowne Road on 31st March, the newspapers warned that the game would start at 3pm sharp as the visitors had a train to catch after the game.

Cussen appeared to adapt to the higher standard of game with ease and scored a try in the first half as Leinster won by 17 points to 9.

## Athletics

In the 1917 Schools athletics championships, which were held at Lansdowne Road on Sunday 27th May, Denis was now too old to compete in the junior events and he was on the young side of the competitors taking part in the senior events. Despite this, he won the 1917 120 yards hurdles in a time of 21.6 seconds. He finished three yards ahead of his schoolmate Michael J Ross who won the 100-yards event that year.

Alongside Ross, Cussen was on the school's relay race that won gold in the 4x400-yards relay. Ross was the winner of the best overall athlete award.

Denis returned to Limerick for his summer holidays with a Leinster Schools Senior Cup medal and a National 120 yards title to show his proud parents.

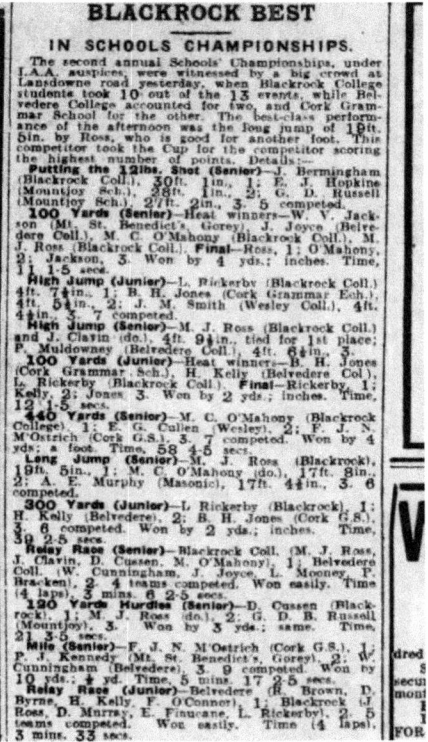

*Irish Independent report on the 1917 Schools Athletics Championships*

*An extract from the Blackrock College ledger showing Denis' account 1917 Charges for Music, Dancing, Cricket, Tennis, Books, Repairs and Doctor visits*
*Courtesy of Blackrock College Archives*

# 1917/1918

Blackrock College reopened after the summer break on 17th September 1917. World War One was raging and in October, just after Denis Cussen returned to Blackrock, Irish born Dave Gallagher, who had captained the 1905 All Blacks Originals who toured the Northern Hemisphere, was killed at the Battle of Passchendaele on the western front.

## Rugby

*Blackrock College Senior Cup Winners 1918*
M Kelly – M McCormick – J Sullivan – T Glynn – J Gilleece – M Broderick – P Walsh
A Browne – T McVicar – J O'Mahony – D Cussen (Capt) – J Cussen – J Carew – M Coghlan
W Healy      A Kelly

*Photo Courtesy of Blackrock College Archives*

For the 1918 rugby season, Denis Cussen was made captain of the Blackrock College senior rugby team. His rapid elevation to the Leinster Schools' team and his athletics achievements adding to his growing reputation for excellence. The majority of the team were still older than he was. There was a lot of change in the team that year.

Most of the cup winning team from the previous season had moved on to university. Only Denis and Thomas Glynn from Galway remained of the team. They were joined by Denis' brother Jack Cussen and a raft of new players.

Ahead of the Leinster Senior Cup, Blackrock took on Belvedere in a schools' league match at Lansdowne Road. The game is notable only because it is certain that Kevin Barry played for the Belvedere team that day. Barry who the previous year had been part of the Belvedere Junior Cup success played on their Senior Cup team in 1918. The game ended in a 3-3 draw.

The opening round of the Leinster Schools' Senior Cup in 1918 saw Blackrock take on High School at Lansdowne Road on 2nd March. Blackrock were easy winners with their captain, Denis Cussen, putting on a show by scoring three tries, a penalty and kicking four conversions (21 points). For good measure, Blackrock played most of the second half down a man after Glynn had to retire injured. Blackrock won the game 29-nil.

In the second round (semi-final), Blackrock took on Wesley and again were easy winners. Their captain Denis Cussen scored two tries but was outshone by his brother Jack who scored three. Denis also kicked two conversions as Blackrock won 31-nil. Mountjoy had defeated Belvedere in the other Cup semi-final 19-nil and so the Cup Final was Blackrock v Mountjoy on 16th March.

Ahead of the Cup final, Cussen took part in the Leinster trial game at Lansdowne Road on 11th March and after scoring two tries, was again selected to play for Leinster. His brother Jack also played in the trial but didn't make the Leinster team.

Denis Cussen captained the Blackrock team to their fourth consecutive Leinster Schools' Senior Cup against Mountjoy. He was again on the scoresheet with two tries and his brother Jack also scored as Blackrock won 12-nil.

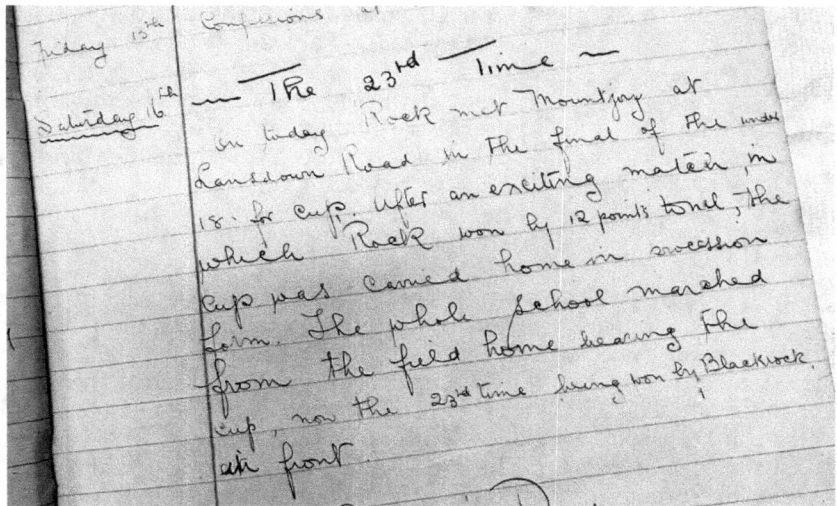

*The Scholastics Diary 16th March 1918*
*Courtesy of Blackrock College Archives*

The Scholastics Diary records the day. "Today Rock met Mountjoy at Lansdowne Road in the final of the under 18's cup. After an exciting match in which Rock won by 12 points to nil, the cup was carried home in procession form. The whole school marched from the field home bearing the cup, now the 23rd time being won by Blackrock".

## Kevin Barry (1902-1920)

Kevin Barry was born six months after Denis Cussen, on 20th January 1902. He was born in Dublin, the fourth of seven children born to Thomas and Mary Barry. The Barry family had a dairy business on Fleet Street which sold products produced primarily on the family farm in Hacketstown, County Carlow.

When his father died in 1908, young Kevin Barry was sent to Carlow where he was taken care of by his mother's family. Barry attended Rathvilly National School and lived in Carlow until 1915 when he

 returned to Dublin where his mother enrolled him in St Mary's College in Rathmines. After two years there, St Mary's College closed to students and Kevin Barry was moved to Belvedere College in 1916.

Being in the politically charged atmosphere that was Dublin in 1916, Kevin Barry developed nationalist sympathies and in 1917 he joined C Company, 1st Battalion of the Dublin Brigade of the Irish Volunteers. He was fifteen.

In mid-September 1920, members of the Irish Volunteers identified an opportunity. A British army lorry guarded by an armed party of soldiers made twice weekly trips to Monk's Bakery at 79-80 Church Street to buy bread. The lorry came every Monday and Thursday morning between 11:00 and 11:15. The party usually consisted of an officer and a driver in the cab with a non-commissioned officer and eight privates in the rear. The officer and one soldier would enter the bakery to purchase bread. Four or five soldiers would stay with the lorry without taking any particular security measures while the others would cross the street to purchase cigarettes or sweets. Within ten to fifteen minutes the bread would be loaded and the lorry would depart. It was decided to attack this truck and to commandeer the soldiers' guns.

On the morning of 20th September 1920, Barry who by now was a medical student at UCD and who had an exam that afternoon, went to mass, then joined a party of IRA volunteers on Bolton Street.

The ambush went wrong, a shoot-out ensued in which three of the troops were killed. Barry's gun jammed and he found safety under a vehicle. While his colleagues escaped, Barry was taken prisoner. He was interrogated and tortured but refused to divulge any information.

A month to the day after he was captured, Barry was tried on three counts of murder. At the opening of his trial, Barry announced, *"As a soldier of the Irish Republic, I refuse to recognise the court"*. The trial proceeded with Barry taking no further part. He was convicted and sentenced to death by hanging with the execution taking place on 1st November.

Kevin Barry was duly hanged, after hearing two Masses in his cell. Canon Waters, who walked with him to the scaffold, wrote to Barry's mother later, "*You are the mother, my dear Mrs Barry, of one of the bravest and best boys I have ever known. His death was one of the most holy, and your dear boy is waiting for you now, beyond the reach of sorrow or trial*".

Because of his young age and the execution taking place during the War of Independence, Barry became an iconic figure. He is remembered by the song written in his name and recorded by Paul Robeson, eminent American baritone.

## Inter Provincial Rugby

Two days after Denis Cussen lifted the Leinster Schools Senior Cup, he turned out in a second Leinster Schoolboys trial game. His school mates were able to come and watch the game. The scholastics' diary record for Monday 18th March reads, "*Half day. Regulation for lunch and dinner. Allowed out to see probables v possibles at Lansdowne Road. After dinner had half an hour study before benediction and bed."*.

Cussen was selected for the representative side and played against his home province at Lansdowne Road a couple of days later. Despite losing the game, Cussen was again on the scoresheet scoring a try against the run of play. Munster won the game 16-6.

A week later Denis and the Leinster team went to Belfast to play Ulster and again came out on the losing side. They lost 17-3. His success with the school team, wasn't translating to provincial success that year.

## Athletics

Just six months after Denis Cussen had won the 120 yards hurdles in the 1917 School Athletics Championships, the 1918 competition was held at Lansdowne Road in September 1918. It was to be a huge success for him; he won two gold, three silver and a bronze medal.

Cussen entered and won the shot-put competition by throwing the 12lb ball 31 feet. He entered and won the High Jump with a jump of four feet and six inches.

He entered the long jump and won the silver medal. Corkman Frederick McOstrich out jumped him by a little over a foot. McOstrich also won the 100-yards with Denis taking the bronze.

In the 120 yards hurdles, Denis just failed to retain his title. He came second behind AJ Eccleston from the Royal Hibernian Military School. Denis was also on the Blackrock College relay team that came second to Belvedere.

McOstrich took the prize for best overall performance. He scored 15 points. Denis' performance only earned him 14 points so he came second.

Denis' younger brother Bertie won the junior high jump competition and came second in the 300 yards for juniors.

## 1918/1919

Blackrock College opened for the new term on 10th September 1918. World War One was almost over. Two months later the armistice was declared and everyone expected peace to be restored. In Ireland it was a prelude to the War of Independence and the Civil War that followed. Peace wouldn't come for another five years.

Spanish flu swept the country as soldiers brought the disease home from the continent. Most of the term up to Christmas was disrupted by students falling to the illness. The scholastics' diary for 24th October reads *"A victim to the epidemic – the remains of a victim to the sickness, is removed from the college today. Anxiety seems to exist on all sides"*. The school broke for Christmas break on December 19th. Denis and his brothers were happy to return home to Newcastle West.

Returning to Newcastle West for that Christmas was an exciting time to visit. Newcastle West were in the All Ireland Hurling final. At the time, the club country champions would qualify to represent their county in the All-Ireland series. Newcastle West were representing Limerick. They had beaten Clare in September to become Munster champions and on 24th January they beat Wexford in the final. Their win was resolute, 9-5 and 1-3. While the Cussen family were not GAA members, Denis would have grown up with captain Willie Hough and the team, around the small town of Newcastle West.

*The Limerick (Newcastle West) Hurling team that won the All Ireland in Jan 1919*

## Rugby

When the students returned from their Christmas break on 14th January it was Senior Cup time. In his final year at Blackrock, Denis again captained the Blackrock team who were now going for their fifth straight Leinster Senior Cup success in a row. As was the case the previous year, there was a lot of change in the senior team. Only two of the previous year's team, Denis and student priest Tom McVicar, remained. With older brother Jack now at Trinity College, younger brother Bertie joined Denis on the team.

**Blackrock College Senior Cup Winners 1919**
J McCabe – P Walsh – M Brosnan – G Comerford – M Quinn – H Hallahan
G O'Hara – H McCormack – D Cussen (Capt) – P O'Mahoney – R Cussen
J Catalao – R Walsh – T McVicker – W Cleary

Photo Courtesy of Blackrock College Archives

The draw for the 1919 Leinster Schools' Senior Cup was made on 21st February and it pitted Blackrock against Castleknock in a preliminary round. Unfortunately, there is no match report covering the game or the first-round game against Kings Hospital. Winning both of those put Blackrock into the semi-final against Belvedere on 19th March.

Cussen played a captain's role in the semi-final, scoring a try and setting up a second as Blackrock qualified for the final for the fifth straight year.

> "Yesterday at Lansdowne Road, Blackrock qualified to meet Mountjoy in the Leinster Schools Cup Final on Saturday next. They beat Belvedere by a goal and 3 tries to nil in a hard game, which was always

a battle between the Blackrock backs and the Belvedere forwards. Belvedere first having the wind, never really looked like scoring, while 'Rock got over twice. D Cussen rounding the opposition after a clever bout of passing, and McVicker, after a clever cut through sending O'Mahony in at the corner.

Blackrock were pressing all the concluding period, but O'Brien, the Belvedere fullback, gave a splendid exhibition of fielding, kicking and tackling, but despite several likely looking movements, Blackrock only crossed their opponents' line twice. McVicker swerved through the opposing backs and converted and then, following passing by Catalao, McVicker and D Cussen, Quinn nipped in at the right corner. All the three-quarters ad halves of the winning lot played well, with McVicker and D Cussen best; while the pick of a level front rank were O'Hara, Larkin and Brosnan. For Belvedere, Byrne at out-half kicked cleverly and the pick of a good pack were Murphy, Crean, Connolly and Devereux."

The final was played on Saturday 22nd March at Lansdowne Road. In front of a large crowd, Denis Cussen won his third Leinster Schools' Senior Cup and Blackrock won their fifth consecutive crown. With his brother Bertie also in the team, Blackrock beat Mountjoy 8-3. The scholastics' diary record for the day read:

"The cup back again for the 24th time. After a most exciting match the result of which for a considerable time was very doubtful. Blackrock succeeded in gaining a complete victory 8 pts-3. All the boys then marched back to the college bearing the coveted trophy. Colloquium at dinner and tea. Benediction 7.40."

Mountjoy had the better of the first half. They had much stronger forwards, and as it was in the semi-final, it was the opposition forwards versus the lightning quick Blackrock backline. There was no score in the first half with Blackrock under siege in their own half for most of the half.

In the second half, both of the Cussen brothers scored tries as Blackrock came into the game. In the final minutes, they clung on for a great win.

## RUGBY FOOTBALL.

### BLACKROCK RETAINS SCHOOLS CUP.

**Blackrock College, 8 pts.; Mountjoy Sch., 3 pts.**

There was a large crowd at Lansdowne road when these old rivals turned out for the final, but once more Blackrock prevailed and retained the cup, scoring a goal and a try to a try. That luck was against Mountjoy must be admitted, as though they lost Langford half-way through the first half and played a man short for the rest of the match they were pressing for three-fourths of the game.

There was no score in the opening period, though the Mountjoy forwards, even when a man short, were always beating the opposing eight both in the loose and tight. For the first 20 minutes of the second period Mountjoy were hammering away at the 'Rock line, and Ives getting away from touch scored an unconverted try. M'Vicker and Cussen raised the siege, and with play hovering about the Mountjoy "25" R. Cussen got hold, and quickly sizing the situation raced behind the posts for M'Vicker to convert. Blackrock were now going great guns, and clever passing by Cataloa, M'Vicker, and the Cussens saw D. Cussen rounding the opposing backs, but he failed to add the extra points. Mountjoy came again in the last five minutes, and things looked bad for Blackrock when Delaghon misfielded. M'Vicker saved the situation. When "no side" went Mountjoy were pressing.

It was a regular battle royal between the Mountjoy forwards and Blackrock backs, and for a long time it looked as if the former would prevail. However, when the Blackrock backs did get a chance they quickly settled the matter, and the principal factor in their win was the splendid all-round display of M'Vicker, who was well served by the young Portuguese, Cataloa, as scrum-worker. The middle line made the most of their opportunities, with D. Cussen and O'Mahony the pick, and the best of a moderate pack were O'Hara, P. Walsh, and H. M'Cormack.

**Bective Rangers, 14pts.; Wanderers, Nil.**

## Schools Inter Provincial Rugby

Two days after he lifted the Leinster Schools' cup, Denis Cussen captained the probables side in the Leinster schools' trail. Playing opposite him was his brother Bertie. Denis' team won the game 31-nil with Denis scoring a drop goal for his side. Following the trial, Denis was named captain of the Leinster side but Bertie was not selected.

Blackrock College

*Denis (Captain) with the 1919 Leinster Schools' team*

Denis captained Leinster to victory in their first Inter Provincial game against Munster in Cork on 5th April. The Irish Independent reported on the game.

> "That Rugby still has a place in the southerners' heart was proved on Saturday when a splendid attendance saw the Leinster boys defeat Munster at the Mardyke in an intensely exciting game by a goal and a try to two tries. The visitors' marrow victory is enhanced by the fact that they were without the clever Blackrock out half McVicker while Gallence had also to declare off, another Blackrock boy in O'Hara taking his place. Leinster owe their win mainly to their cleverness and finish, but so can be said in the losers' favour that they have had very little match play this season owing to various causes, while they had only two schools to pick their side from. With ground and weather favourable, a fast game resulted ad with each side scoring in turn, and Munster within a pip of pulling the game out of the fire in the last few minutes, interest was kept up right to the end.
>
> Leinster were the first to find their feet, and after being pulled up a couple of times by Murphy-O'Connor, Hurst finished off passing by

*Catalao and Houghton by dashing over, but Murphy failed to improve. After this play swung up and down till Canty scored an unconverted try in a forward scramble, and the sides changed over on equal terms.*

*Leinster were again the first to get going, Hurst finding touch inside the Munster 25, with a huge punt. Play was at the home 25 when Cussen picking up, threw wide to Hurst, who failed to gather at first attempt but recovering swerved through a couple of opponents to score a topping try and Murphy capped the effort by landing a goal from the touch lin. Crean might have put Leinster further ahead but threw away a nice chance. From this till the end the heavier Munster pack kept Leinster on the defensive. Good tackling by the backs and stopping of rushes by Murphy kept them at bay until the last few minutes, when Murphy-O'Connor got on from a line out, but though the charge was disallowed he failed to convert from an easy position.*

*The Munster forwards had the better of the deal in the straight, shoving and rushing but were not as clever with their feet as Leinster, in which particular line Hanna and Bell were at times really brilliant, while Murphy, Walsh and Speedy were all hard workers. Catalao was hurt early on, but played up pluckily and if Houghton did not open up the game he kicked well. The three-quarters all did well. Hurst excelling himself on the left wing, and O'Brien played a sound game at full. Murphy-O'Connor carried the Munster back division on his shoulder, and they would have been queer street without him. Kinmouth ran fast on the right win, and Dorgan, the scrum half kicked cleverly, while the pick of a hefty pack were Browne, O'Callaghan, Roche and Keating."*

Cussen's second game as captain of the Leinster Schools' team was played against Ulster at Lansdowne Road on 12th April. On this occasion he couldn't steer his side to victory. Leinster lost 13-nil.

Leinster were missing Catalao and McVicker from their first choice and *"for nearly three-fourths of the game were on the Ulster side of half-way, but they never inspired confidence, and, except on a couple of occasions, were never really dangerous"*.

There were no further Inter Provincial games and so the season ended as did Denis' secondary school education. His school's rugby career had ended with an impressive three Leinster Senior Cup wins, two as captain and six Leinster Schools Caps with two as captain and two tries.

## Athletics

By the time the IAAA Schoolboy Athletics championships came around later in the year, Denis had graduated from Blackrock College and so didn't take part.

Denis Cussen graduated from Blackrock College on 17th June 1919. He returned home to Newcastle West for a summer break before starting his university education at Trinity College. While at Blackrock College, he had won three Leinster Schoolboys Senior Cup medals. He had represented and captained Leinster schoolboys. He had become National Champion in 120 yards hurdles, high jump, long jump and 4x400-yards relay. He had also won silver and bronze medals at a national level. His sports career was just getting started.

The Cussen brothers had been stars of the Blackrock College rugby team while attending the school. However, after they left to go on to Trinity College, they were notably absent from the Blackrock College annual. The president of the college at the time was Archbishop John Charles McQuaid was questioned by eldest Cussen, Jack, as to why and he got the response that, indeed McQuaid had left their name from the annuals because he did not approve of their attending Trinity College, a protestant institution. Subsequently the Catholic Church banned attendance at Trinity for Catholics without the approval of the bishop.

| 1916/17 Leinster Schools Senior Cup | | | | | |
|---|---|---|---|---|---|
| | Result | For | Against | Date | Comment |
| Wesley | Win | 52 | Nil | 24th Feb | Cussen scored two tries |
| Mountjoy | Win | 23 | 5 | 21st Mar | Cussen scored three tries |
| Belvedere | Win | 21 | Nil | 24th Mar | Cussen scored |

| 1917/18 Leinster Schools Senior Cup | | | | | |
|---|---|---|---|---|---|
| | Result | For | Against | Date | Comment |
| High School | Win | 29 | nil | 2nd Mar | Cussen scored 3 tries, a penalty and kicked 4 conversions |
| Wesley | Win | 31 | nil | 6th Mar | Cussen scored 2 tries and kicked 2 conversions |

# Blackrock College

| | | | | | |
|---|---|---|---|---|---|
| Mountjoy | win | 12 | nil | 16th Mar | Cussen scored 2 tries |

### 1918/19 Leinster Schools Senior Cup

| | Result | For | Against | Date | Comment |
|---|---|---|---|---|---|
| Castleknock | Win | | | 1st Mar | No match report |
| Kings Hosp | Win | | | 12th Mar | No match report |
| Belvedere | Win | 14 | Nil | 16th Mar | Cussen scored a try. Probably played against Kevin Barry. |
| Mountjoy | Win | 8 | 3 | 22nd Mar | Cussen scored a try |

*Denis Cussen – Blackrock College Senior Cup Record*

### 1916/17 - Leinster Schools Inter Provincial

| | Result | For | Against | Date | Comment |
|---|---|---|---|---|---|
| Munster | Win | 6 | 3 | 17th Mar | |
| Ulster | Win | 17 | 9 | 30th Mar | Cussen scored a try |

### 1917/18 - Leinster Schools Inter Provincial

| | Result | For | Against | Date | Comment |
|---|---|---|---|---|---|
| Munster | Loss | 6 | 16 | 23rd Mar | Cussen scored a try |
| Ulster | Loss | 3 | 17 | 30th Mar | |

### 1918/19 - Leinster Schools Inter Provincial

| | Result | For | Against | Date | Comment |
|---|---|---|---|---|---|
| Munster | Win | 8 | 6 | 5th Apr | Captain |
| Ulster | Loss | Nil | 13 | 12th Apr | Captain |

*Denis Cussen – Leinster Schools Record*

# Trinity

Having graduated from Blackrock College, Denis entered Trinity College to study medicine in the autumn of 1919. The move to Trinity would have been viewed as unusual for a catholic family at the time. The family oral history is that Bob Cussen was advised by a friend that if he sent his boys to "National" (UCD) that they might get involved in nationalistic politics. On that basis Bob had sent older brother Jack to Trinity and Denis followed suit. Denis and Jack took up residence in the student rooms on campus and both continued their sporting endeavours. Younger brother Bertie followed two years later.

## 1919/1920

### Rugby

Trinity's rugby team, Dublin University Football Club, is the oldest rugby club in Ireland. Established in 1854, it has a long and proud history in Irish rugby. DUFC were prominent in the establishment of the Leinster Cup in 1881 and were the inaugural winners beating Kingstown in the final. From that point until the outbreak of World War One, Trinity won the Leinster Senior Cup on seventeen occasions and were runners up another seven. Rugby was put on hold during the war years and the Leinster Senior Cup restarted in 1920.

Having joined DUFC as the captain of the Leinster schoolboys' team, Denis couldn't initially break into a strong first XV and so played the 1919/20 season in the DUFC second team. As he did so, the DUFC first team won the first Leinster Senior Cup to be played after the war years, beating Wanderers in the final.

### Boxing

Towards the end of his first year at Trinity, Denis Cussen took part in Trinity Week's Sports Competitions. In May 1920, he entered the boxing championships at the OTC Training Square. Weighing in at eleven stone and six pounds, Denis competed in the heavy weight division.

Cussen won the title of Trinity Heavy Weight Champion by knocking out fellow competitor JC Collins. In the third round of their four-round bout, Cussen launched a left hook which caught his opponent square on the chin and knocked him out. Collins had to be helped back to his feet.

*Left: Denis Cussen landing a right hook on the jaw of JC Collins and below, the aftermath*

**HEAVY-WEIGHTS—FINAL.**
**J. C. Collins v. D. Cussen.**
**Four Rounds**—In the first round the exchanges were heavy, and both scored heavily with the right, but Cussen conserved his energy, and was the stronger at the close.—Heavy punishment was dealt out by both in the second round. Collins was wild, and still wasted his energy. In the third round Cussen caught his man with a left uppercut, and Collins rose groggy. Cussen again swung the left to the point, and knocked his man clean out.

*Newspaper report of the fight*

A few days later, the Trinity boxers took on the College of Science boxers. Cussen was drawn against T Foley. *"This was a hard-hitting* contest and the varsity champion, with good two-handed work, piled up points and made his opponent do a lot of covering. Foley forced matters in the closing rounds but was not able to wipe off the arrears". Cussen won again.

## Athletics

As Denis was competing in the boxing competition during Trinity Week, he was unable to compete in one day of the athletics competition. 1920 was an Olympic year and the day Denis missed was the Olympic trials day. The newspaper report said afterwards *"The standard reached in all the events was very high; but chief honours fell to Denis Cussen, an all-round athlete, who, through engaging in the boxing competitions, did not appear in any of the athletics contests on Wednesday. Had he done so, he would most certainly have qualified in the Olympic trial for the Long Jump".*

*Denis Cussen competing in the long jump at Trinity 1920*

Having won the boxing competition, Denis took part in the second day of the athletics carnival. It was his performance on this day that led to the newspaper rueing his absence from the Olympic trial. Denis put in an all-round display and won the long jump with a leap of twenty-one feet and nine inches. He won the freshman 100-yard race and followed that up by winning the main 100-yard race in a time of 10.2 seconds. In that race he beat Hedges Worthington-Eyre who competed in the 1920 Olympics a few months later. Cussen also won the silver medal in the high jump and won the relay race. With such an outstanding display, Cussen was awarded the vice-chancellors cup for best performance.

## A FINE ATHLETE.

### D. CUSSEN TRINITY CHAMPION

#### COLLEGE RACES—YESTERDAY.

It was quite like old times in the College Park yesterday, as, with glorious weather favouring the concluding day of the races, there was the biggest attendance for years. The performances were very good, D. Cussen in particular proving himself a very useful all-round athlete. He won the long jump with the fine distance of 21 ft. 9 in., only 3 in. lower than standard, and created a big surprise by taking the 100 yards championship, in which he defeated Pienaar and Worthington-Eyre by inches. Here he gained a standard medal by doing 10 1-5, just 1-5 sec. inside, while previously he had put the 100 yards scratch Freshmens' to his credit. In the high jump, with a handicap of 3 in., he participated in a three-cornered dead heat. In the hurdles he was winning easily when he burst through the last obstacle and was disqualified.

The mile handicap proved very interesting, the scratchman, Mein, leaving his effort very late, and only suffered defeat by 2 yards by Glasgow. The international wing three-quarter, Dickson, won the hurdles handicap, and also got first prize in the high jump for the best nett jump of 5 ft. 4 in. The Rugby captain, W. L. Smith, also had a very successful afternoon, winning the 16lb. shot and discus events, while he got second in the long jump, and was also one of three dead-heating in the high jump.

D. Cussen was awarded the Vice-Chancellor's Cup for the best performance. This splendid athlete also won the heavy-weight boxing championship of the College recently.

*Irish Independent – 4th June 1920*

The IAAA Nationals Championships had been held a week before the Trinity Week athletics championships where Cussen announced himself on the national stage. Had they been held after the Trinity Week competitions, Cussen would no doubt have been involved and could possibly have medalled. Worthington-Eyre, who Cussen had just beaten, came second in the 220-yards and won the 400-yards national title.

It was too late for the IAAA National Championships but Denis' performance at the Trinity event, in particular in the long jump, led to him being selected for the Ireland team that took part in a tri-nations championship against Scotland and England. Cussen's first Irish athletics cap came on 10th July at Crewe where he competed for Ireland in the long jump. He came a very respectable second place.

## 1920/1921

### Rugby

At the commencement of the 1920/21 season, Denis Cussen was with the Dublin University second XV. By the season's conclusion, however, he had not only secured promotion to the first XV but had also earned international honours with Ireland.

The publication "Dublin University Football Club 1866–1972" chronicles the club's history and includes photographs of the first XV for most seasons. Notably, the 1920/21 team photograph does not include Cussen, confirming his absence from the senior side at the outset. The line-up featured future Ireland internationals Robert Crichton, James Dickson, and Reuben Owens, alongside future Springbok Jan van Druten, illustrating the high calibre of players Cussen was competing with to earn his place.

Also among the squad was William James O'Donel from Mayo, an engineering student who had served briefly during the war; he passed away in Brazil in 1925. Medical student Richard Dowse, another teammate, was the younger brother of John Dowse, who had represented Ireland prior to the conflict. The brothers had lost a sibling, Charles, in the war, underscoring the lingering impact of the Great War on the era.

As defending champions of the Leinster Senior Cup, Dublin University began the season strongly with six domestic fixtures preceding their traditional series of varsity matches. That year, the itinerary included a tour of Britain for encounters against Liverpool, Cambridge, London, Queens, and Oxford universities. Cussen did not appear in the initial six games but joined the varsity tour, making his first XV debut against London University at the end of November, where he scored two tries. Upon returning to Ireland, he maintained his momentum, notching a drop goal against Blackrock and two further tries against Edinburgh University in the pre-Christmas fixtures. These displays propelled him into contention for Leinster and Ireland selection, culminating in his inclusion for both in January 1921.

*The DUFC First XV at the start of 1920/21*
*Inset: JE McCormick and Nathaniel Tipping*
Standing: T de Bruijn, William O'Donel, Reuban Owens, Jan van Druten, DJ Malan, Richard Dowse, JD Leahy
Sitting: Robert Crichton, WL Smith, James Dickson, Edward Rollins, JF Stewart

Cussen's performances for the rest of the season were astounding. He played in five games between 18th December and 2nd April and scored two tries in each of them as Trinity beat Monkstown, Bective and the 2nd Welsh Regiment on a Leinster Cup run that took them to the final against University College Dublin. Cussen scored twice against Monkstown in the opening round of the Leinster Senior Cup on 5th March. As a reminder that these were troubled times, the following day, Limerick mayor George Clancy and the previous mayor, Michael O'Callaghan, were murdered by the Black and Tans.

Cussen didn't score in the cup final on 4th April but a try by future Springbok, Jan Van Druten, gave Trinity back-to-back cup successes. Denis Cussen was a Leinster Senior Cup winner. He had played in nine games that season for the first XV and Trinity had won all nine.

It is evident how explosive his appearance on the scene was that his first game for Trinity was on 27th November. On 5th January, there was a Combined Universities v The Rest of Leinster game played for charity and Cussen wasn't selected, however just two weeks later he was on both the Leinster and the Irish national team.

## RUGBY "CAPS."

### Eight Leinster; Four Ulster; One Munster.

#### CUSSEN'S METEORIC RISE.

After a rather thorough series of trials the Irish Rugby team has been selected, and hopes are entertained that we will be handing back the "wooden spoon" to some of the other countries this year. A youthful leavening of the team should bear fruit. The big surprise of the selection is D. Cussen, the Dublin University champion boxer and Irish international jumper. He played himself on to the team in Saturday's match, scoring one grand try after beating four of the opposition in a swerving run. Cussen and N. Purcell (Lansdowne) are double internationalists, the latter hav-

Trinity

| 1920/21 | | | | | |
|---|---|---|---|---|---|
| | Result | For | Against | Date | Comment |
| Clontarf | Won | 6g, 1dg, 3t | nil | 16th Oct | Not in the team |
| Wanderers | Drew | 1pg | 1t | 23rd Oct | Not in the team |
| Old Wesley | Won | 4t | 1dg | 30th Oct | Not in the team |
| Lansdowne | Lost | 1t | 1g | 6th Nov | Not in the team |
| Bective | Won | 2t | nil | 13th Nov | Not in the team |
| Lansdowne | Won | 1pg, 2t | 1t | 20th Nov | Not in the team |
| Liverpool | Won | 1g, 1pg, 1t | 1dg, 1t | 22nd Nov | Didn't play |
| Cambridge | Lost | 1g | 2g, 1dg | 25th Nov | Didn't play |
| London | Won | 3g, 3t | nil | 27th Nov | Debut. Cussen scored 2 tries |
| Queens Uni | Lost | 1t | 1dg, 1t | 3rd Dec | Didn't play |
| Oxford Uni | Lost | 2g, 2t | 1dg, 5t | 9th Dec | Didn't play |
| Blackrock | Won | 1g, 2dg, 2t | nil | 11th Dec | Cussen scored a drop goal |
| Edinburgh | Won | 1g, 1dg, 5t | nil | 18th Dec | Cussen scored 2 tries |
| NIFC | Lost | nil | 1t | 16th Jan | On International duty - Didn't play |
| Wanderers | Lost | 2t | 1g, 1t | 19th Jan | On International duty - Didn't play |
| Old Wesley | Won | 1g, 3t | 1t | 26th Jan | On International duty - Didn't play |
| UC Dublin | Won | 2g, 2t | 1t | 2nd Feb | Cussen scored 2 tries |
| Queens Uni | Lost | nil | 2g, 2t | | On International duty - Didn't play |
| Clontarf | Won | 1g, 1t | nil | 19th Feb | On International duty - Didn't play |
| Garryowen | Game Not Played | | | | |
| Monkstown (Cup) | Won | 6g, 1t | 1g | 5th Mar | Cussen scored 2 tries |
| Bective (Cup) | Won | 3g, 3t | 1t | 26th Mar | Cussen scored 2 tries |
| 2nd Welsh Regiment (Cup) | Won | 1g | nil | 2nd Apr | Cussen scored 2 tries |

| UC Dublin (Cup Final) | Won | 1g | nil | 4th Apr | Van Druten scored the try |

*Dublin University FC games 1920/21 Season*

## Athletics

Having missed the opportunity to compete in the 1920 IAAA Championships, Denis was very much in the frame by the time twelve months had passed. In the intervening year Denis had gone from Trinity's second XV in rugby and being an athletics relative unknown, to a Leinster Senior Cup winner with Trinity, a Leinster provincial starter and he had four international caps to his name. Just as he had exploded into the rugby headlines, Cussen made a huge athletic statement at the IAAA Championships on 17th May 1921. He won the three national titles; the 100-yards, the 220-yards and the long jump.

A week later on 23rd May, Cussen competed in the Dublin University Championships and again won the 100-yards and long jump competitions easily. In his heat in the 100-yards, he clocked a time of 10.4 seconds and won easily by three yards. The other heat was won by Olympian Worthington-Eyre in the same time. The two squared up in the final and Cussen won by a foot. Their positions were reversed in the 220-yards with Cussen coming second. In the long jump, Denis jumped twenty-one feet and three inches to win gold. He was a full three feet ahead of his nearest competitor.

Denis had achieved huge success in May 1921. However, as a reminder that this was a very troubled time in Ireland, two days after the Dublin University Championships (on 25th May), the IRA stormed the Customs House. The British Army surrounded the building and five IRA members were shot dead. Another eighty were captured. All this happened just across the river from Trinity College where Denis was living. He would have been happy to escape home to Newcastle West for his summer break a month later.

# 1921/1922

Over the summer while Denis was home in Newcastle West, political instability continued. By the time he returned to Trinity for the next term, Michael Collins and Arthur Griffith had been invited to London

Trinity

to discuss *'limited sovereignty for Ireland within the British Empire'*. Those negotiations were ongoing as the new rugby season started.

*7th December 1921*

## Rugby

**Dublin University 1st XV 1921/22**
Back row: John Thompson, C McCalden, Reuban Owens, J Shepherd, Joseph Gillespie, Allan Troughton
Sitting: Jan van Druten, W Smith, Robert Crichton, J Stewart, J McCormick, Denis Cussen, DJ Malan
Front: J Steele, Ivan Marais

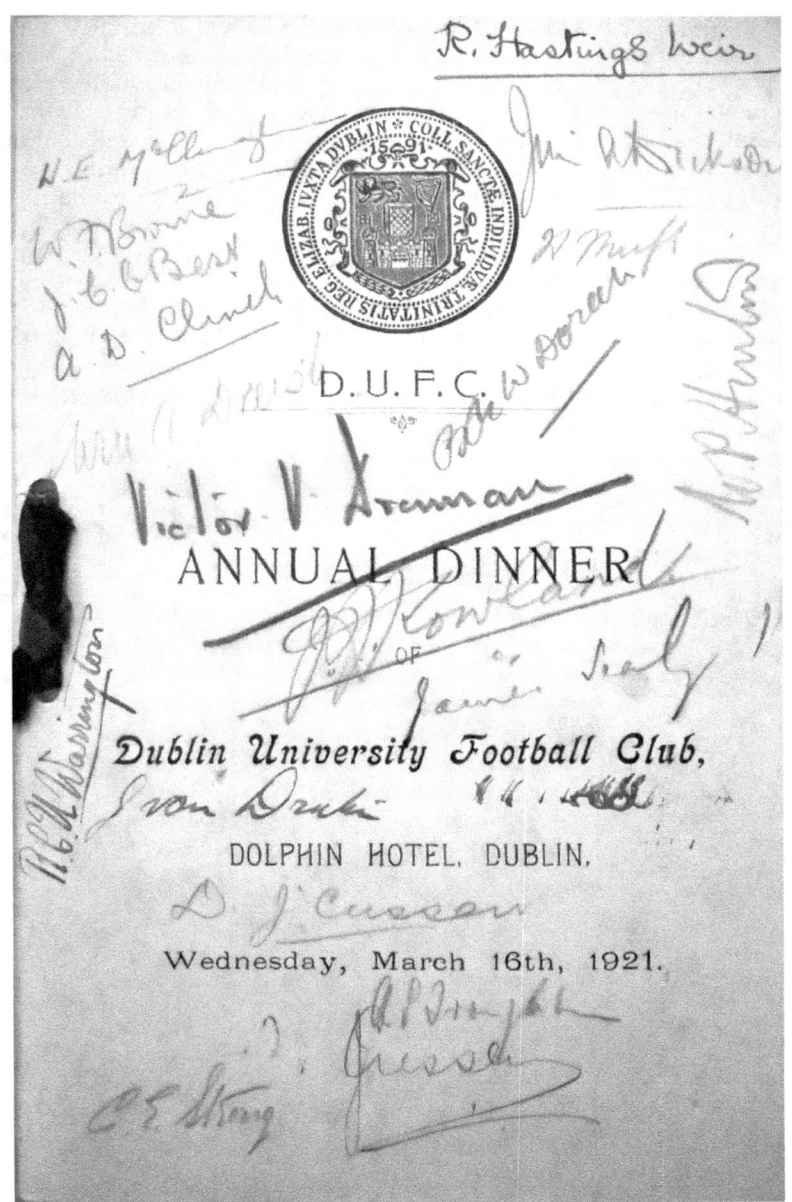

*Autographed dinner menu from DUFC Annual Dinner 1921*

For the 1921/22 season, Denis Cussen was a locked in first XV player. He was now an international player and one of the more senior players in the team. As was always the case, some students graduated and so there was inevitable change in the team. Gone were Tipping, de Bruijn, O'Donel, Leahy and Rollins. Newcomers to the team included American born John Thompson who would later captain Ireland, Allan Troughton, Joseph Gillespie who would be capped once for Ireland and big South African Ivan Marais.

Cussen scored in three of the first four games of the season as Trinity went in search of a third Leinster Senior Cup in a row. In the ten games that he played before Christmas, he scored in all but two. He scored twice against Clontarf on 5th December. The following day the announcement came from London that a deal had been reached for an Anglo-Irish Treaty.

The season proved difficult though as Cussen struggled with injury. He played in twelve games, scoring eleven tries before straining his thigh in the international game against England at the start of February. He missed the rest of the season. In his absence, Trinity got to the semi-final of the Leinster cup but lost to Lansdowne after a replay. Lansdowne went on to lift the cup when they beat Monkstown in the final.

| | Result | For | Against | Date | Comment |
|---|---|---|---|---|---|
| | | **1921/22** | | | |
| Monkstown | Won | 4g, 2pg, 2t | Nil | 17th Oct | Cussen scored 1 try |
| Lansdowne | Lost | Nil | 1t | 22nd Oct | Played |
| NIFC | Lost | 1g, 1pg, 2t | 4g | 31st Oct | Cussen scored 1 try |
| Cork Con | Won | 2g, 4t | nil | 3rd Nov | Cussen scored 1 try |
| Wanderers | Lost | 2t | 1g, 1t | 7th Nov | Didn't play |
| Welch Regiment | Won | 1g, 2t | 1t | 14th Nov | Didn't play |
| Bective | Won | 3g, 2t | nil | 21st Nov | Cussen scored 1 try |
| UC Dublin | | | Game Not Played | | |
| Oxford | Lost | 1t | 4g, 1t | 26th Nov | Didn't play |

# Trinity

| | | | | | |
|---|---|---|---|---|---|
| Edinburgh | Lost | 1t | 2g, 1t | 30th Nov | Didn't play |
| Clontarf | Won | 3g, 2t | 2g, 1t | 5th Dec | Cussen scored 2 tries |
| Cambridge | Won | 2g, 1t | 1t | 11th Dec | Cussen scored 1 try |
| Liverpool | Won | 3g, 4t | nil | 15th Dec | Played |
| Queen's | Won | 2t | 1g, 1t | 19th Dec | Cussen scored 1 try |
| UC Cork | Won | 1g, 5t | nil | 22nd Dec | Played |
| Wanderers | Won | 6t | 1g | 21st Jan | On International duty - Didn't play |
| Welch Regiment | Won | 1g, 2t | 2t | 19th Jan | Cussen scored 2 tries |
| Clontarf | | | Game Not Played | | |
| Blackrock | Won | 1g, 4t | nil | 2nd Feb | Cussen scored 1 try |
| Bective | Won | 4g, 4t | 1t | 4th Feb | On International duty - Didn't play |
| UC Dublin | Won | 2g, 2t | 1t | 15th Feb | Injured |
| Lansdowne | Won | 1g, 1pg, 2t | 1t | 20th Feb | Injured |
| Monkstown | Won | 4g, 1t | 1t | 1st Mar | Injured |
| Cork Con | Lost | nil | 2g, 1dg, 1t | 3rd Mar | Injured |
| UC Cork | Won | 1g, 1t | 1g | 5th Mar | Injured |
| Old Wesley | Lost | 1t | 1pg, 1t | 11th Mar | Injured |
| Instonians | Drew | 2g, 1mg, 2t | 2g, 1pg, 2t | 14th Mar | Injured |
| Blackrock (Cup) | Won | 1g, 1pg, 3t | Nil | 18th Mar | Injured |
| Lansdowne (Cup Semi Final) | Drew | 1pg | 1t | 25th Mar | Injured |
| Lansdowne (Cup Semi Final Replay) | Lost | 1t | 1pt | 29th Mar | Injured |

*Dublin University FC games 1921/22 Season*

## Athletics

Having missed a lot of the rugby season through injury, Denis was recovered sufficiently to take part in the athletics season which started in April of 1922. In the annual Dublin University Athletics

Championship, Denis was defending champion and the man to beat. The competition was held on Tuesday 16th May at College Green, the same day that the final British troops withdrew from the Curragh Camp and handed it over to the new Irish army.

In the 100-yards Cussen had competition. Robert Rowan Woods, the son of doctor Sir Robert Henry Woods from Tullamore, had received his education at Shrewsbury College in England. While there he had won the English schoolboys' national championship the previous year. He returned to Ireland and entered Trinity to study medicine. Woods would be one of Cussen's main challengers over the next few years.

Both Cussen and Woods won their heats easily and were paired in the final. In that race, Cussen was leading after eighty yards but Woods put in a strong finish. The two tumbled over the finish line and Cussen had only just won. His winning time was 10.5 seconds.

Cussen sat out the 220-yards competition which Woods won. In the long jump, Denis cleared 21 feet and 9 inches to retain his title. As it was the previous year, his jump was over two feet longer than his nearest competitor.

Later in the month, Trinity took on Queens University in an athletics challenge. Cussen won the 100-yards with Woods coming second. He also won the long jump with a jump of 21 feet 7 ½ inches.

At the IAAA National Championships held at Lansdowne Road on 5th June, Denis retained both the National 100-yards and long jump titles. He then returned home for the summer as Dublin erupted into Civil War.

## 1922/1923

The summer of 1922 saw the IRA assassinate Sir Henry Wilson in London, anti-treaty forces occupy the four courts and across the country there was fighting as the new National Army struggled to control the uprising of anti-treaty forces. August saw the death of Arthur Griffith and the assassination of Michael Collins at Béal na Bláth. By the time Denis Cussen returned to Trinity, Ireland was in a very dark place.

Trinity

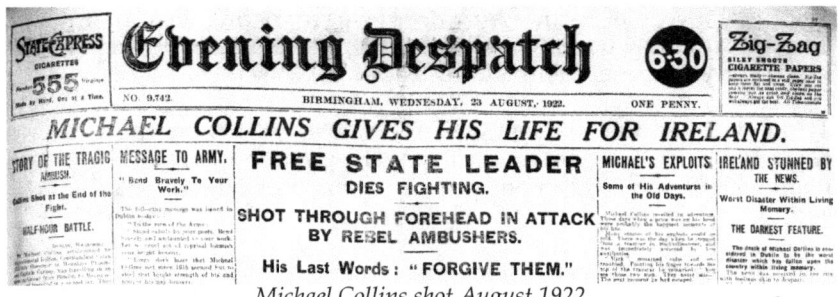

*Michael Collins shot August 1922*

## Rugby

Going into the 1922/23 season, Cussen was joined in the Trinity first XV by Jammie Clinch. Clinch, whose father Andrew Clinch was an Irish International and who was one of the first Irish men to play for the British and Irish Lions in 1896, would be a major presence in the Irish team for the next ten years. A flanker, he was capped thirty times and followed his father into the British and Irish Lions team in 1924.

*Dublin University 1st XV 1922/23*
*Denis Cussen is standing, middle row, third from the left*

Another newcomer to the Trinity team was Mark Sugden. An England born scrum-half, Sugden would play twenty-nine times for Ireland and would be long-time friend and colleague of Cussen.

Trinity opened their season on 7th October by hammering Clontarf. Unfortunately, there was no newspaper report on the game. It is very likely that Cussen scored one or more of the tries they scored that day. Trinity won by two goals, one penalty goal and six tries to a try.

Trinity went on to have a magnificent season. They played twenty-three games and lost only two. Denis Cussen missed three games as he was with the Irish national team. In the twenty games he played, he scored twenty-four tries, including a seven-match streak in which he scored in every game.

*The Trinity and Cambridge Teams from November 1922*
*Cussen, who scored two tries that day, is standing fourth from right*

In December, the Edinburgh University team came to Dublin. Trinity won the game but it was notable more for who Denis was marking. Scottish international, Eric Liddell played for Edinburgh. Liddell scored a try but the match report mentions numerous times Cussen prevented other scores. Like Cussen, Liddell went on to be an Olympian and set a world record time in the 400m at the 1924 Olympics. This feat was one of the plot lines in the movie Chariots of Fire.

## Eric Liddell (1902-1945)

Eric Liddell was born in Tianjin, China in January 1902. His parents were Scottish Christian missionaries. When he was six years old, he and his older brother were sent back to the United Kingdom where they were enrolled in Eltham College, South London. As he grew up, he had little contact with his parents who stayed in China. It is said that he met them only once in the following eleven years but kept in touch with weekly letters.

While at Eltham, Liddell like Denis Cussen, showed great athletic ability. At the 1918 school sports day, he won the long jump, the 100-yards and the quarter mile titles and came second in the cross country, high jump and hurdles competitions. He went on to captain both the school's rugby and cricket teams.

Liddell went on to study science at the University of Edinburgh and continued his sporting activities. He was selected to play for the University's rugby team and went on to be selected for the Scottish national team. He made his debut in Edinburgh in Scotland's 6-3 win over Ireland in 1922. Liddell scored a try that day but it was his only outing that year. The following season he scored in the games against France, Wales and Ireland meaning he scored in each of his first four international tests. With Scotland he won seven caps, winning all but one game. His opposite number in the 1923 Ireland Scotland game was Denis Cussen against whom he scored a try.

Liddell also continued his athletic career while in Scotland. He competed in the 1923 AAA championships and became British Champion by winning both the 100-yards and 220-yards. He set a British record in the 100-yards of 9.7 seconds and was a strong medal candidate for the 1924 Paris Olympics.

# Trinity

*Eric Liddell sitting on the ground on right in 1922*

*Eric Liddell winning the 400m at the Paris Olympics 1924*

When the schedule for the 1924 Olympic Games was announced, the 100m heats were scheduled for a Sunday. A devout Christian, he refused to run on his holy day and so dropped out of the 100m. A perceived medal hope in both the individual and relay races, he was put under tremendous pressure to compete but he steadfastly refused. Instead, he competed in the 200m and the 400m, a distance where he wasn't as strong.

At the games he won bronze in the 200m behind Jackson Scholz and Charles Paddock (both of USA). On 11th July 1924, Liddell ran in the Olympic 400m. Selected in the outside lane where he was unable to see his competitors, Liddell ran the entire race as if it was a 100m sprint. With a distinctive running style where he looked up towards the sky, Liddell won gold and broke both the Olympic and World Record in a time of 47.6 seconds.

A few days after he won the Olympic gold, Liddell graduated from university and in 1925, he walked away from sports and travelled to China to do missionary work like his parents.

In China he married Canadian Florence Mackenzie and they had three children. In 1941, the Japanese invaded China and it became dangerous for westerners, so Liddell moved his family to Canada but he himself stayed to continue his missionary work in the dangerous surroundings.

In 1943, Liddell was interned by the Japanese at Weihsien Internment Camp. He was subjected to terrible conditions and forced labour. Liddell died of a brain tumour in 1945 while still in captivity.

As he was born in China, he is revered as their first Olympic champion. His story was one of the plots of the Hollywood movie, Chariots of Fire.

Despite such a strong season, Trinity came up short when they were beaten by Bective in the Leinster Senior Cup semi-final at Lansdowne Road. Bective scored a goal and a penalty goal in the *"biggest rugby surprise of the season"*. They went on to beat UCD in the Leinster Senior Cup final 18-nil.

Trinity

Back-to-back defeats in the Leinster Senior Cup semi-final was a disappointment. Denis Cussen still had his athletics season to come and a chance for some medals.

| | Result | For | Against | Date | Comment |
|---|---|---|---|---|---|
| | | **1922/23** | | | |
| Clontarf | Won | 2g, 1pg, 6t | 1t | 7th Oct | No match report |
| Bective | Won | 3g, 2t | nil | 16th Oct | Cussen scored 2 tries |
| Monkstown | Won | 3t, 6t | 1dg | 18th Oct | Cussen scored a try |
| Wanderers | Won | 3g, 2t | 1g, 1t | 23rd Oct | Cussen scored a try |
| Lansdowne | Won | 1g, 2t | 1pg, 1t | 30th Oct | Played. Didn't score |
| NIFC | Won | 6g, 4t | 3t | 11th Nov | Cussen scored 3 tries |
| Queen's | Won | 3g, 2t | 1pg | 13th Nov | Cussen scored 2 tries |
| Instonians | Won | 2g, 1t | nil | 19th Nov | Cussen scored a try |
| Liverpool | Won | 3g, 2t | 1t | 21st Nov | Cussen scored a try |
| Cambridge | Won | 1g, 3t | 1g | 23rd Nov | Cussen scored 2 tries |
| Aldershot | Won | 1t, 1dg, 5t | 1g, 1t | 27th Nov | Cussen scored 2 tries |
| Bective | Won | 4g, 4t | 1t | 30th Nov | Cussen scored a try |
| Blackrock | Won | 1g, 3t | nil | 2nd Dec | Not mentioned in match report |
| Edinburgh | Won | 1g | 1t | 12th Dec | Played. Eric Liddell scored for Edinburgh |
| Oxford | Won | 1g, 4t | 2pg, 1t | 20th Dec | Cussen scored 3 tries |
| Lansdowne | Won | 2t | 1g | 18th Dec | Cussen scored a try |
| Loyola | | Game Not Played | | | |
| Welch Regiment | | Game Not Played | | | |
| Blackrock | | Game Not Played | | | |
| Old Wesley | Won | 1pg, 2t | 1g | 10th Feb | On International duty - Didn't play |
| UC Dublin | Lost | 1g, 1t | 1pg, 2t | 14th Feb | Cussen scored a try |
| Wanderers | Won | 4g, 4t | 1t | 17th Feb | Cussen scored 2 tries |

# Trinity

| | | | | | |
|---|---|---|---|---|---|
| Monkstown | Won | 4g | 1g | | On International duty - Didn't play |
| Monkstown | Won | 4g, 1pg | 2t | | On International duty - Didn't play |
| Blackrock (Cup) | Won | 2g, 4t | nil | 4th Mar | Cussen scored a try |
| Bective (Cup) | Lost | nil | 1g, 1pg | 24th Mar | Played well |

*Dublin University FC games 1922/23 Season*

## Athletics

*Cussen winning the long jump in May 1923 just before his injury*

Denis Cussen had survived the 1922/23 rugby season without injury and was in good form going into the athletics season. At the end of May, Dublin University took on the Rest of Leinster in an athletics competition. It was held at Croke Park on 21st May. Denis' form was on display as he won the 100-yards ahead of MJ Stafford and RR Woods in a time of 10.8 seconds. He also won the long jump competition with a jump of 20 feet and 9 inches.

A week later the newspapers carried an article saying he was going to miss the Trinity Athletics Championships which were on 30th. A few days later another article appeared saying he would appear.

When the Trinity Championships were held, Cussen was a no-show. He had injured his ankle and was quoted as saying that while he could run, he wouldn't do himself justice so opted to skip it. In his absence RR Woods won the 100-yards, 220-yards and long jump. The injury would hamper Cussen's performances for the best part of eighteen months.

## 1923/1924

Over the summer of 1923 Denis returned to Newcastle West and recovered from his injury. 1924 was an Olympic year and Ireland would, for the first time, compete as an independent country.

### Rugby

In the 1923/24 season, Denis was joined at Trinity by his younger brother Robert (Bertie). Bertie started that season in the second XV but would quickly join Denis in the Trinity first team. A new addition to the Trinity XV in the season was Jonathan Fredrick Wilde, a relative of Oscar Wilde. Another was Ian Malcolm Bowen (IMB) Stuart who would become a firm friend of Denis. Allan Troughton, who had been on the team the previous year and had played for Leinster, was diagnosed with TB and had to retire. He moved to South Africa for a warmer climate and became a priest.

As 1924 was an Olympic year and as he was nursing his ankle injury Cussen opted out of international rugby for the year and was sparing in his availability for the Trinity team. He sat out the first three games of the year and then exploded into action by scoring five tries as Trinity hammered Wanderers on 20th October.

Cussen was selected for the Rugby Centenary game played in late October and travelled to that historic game which was played at Rugby School, missing some Trinity games.

As the season progressed and his ankle recovered, Cussen made himself available for more important games and more often than not, scored when he played. He played in the final six games of the season in February and March 1924, scoring eight tries.

**NORTH'S GOOD WIN**

**SOME RUGBY SURPRISES IN DUBLIN**

**D. CUSSEN'S FIVE TRIES**

There was a big list of matches in Dublin on Saturday, half a dozen senior games being decided. The ten Dublin clubs were supplemented by two visitors from Belfast. "North" defeated Monkstown at Sydney Parade by 12 pts. to nil, but Malone lost at Miltown to Palmerston by 11 pts. to 3 pts. Wanderers, though beaten by 6 tries to 2 goals, put up a splendid fight against Trinity at Lansdowne Road. D. Cussen, the Irish international, re-appeared, and scored 5 tries. At Castle Avenue, Lansdowne led by 6 pts. to nil at

D. Cussen

*Dublin University 1st XV 1923/24*
Back: C Loubser, J Steele, O Chance, M Sugden, J Shepherd, T Millin, J Wilde
Front: J Clinch, D Cussen, J Thompson, R Dowse, I Stuart

Trinity

His final game of the season was a Leinster Senior Cup tie against UCD. He scored both of Trinity's tries but they lost narrowly. As had happened on the two previous seasons, Trinity's vanquishers went on to lift the cup. UCD beat Monkstown 12-3 in the final. Trinity did lift the Dublin Metropolitan Cup that year.

| 1923/24 | | | | | |
|---|---|---|---|---|---|
| | Result | For | Against | Date | Comment |
| Lansdowne | Won | 3t | 1pg | 6th Oct | Didn't play |
| Palmerston | Won | 1g, 4t | 1t | 11th Oct | Didn't play |
| Bective | Won | 2t | 1t | 13th Oct | Didn't play |
| Wanderers | Won | 6t | 2g | 20th Oct | Played and scored 5 tries |
| UC Dublin | Drew | 1g, 1t | 1g, 1t | 25th Oct | Played. Didn't score |
| Blackrock | Won | 2t | Nil | 29th Oct | Cussen away at Centenary Game |
| Old Wesley | Won | 2g, 1t | nil | 31st Oct | Cussen away at Centenary Game |
| NIFC | Won | 2t | 1pg | 3rd Nov | Cussen scored a try |
| Bective | Won | 1g, 1t | 1pg, 1t | 7th Nov | No match report |
| Blackrock | Won | 1g, 2t | 1t | 14th Nov | Didn't play |
| Instonians | Won | 1t, 2t | 3t | 17th Nov | Not mentioned in match report |
| Edinburgh | Won | 1g | 1t | 23rd Nov | Cussen scored a try |
| Oxford | Lost | nil | 3g, 1dg, 1t | 24th Nov | Not mentioned in match report |
| Queen's | Won | 2g, 1pg, 1t | 1g, 1dg | 3rd Dec | Cussen scored a try |
| Monkstown | Won | 1g, 1dg, 3t | 1pg | 10th Dec | Cussen scored 3 tries |
| Clontarf | Won | 5g, 1dg, 4t | nil | 15th Dec | Didn't play |
| Cambridge | Lost | 1g, 1pg, 3t | 3g, 1dg, 1t | 22nd Dec | Cussen scored a try |
| Old Wesley | Won | 3g, 1t | nil | 14th Jan | Denis didn't play |
| Wanderers | Won | 1g, 3t | 1g, 1dg, 1pg | 23rd Jan | No match report |

# Trinity

| | | | | | |
|---|---|---|---|---|---|
| Liverpool | Won | 2g, 1pg, 3t | nil | 4th Feb | Denis didn't play |
| Monkstown | Won | 5g, 6t | nil | 13th Feb | Cussen scored 2 tries |
| UC Dublin | Won | 3g, 1pg | 1t | 16th Feb | Not mentioned in match report |
| Cork Con | Lost | 1g, 1t | 3t | 18th Feb | Cussen scored a try |
| UC Cork | Won | 1g, 2t | 2t | 23rd Feb | Cussen scored a try |
| Lansdowne | Won | 2g, 2t | nil | 10th Mar | Cussen scored 2 tries |
| UC Dublin (Cup) | Lost | 2t | 1g, 2t | 17th Mar | Cussen scored both tries |

*Dublin University FC games 1923/24 Season*

*The Cussen Brothers – Jack, Denis, Bertie and Michael (sitting)*
*Photo taken at Trinity College*

## Athletics

Having missed most of the athletic season the previous year, Denis Cussen was back by the time the 1924 competition season started. He wasn't at his best though and it cost him. Ahead of him was the Trinity Championship and the IAAA Championship which that year was the qualifier event for both the Olympic team and the Tailteann Games team.

In the annual Trinity Athletics Championship, Denis and Robert Rowan Woods went head-to-head. Cussen had missed the previous year giving Woods an open run at the title. Denis wanted it back. The 1924 competition was held at College Park on Wednesday 21st May.

In the 100-yards, Woods won the first heat in a time of 10.8 seconds. Cussen won the second heat in 11 seconds which was slow for him at this stage in his career and an indication that he wasn't fully recovered from the problem ankle. In the final Cussen beat his opponent by inches. The winning time was 10.8 seconds. Woods won the 220-yards and 440 yards, neither of which Cussen competed in. In the long jump, Denis Cussen had to settle for second place. His jump of 19 feet and 5 inches was beaten by his little brother Bertie who managed an inch and a half more than him.

At the National Championship at Croke Park on 7th and 8th June, Cussen's poor form continued. He didn't place in the 100-yards and could only manage third in the long jump. He needed more time to fully recover from his injured ankle. He would miss out on the Olympic Games but had qualified for the Tailteann Games.

# 1924/1925

In the 1924/25 rugby season, Denis was joined full time in the Trinity first team by his brother Bertie. Bertie had been a star at centre for the Blackrock College team and it soon became apparent that he was stronger in that position than the incumbent Mark Sugden. Sugden was moved to scrum half to facilitate Bertie and went on to be capped at scrum half by Ireland and is regarded as one of the best scrum halves ever to play the game.

Left out of the international team after his poor form the previous year, Denis focused on the Trinity team. Also joining him on the team was Arthur Odbert with whom he had won the Leinster Schools Senior Cup in 1917 and Edward Bingham. Bingham, from Dungannon, went on to be a polar explorer and has a glacier in Antarctica named after him.

Cussen had a strong start to the season. He played in nine of the first ten games and scored ten tries. From the match reports that are available for the season, he went on to score at least twenty-seven tries in twenty-two games.

In the Leinster Senior Cup, Trinity's sequence of losing to the eventual winners continued. The came up against Bective on 23rd March and narrowly lost 5-6. Bective went on to win the cup by beating UCD in the final 3-nil.

Dublin University 1st XV 1924/25
Back: J Wallace, R Cussen, O Chance, A Pike, R Dowse, I Stuart, J Clinch
Front: M Sugden, T Millin, E Bingham, R Crichton, D Cussen, C Nunns, A Odbert

| 1924/25 | | | | | | |
|---|---|---|---|---|---|---|
| | Result | For | Against | Date | Comment | |
| Lansdowne | Won | 3g, 1t | 1g | 6th Oct | Didn't score. Poor game as per reports | |

# Trinity

| | | | | | |
|---|---|---|---|---|---|
| Bective | Won | 2g, 1pt, 1t | 1g | 13th Oct | Cussen didn't score |
| Palmerston | Won | 7g, 1pg, 6t | nil | 16th Oct | 56-nil. Cussen scored 3 tries |
| Old Wesley | Won | 1g, 1pg, 2t | nil | 20th Oct | Didn't play |
| Monkstown | Won | 3g, 3t | 1pg, 1t | 23rd Oct | Cussen scored a try |
| Blackrock | Lost | 1g | 1g, 1t | 27th Oct | Cussen scored a try |
| UC Dublin | Won | 3g, 1t | nil | 30th Oct | Cussen scored a try and hit the post with a drop goal |
| Queens | Won | 1g, 6t | 1g, 3t | 10th Nov | Cussen scored 2 tries |
| NIFC | Lost | 1pg, 1t | 1g, 3t | 17th Nov | Cussen scored a try |
| Glasgow | Won | 2g, 4t | 1g | 20th Nov | Cussen scored a try and also kicked a conversion |
| Instonians | Lost | nil | 1dg, 1t | 24th Nov | Didn't score |
| Cambridge | Lost | nil | 3g, 1pg, 1t | | No match report |
| Liverpool | Won | 2g, 4t | 1t | 29th Nov | Cussen scored 2 tries |
| Edinburgh | Won | 3g, 4t | nil | 9th Dec | Cussen scored 2 tries |
| Oxford | Lost | 3t | 3g | 16th Dec | Cussen scored a try |
| Wanderers | Won | 4g, 1t | 1pg | 10th Jan | Cussen scored 2 tries |
| Monkstown | Won | 2g, 10t | nil | 21st Jan | Cussen scored a try |
| Clontarf | Drew | 2t | 2t | | No match report |
| Wanderers | Won | 2g, 3t | 1g | 7th Feb | Cussen scored 3 tries |
| Palmerston | Lost | 1g | 1pg, 3t | 14th Feb | Cussen scored a try and converted it |
| UC Dublin | Lost | nil | 1t | 21st Feb | Played. Didn't score |
| Bective | Lost | 1g | 2g, 1t | 25th Feb | No match report |
| Cork Con | Won | 1g, 1dg, 2t | 1t | 27th Feb | Cussen scored a try and kicked a drop goal |
| Lansdowne | Won | 2t | 1dg | 5th Mar | Cussen scored a try |
| Garryowen | Won | 1g, 5t | 1g | 15th Jan | Cussen scored 3 tries and kicked a conversion |
| Bective (Cup) | Lost | 1g | 2pg | 23rd Mar | Cussen didn't score |

*Dublin University FC games 1924/25 Season*

## Athletics

Cussen's performances on the rugby field in the spring of 1925 showed that he was back to full fitness and speed. He scored in almost every game he played from January onward. He was fit and ready to defend his 100-yard Trinity title when the championships came around in May.

This would be his last time competing in the competition as he would graduate at the end of the calendar year. He had a remarkable record; he had won the 100-yards every time he competed; he won four out of five times and didn't compete due to injury on the other occasion. When the competition was held on Wednesday 27th May, Cussen won again securing his fifth Trinity 100-yard title.

In the heats, Cussen won easily. He finished four yards ahead of his competition in a time of 10.6 seconds. In the other heat, Muirceartach Gregan beat RR Woods. Gregan clocked the same time as Cussen had. In the final, Cussen exploded from the start line. Gregan ran a strong race and kept up with Cussen but nearing the tape, he faded and lost by a couple of feet. RR Woods took third place. Denis' winning time was 10.4 seconds.

In the 220-yards, Woods won the first heat. Gregan won the second, just ahead of Cussen. In the final, Gregan came first, Woods second and Cussen claimed the bronze.

Cussen also claimed the shot-put and discus titles. He threw the sixteen-pound weight thirty-five feet and four inches. In the discus event, almost nonchalantly, his first throw of 115 feet and 2 inches set a record for the championships. He didn't have to throw again and took the gold medal.

*Denis Cussen throwing a record in the discus in 1924*

## 1925/1926

1925/26 was Denis Cussen's final year at Trinity and it would be his most successful on the rugby field. He also regained his place in the Irish international team during a year in which Trinity won the Leinster Senior Cup and the Bateman Cup.

Denis should have been named captain of the Trinity team that year but was overlooked due to residual anti-Catholic culture that still existed at the college. The Pike brothers from Tipperary were vocally anti-Catholic and so Terence Millin was named captain. Cussen's brother Bertie had to overcome the same culture before becoming captain the following year.

**Dublin University 1st XV 1925/26**
Back: J Hewitt, C Nunns, O Chance, J Wallace, A Buchannan, P O'Donovan, R Pike, R Flood
Front: D Cussen, R Dowse, M Sugden, T Millin, R Cussen, A Pike, E Bingham

As usual there were some new faces in the team. Allan Buchanan joined. He would go on to win six caps for Ireland in the front row. Sadly, he died in a car accident on his way home from a game at Twickenham in 1952. Also in the team for the year were two of four Pike brothers. There were four Pike brothers in all. From Thurles Andrew and Robert were on the Trinity team this year. While they had success this year with Trinity, neither were capped. Their brothers

Trinity

Victor and Theodore were both capped and also both knighted. Theodore won seven Irish caps and was knighted as a Governor of British Somaliland. Victor was capped thirteen times and knighted for services as a priest in the British army in WW2.

Denis opened the season in style, scoring six tries in the first three games against Bective, Old Wesley and Wanderers. By the time Trinity went on their tour of the British Universities at the end of November he had scored three more. On the tour, he played the game against Oxford University but didn't score. He then returned home to sit his final surgery exams. After his exams he went on a four-game scoring spree, scoring tries against Monkstown, Queens University, UCD and Cambridge.

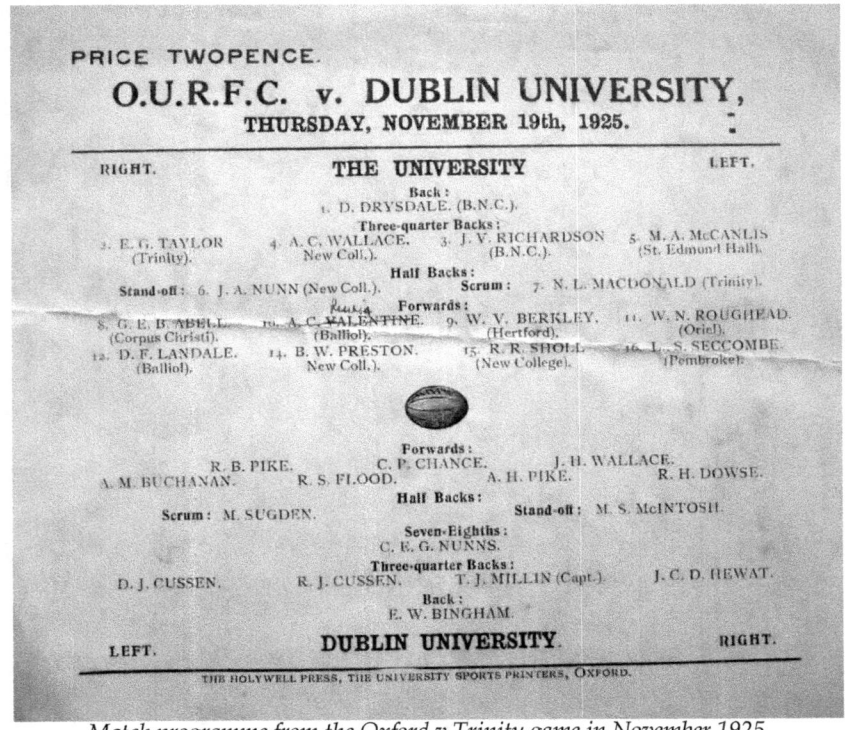

*Match programme from the Oxford v Trinity game in November 1925*

In December, Denis passed his final exams and was now a qualified doctor. He sent a telegram home to inform his parents at the start of December and was home in person to celebrate for Christmas.

After a break for the internationals, he returned for the Leinster Senior Cup. In the semi-final Trinity were drawn against Bective. Cussen scored two tries as Trinity easily won the game.

In the Leinster Senior Cup final, played on 12th April at Lansdowne Road, Cussen again scored as Trinity lifted the cup by beating UCD. The final pass that put him through for the try came from his brother Bertie. Denis Cussen had won the Leinster Senior Cup twice, in his first year at Trinity and again in his last.

*The Trinity team that won the Leinster Senior Cup in 1926*
Back row: AH Pike, DJ Cussen, RH Dowse, AM Buchanan, M Sugden, TJ Millin, R Flood, C Nunns, JT Paul, RB Pike, JC Cherry
Front row: N McIntosh, RJ Cussen, E Bingham, JH Wallace

*Denis Cussen in to score his try in the Leinster Senior Cup Final. Bertie who passed the ball to him is extreme right.*

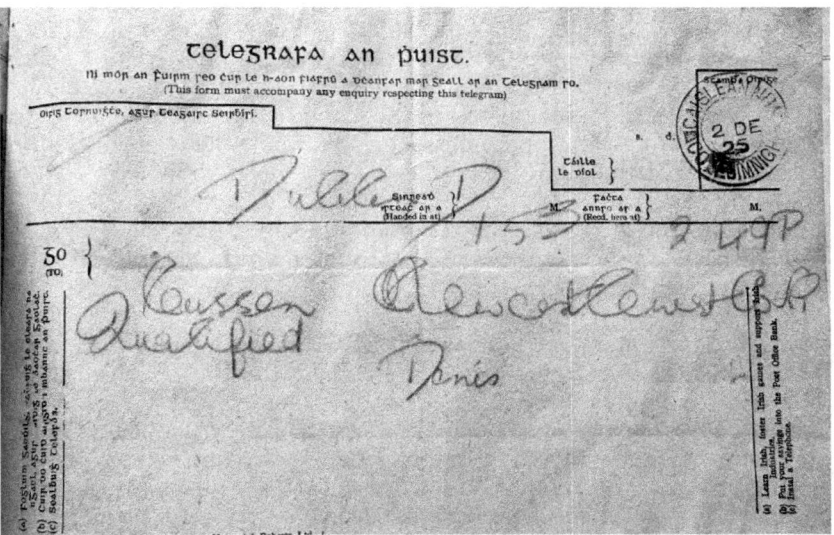

*The telegram Denis sent home when he graduated in December 1926*

## Bateman Cup winners 1926

Victory in the Leinster Senior Cup secured Dublin University's qualification for the Bateman Cup. The Great War had claimed the lives of numerous medical professionals, including Captain Arthur Cyril Bateman and his brother, Major Reginald Bateman. Both were Irishmen and the sons of Godfrey Bateman, who served as Inspector of Schools in Ireland prior to the establishment of the Irish Free State.

Arthur, a proficient rugby player, represented Trinity during his medical studies and also earned international caps for Ireland in cricket. Upon the outbreak of war, he joined the Royal Army Medical Corps and served at Ypres, where he was awarded the Military Cross *"for conspicuous gallantry and devotion to duty in repeatedly going round the front line and attending to the wounded, who had been lying out in some cases for two days. Although continually exposed to hostile sniping and machine gun fire, he displayed the utmost disregard of danger."* Eight months later, on 28th March 1918, Bateman *"manfully stuck to his post until the Germans were within a few yards of him, when he started to retire along with his orderlies. Unfortunately, he was hit, and fell into the hands of the enemy."* His body was never recovered.

Arthur's elder brother, Reginald, had likewise played for Trinity during his university years. He subsequently emigrated to Canada, taking up a professorship in English at the University of Saskatchewan. At the war's outset, he enlisted in the Canadian Expeditionary Force. Serving with the 46th Canadian Infantry Battalion, he was killed when a shell struck battalion headquarters at Dury, near Amiens.

In memory of his sons, Godfrey Bateman instituted the Bateman Cup in 1922. The competition featured the four provincial cup winners in a knockout format.

The inaugural Bateman Cup was claimed by Lansdowne, who defeated Cork Constitution 6–5 at Lansdowne Road. Bective Rangers secured the title in 1923, while Queen's University became the first Ulster side to win in 1924. Young Munster achieved a notable victory in 1928 beating hot favourites Lansdowne in the final. Their win still remembered in their club son Beautiful Beautiful Munsters – *"But they all gave it up for the Bateman Cup was won by the Yellow Road"*.

The 1926 provincial champions were Trinity, Garryowen, Collegians, and Galwegians. Trinity were drawn against Galwegians in the semi-final on 15th April 1926; Denis Cussen did not feature in the match, which Trinity won convincingly, scoring three goals and three tries to a single try.

The final took place on 17th April 1926 at Lansdowne Road, with Garryowen having prevailed in the other semi-final. Cussen who was by then living in London, returned for the final and scored two tries as DUFC beat Garryowen 13-nil to win the title.

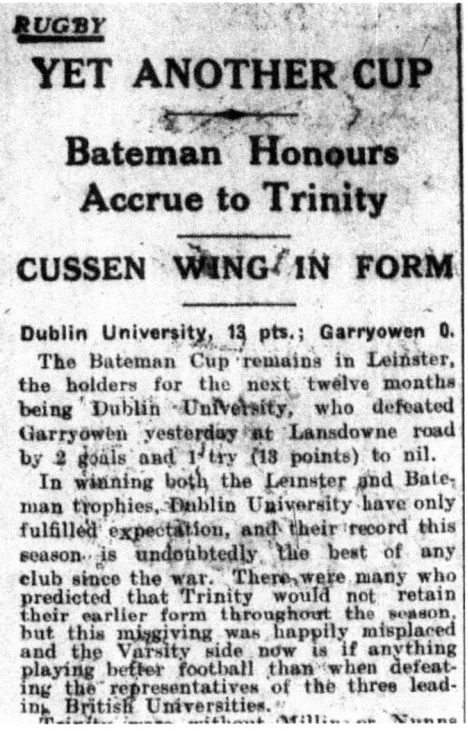

| 1925/26 | | | | | |
|---|---|---|---|---|---|
|  | Result | For | Against | Date | Comment |
| Bective | Won | 4g, 2pg, 2t | 1g, 1t | 3rd Oct | Cussen scored a try |
| Old Wesley | Won | 3g, 1dg, 5t | 1pg, 2t | 10th Oct | Cussen scored 4 tries |
| Wanderers | Drew | 1pg | 1pg | 15th Oct | Cussen scored a try |
| Blackrock | Won | 2g, 6t | nil | 24th Oct | Played. Didn't score |

# Trinity

| Opponent | Result | For | Against | Date | Notes |
|---|---|---|---|---|---|
| Liverpool | Won | 4g, 2pg, 2t | nil | 28th Oct | No match report published |
| Lansdowne | Won | 3g, 1t | 1g, 2t | 1st Nov | Cussen scored 2 tries |
| NIFC | Lost | 1pg | 1g, 1t | 14th Nov | No match report published |
| Oxford | Won | 4g, 1pg | 1t | 19th Nov | Played. Didn't score |
| Edinburgh | Won | 1g, 1pg | 1t | | Denis returned to Dublin for Surgery Exam and didn't play Edinburgh or Glasgow |
| Glasgow | Won | 1g, 2t | 1g, 1t | | |
| Monkstown | Lost | 1g | 1g, 2t | 30th Nov | Cussen scored a try |
| Queens | Lost | 2t | 2g | 7th Dec | Cussen scored a try |
| UC Dublin | Won | 2t | 1t | 10th Dec | Cussen scored a try |
| Cambridge | Won | 2t | 1g | 18th Dec | Cussen scored a try |
| Palmerston | Won | 1g, 3t | 1pg, 1t | | No match report. |
| Instonians | Lost | 1g, 1t | 3g, 1t | 16th Jan | Disallowed try for foot in touch |
| Wanderers | Won | 4t | 1g, 1t | 20th Jan | didn't play |
| UC Cork | Won | 4g, 1pg, 1t | Nil | 12th Feb | On International duty - Didn't play |
| Garryowen | Won | 4g, 1pg | 1g, 1t | | No match report. |
| UC Cork | Won | 4g, 1pg, 1t | Nil | 17th Feb | No match report. |
| Cork Con | Won | 3t | 1t | 20th Feb | Didn't play |
| Bective | Won | 1g, 1pg, 4t | 1dg | 1st Mar | Didn't play |
| UC Dublin | Lost | 1t | 1g, 1t | 3rd Mar | Didn't play |
| Bective (Cup) | Won | 4g, 3t | Nil | 15th Mar | Cussen scored 2 tries |
| **UC Dublin (Cup Final)** | Won | 1g, 2t | 1t | 12th Apr | Cussen scored a try |
| Galwegians (Bateman Cup) | Won | 3g, 3t | 1t | 15th Apr | Didn't play |
| **Garryowen (Bateman Cup Final)** | Won | 2g, 1t | Nil | 17th Apr | Cussen scored 2 tries |

*Dublin University FC games 1925/26 Season*

By the time the athletics season started in the late spring of 1926, Denis had already graduated from Trinity and was working in London. He didn't take part.

# Hospitals Rugby

Rugby has had a long association with the medical community. Guy's Hospital RFC is the oldest rugby club in the world, having been established in 1843. The oldest Rugby competition is the London Hospitals Cup who's first final was played between Guys Hospital and St Georges Hospital in 1875. The same applies in Ireland. Ireland's first ever international, played against England in 1875 featured five medical students. Of the first two hundred players capped for Ireland, forty-four had medical backgrounds or had trained in Dublin hospitals.

## Dublin Hospitals Rugby

The Dublin medical community put together a Dublin Unified Hospitals team in 1878. Featuring players from each of the Dublin teaching hospitals, they started playing an annual fixture against "The Rest". "The Rest" being a team made up from the various rugby clubs around Dublin. This annual game continued to be played up until the 1930s.

The Dublin Hospital Challenge Cup was inaugurated in 1881. Among the committee members that put the competition together was Henry Stoker. A nephew of Bram Stoker who wrote Dracula, Henry had two brothers Frank and Earnest who would both go on to play for the Irish rugby team. Frank Stoker would also go on to win the Wimbledon Doubles title on two occasions 1890 and 1893.

The first competition featured Richmond, Jervis Street, Sir Patrick Duns, Royal City of Dublin (Baggot St), Adelaide, Mercers, Dr Steevens and Meath Hospitals. Duns and Meath played the final at Lansdowne Road on 14th March 1882. The Meath Hospital won 5-3. Eligibility to play in the competition was that you had to be a medical student, intern or qualified doctor.

The cup itself was originally a hunting trophy crafted in 1812 and was purchased by the Hospitals Committee for £50 in 1881 and is still used today.

Over the years some of Ireland's greatest players, had played Hospitals Rugby. Karl Mullen, Jammie Clinch, Tom Crean, Limerick's two-time Lion Bill Mulcahy and Ireland's first ever Olympic gold medal winner Pat O'Callaghan had all played Hospitals rugby during their university years.

There was no Hospitals Cup played during the first world war. It restarted again in 1920, coinciding with Denis Cussen entering Trinity and becoming eligible to play in the competition. Cussen opted to play for the Royal City of Dublin Hospital (aka Baggot Street Hospital) as did his older brother Jack.

*Baggot Street Hospital*

## 1920 Dublin Hospitals Cup

**Baggot St Hospital 11 – Dental Hospital Nil**

# Hospitals Rugby

Denis Cussen's first game in the Hospitals Cup was a 2nd Round tie against the Dental Hospital at Lansdowne Road on 13th February 1920. Baggot St had received a bye in the first round. The Dental Hospital had played Mercers in the first round and had won to progress in the knock out competition.

The game was on the same weekend as the Five Nations game between England and Ireland and so there was no match report published but Baggot Street won the game 11-nil and progressed to play St Vincent's Hospital in the third round which was also the semi-final.

### Baggot St Hospital Nil – St Vincent's Hospital 27

In the third round, Baggot Street Hospital came up against St Vincent's Hospital and were hammered 27-nil. St Vincent's went on to win the competition by beating Dun's Hospital in the final 9-nil on 9th March.

## 1921 Dublin Hospitals Cup

In the draw for the 1921 competition, Baggot Street again received a bye in the first round but were drawn against reigning champions and their conquerors of the previous season, St Vincent's in the second round.

### Baggot St Hospital 8 – St Vincent's Hospital Nil

The game was played at Donnybrook on 17th February. St Vincent's had a very strong team. They had a dozen players who were playing for senior clubs, including ten who were currently playing for UCD. The newspaper reports said that overconfidence ruined their chances. Baggot St won the game 8-nil in a surprise result.

Cussen had a hand in the try:

> "Cussen on resuming, put Baggot St pressing with a fine kick that got touch near the St Vincent's line, and Crawford was only held up on the line. The St Vincent's backs and forwards came away two or three times, but were held up, and after Cussen had made a fine attempt to drop a goal, Deane picked up in the loose and raced through between the posts for Westropp to convert.

## Hospitals Rugby

*For the winners, Malam played a great game at stand-off and was well partnered by Westropp, Deane and Cussen was the pick of the three quarters."*

That victory, avenging their defeat the previous year, put them into a semi-final against Meath Hospital.

*Cussen Brothers Jack and Denis with the Royal City of Dublin Hospital 1920-21*

### Baggot St Hospital Nil – Meath Hospital Nil

A week later they played the semi-final at Donnybrook. The game ended normal time at nil all, in what was described as hard and strenuous game.

Meath pressed for most of the first half, and at one point it looked like one of their players, Kelly, was in but Denis Cussen running from the far wing brought off a great tackle to keep him out. In extra time, Meath proved to be stronger and they scored two tries; one by Cussen's Trinity team mate Jan van Druten.

As had been the case the previous year, the team that defeated Baggot Street Hospital, went on to win the competition. They beat Dun's Hospital in the final 11-3.

*Cussen Brothers Jack (sitting 1st left) and Denis (with the ball)
Royal City of Dublin Hospital*

## 1922 Dublin Hospitals Cup

The draw for the 1922 Hospitals Cup pitted Baggot Street against Richmond Hospital in the first round. That game was played at Terenure Park on 16th February. Denis injured his leg in the Five Nations game against England on 11th February and so missed the entire Hospitals Cup campaign that year.

Baggot Street won their first-round game against Richmond 14-6. In the second round they played Mater Hospital at Lansdowne Road and won decisively 17-0. In the semi-final they came up against Dun's Hospital who had been beaten finalists the previous two years.

Continuing the pattern of losing to the eventual winners, Baggot Street lost to Dun's who went on to win the competition.

## 1923 Dublin Hospitals Cup

### Baggot St Hospital 3 – Dental Hospital 16

With Denis Cussen recovered from injury and back in the team, Baggot Street were drawn to play Dental Hospital in the first round of the Hospitals Cup. The game was initially scheduled for 23rd January but, at the request of Dental Hospital, the game was postponed.

The game was played on 31st January at Donnybrook. Baggot Street were favourites however, despite a strong game from Cussen, Dental Hospital won the game 16-3. Remarkably, for the fourth season in a row, the team that beat Baggot Street went on to win the competition. Dental Hospital won their first ever Hospitals Cup when they defeated Dun's Hospital on 20th March. They won 8-7.

## 1924 Dublin Hospitals Cup

### Baggot St Hospital 3 – Duns Hospital 7

In the 1924 competition, Baggot Street were drawn against one of the strongest teams in Sir Patrick Dun's Hospital. On Tuesday 29th January, the teams paired off at Lansdowne Road in the first round. At this time, Cussen was still recovering from his ankle injury and, while playing, wasn't at his best.

Dun's won the game by a drop goal and a try to a try (7-3). Seven of the Dun's team were colleagues of Denis' from Trinity's first team and medical school.

Terence Millin dropped a goal in the first half to give Dun's a lead. Denis scored a try in the second half, picking up a loose pass and sprinting over the line, to give Baggot Street a lead. Late in the game, Jammie Clinch scored a winner for Dun's. Cussen was again out of the Hospitals Cup early. That year Richmond Hospital won the competition. It was the first of three in a row for them.

## 1925 Dublin Hospitals Cup

### Baggot St Hospital Nil – Dental Hospital 3

In Denis' final year of Dublin Hospitals Cup, Baggot Street were drawn to play against the Dental Hospital. On 29th January, Denis played his final Dublin Hospitals game as Baggot Street were beaten 3-nil.

Denis graduated in December 1925 and was living in London when the 1926 competition was played.

# London Hospitals Rugby

The London Hospitals Cup is the oldest rugby cup competition in the world. Ireland played their first ever rugby international, against England at the Oval in London in February 1875. A month later the same ground hosted the first ever London Hospitals Cup final. Similar to the Dublin version, the London Hospitals Rugby Cup was and remains an annual rugby knockout championship played between the teaching hospitals in London.

St Mary's, now Imperial Medicals, are the most successful team in the competition, however, when Denis was competing in it, Guys Hospital was dominant. Between 1900 and 1930, Guys Hospital won eighteen of the twenty-four competitions.

## 1926 London Hospitals Cup

Traditionally the London Hospitals Cup took place in the spring of the year. Denis moved to London in the spring of 1926 and, while playing a lot of rugby at the time, he wasn't part of the competition that year.

## 1927 London Hospitals Cup

By the time the 1927 London Hospitals Cup was played, Denis was settled in London and part of the St Mary's Hospital team where he worked. When the draw for the first round was made, St Mary's were drawn to play London Hospital.

## St Mary's Hospital 3 – London Hospital nil

Denis' first experience of the London Hospitals Cup was on 8th February 1927 at Richmond. This was six days before Denis played his final international game against England at Twickenham in the Five Nations.

The London Hospital team had two Trinity old boys James Vincent O'Sullivan from Galway and John Macdonald. They also had a couple of South Africans Edwards Rivers Greathead and Johannes Davel. Also on the team was John Kirkpatrick Monro who would later suffer the misfortune of being held prisoner by the Japanese during WW2.

Playing with Denis Cussen were team captain, Indian born Harry Silvester Waters, Nathan Rocyn Jones who had been capped for Wales against Ireland in 1925. Another on the team was Stuart Craddock who was at the time researching penicillin at St Mary's alongside Ian Fleming. Craddock was one of the first people in the world to be treated with the

Going into the game St Mary's were underdogs. London Hospital were one of the favourites for the competition that year. However, the St Mary's forwards played an unexpectedly strong first half that allowed them to get a strong footing in the game.

The highlight of a dull first half was a burst by Cussen which looked dangerous but he was tackled by Stanley and the only real chance of the half was gone. The teams went into the break nil all.

The tightness of the game was evident in the match report the following day which said that *"the feature of the game was provided by the saving and tackling of both teams. The two-star players Stanley (London) and Cussen (St Mary's) were both well marked and weren't given any opportunity to get away".*

Hospitals Rugby

LONDON HOSPITAL BEATEN BY ST. MARY'S

In the second half, St Mary's had a slight breeze at their backs and after an hour scored the winning try. Goldstone scored an unconverted try from a chip ahead that gave St Marys a 3-nil win.

The win set up a second-round tie against the powerhouse of the competition Guys Hospital who had beaten St George's Hospital in their first-round tie.

**St Mary's Hospital nil – Guys Hospital 13**

St Mary's second game was against Guys Hospital in what was the semi-final of the competition. The game was played on Thursday 24th February.

Poor weather in the days before the game meant that the pitch was not in great condition. St Mary's started strongly and their forwards got unexpected front foot ball. Unfortunately, they couldn't capitalise as the ball was greasy from the damp and a lot of passing went astray. Gradually Guys Hospital came into the game and after nineteen minutes they scored a try which gave them a 5-nil half time lead.

When the game restarted in the second half, the weather had deteriorated and it was raining heavily. Guys handled the conditions better and extended their lead after ten minutes of the second half. St Marys never got going in the second half and ended up losing 13-nil. Denis' first experience in the London Hospitals Cup was over for the season. Guys Hospital went on to win the final.

## 1928 London Hospitals Cup

### St Mary's Hospital 3 – St Thomas' Hospital nil

Denis and St Mary's were drawn against St Thomas' Hospital in the opening round of the 1928 Hospitals Cup. The game was played at Richmond on 1st February.

St Thomas' had won the cup two seasons prior so had a strong team. In a game described as fast and vigorous, St Marys opened very strongly *"their three-quarters displayed plenty of enterprise, and the wing men, Jennings and Harvey, ran with fine resolution, but their movements always broke down at the critical stage"*.

Before half time, *"a perfect pass set Jennings in motion, and he ran so hard and with such determination that he swept through the defence and crossed in the corner, rather too wide out for Rocyn-Jones to place a goal"*. St Marys went into the break 3-nil up. In the second half St Thomas' team attacked relentlessly but the St Mary's defence stood firm and they held out for a 3-nil win.

### St Mary's Hospital nil – St Barts' Hospital 10

The win over St Thomas' gave St Marys a semi-final tie against St Barts Hospital. That game was played on valentine's day 1928 at Richmond.

St Mary's lost a player to injury in the first half and had to complete the game down a man. They tired as the game progressed and lost the game 10-nil. St Bartholomew's Hospital went on to win the competition that year.

## 1929 London Hospitals Cup

### St Mary's Hospital 71 – Charing Cross Hospital nil

In a remarkable result, St Mary's smashed Charing Cross in the opening round of the 1929 London Hospitals Cup. The game was played at Richmond Athletic Ground on 7th February.

Cussen scored the first of three tries in the first half as St Mary's got out to a 24 nil half time lead. In the second half, rather than take their foot off the pedal, St Marys continued to put their opponents to the sword. Within the first five minutes of the second half, Cussen scored one of two St Mary's tries. By the end of the game Denis Cussen had scored three and St Mary's were through to the second round of the competition.

## St Mary's Hospital 5 – King's Hospital 16

On 12th March, Denis played his final Hospitals Cup game in the second round against Kings Hospital.

St Mary's were outplayed and lost the game 16-5. The St Mary's try was scored in the second half by Harvey and converted by Marshall. The 1929 competition was won by Guy's Hospital. Denis had retired before the 1930 Hospitals Cup competition was played.

# Dublin v London Unified Hospitals Rugby

Beginning in 1894 and played up until the 1980s, an annual challenge game was played between a team representing the Unified Dublin Hospitals and an equivalent representing the Unified London Hospitals.

There were no games played during World War One and it wasn't until November 1923 that the fixture was put back on the calendar. The first of the re-instated games was played in Dublin at College Park on 13th November 1923.

Denis Cussen was selected for the Dublin team that year and played alongside some of his international team mates. Jammie Clinch, Millen, Crichton Courtney and Cunningham. All doctors. All Irish internationals.

## 1923

The Dublin Hospitals team selected in 1923 had no fewer than seven players who were or would be Irish internationals. Denis Cussen, Terence Millen (Duns), Bill Cunningham (Dentals), Jammie Clinch (Duns), Robert Crichton (Duns), Alex Spain (Mater) and Tony Courtney (St Vincent's) were all either practicing medicals or, like Denis, medical students.

Dublin: Bingham (Duns), Cussen (Baggot St), O'Meara (Dental), Millen (Duns), Steele (Duns), Cunningham (Dental), Magowan (Mater), Crichton (Duns), Spain (Mater), Courtney (St Vincent's), Clinch (Duns)

R Crawford (Baggot St), Godfrey (St Vincent's), Smith (Mater), Loubser (Adelaide)

London: Gaisford (Barts), Neville, Fitzgerald, Miller (Thomas), Bester (Thomas, McGregor (Barts), Malan (RCD), Carnegie-Brown Captain), Parker, Berth, Archer, Allen, Biggs, Collis, McLeod

As well as his international team mates, Edward Bingham had been on the Trinity team previously with Denis, as had South African Cornelius Loubser.

On the London Hospitals side were Wilfred Gaisford who played for the British and Irish Lions in 1924, South African Christiaan Bester, Harold Allen who would later become a Member of Parliament, and Irishman William Robert Collis. Collis won seven Irish caps. After he qualified, he returned to Ireland and was Christy Brown's doctor. He founded Cerebral Palsy Ireland which is now Enable Ireland.

**RUGBY FOOTBALL.**

COME AND SEE THE CELEBRATED LONDON HOSPITALS TEAM PLAY THE DUBLIN HOSPITALS IN COLLEGE PARK TO-DAY, AT 2 45. ADMISSION, 1 3.

The game was fast and interesting according to the reports. Dublin got off to a good start and O'Meara scored early. London drew level after *"A cross-kick from O'Meara to Cussen went astray, and Dublin were lucky to get off as a London man knocked on over the line. London were pressing when Malan got the ball back, and it travelled along the whole three-quarter line for Bester to score a perfect try in the corner but Miller found the kick too difficult".*

Neville scored to give London a lead but Steele levelled again for Dublin. Just as half time was called, McGregor scored the first of his hattrick to give London a 9-6 lead at the break.

The second half started in the same fashion as the first when Dublin scored early. A try by Steele drew the teams level again. A try by Alex Spain for Dublin was cancelled out by a second McGregor try. In the last ten minutes McGregor got his third and London had pulled away to a 17-12 win.

## 1924

The 1924 game was scheduled to be played in the second week of November. Denis was again selected in the team but an announcement was made a week before the game to say that he was one of three players who were unable to travel to London for the game.

## 1925

The 1925 game was played in Dublin on 10th November. Denis Cussen was again announced to play but was replaced at the last minute by John Cherry. London won the game 3-nil.

1925 was Denis' last year playing Hospitals Cup in Dublin and so he was no longer eligible to be picked for the unified Dublin team from 1926 onwards.

## 1927

After Denis moved to England in the spring of 1926, he began playing for St Mary's Hospital which made him eligible to play for the United London Hospital team in the Inter-City Hospitals fixture. In 1927 he was selected and travelled to Dublin for the game which was played at College Park on 8th November.

The London team featured Ernest Frederick, R Stanley, William Prowse, FJ Bellby, Thomas Garland (captain), Daniel Jenkins, Rodney Popplewell, JM Durr, Willem Myburgh, CD Malone, George Greaves Cameron and Harold Robertson. Denis had two fellow Irishmen on the team with him, Harry Waters from Dublin and Daniel Ryan from Wexford.

Dublin was represented by Harold Knott (Bective), Thomas Morris (UCD), Patrick Cremin (UCD), John Cherry (DUFC), Claud Nunns who had played with Cussen at Trinity, Fred Bardley, Michael Joseph Brosnan (UCD), A Smyth (Mater), Myles Shelly (UCD), S Flynn (UCD), James Liddy (Richmond), HV Tighe (DUFC) and Florence O'Driscoll (UCD). Also on the Dublin team were Morgan Crowe who played centre. He made his debut for Ireland in 1929 and won thirteen caps.

## Hospitals Rugby

### RALLY THAT PAID
#### London Hospitals Gain Narrow Win Over Dublin

Making a strong rally in the closing stages at Dublin yesterday afternoon, the United London Hospital's gained a narrow Rugby football victory by 9 points to 8 in their annual encounter against a team representing Dublin Hospitals.

The sides were on equal terms at the interval. Garland scored an unconverted try for London in five minutes and Cherry replied with a try for Dublin. Afterwards Dublin pressed strongly for a time, and a good movement resulted in Crave getting over between the posts.

Murray converted, but an injury subsequently caused his retirement, and for the remainder of the game London attacked spiritedly. Cussen crossed for a try and Durr kicked a penalty goal to give London the victory by one point.

Another international on the team was Paul Murray who was capped by Ireland nineteen times at scrumhalf.

First half tries from London scrumhalf Garland and Cherry (Dublin) had the sides level at half time. Denis Cussen scored a second half try to give the victory to London over his old team. This was Denis Cussen's final Inter-City Hospitals game. He played on in the London Hospitals competition with St Mary's Hospital for another two years.

*The Dublin and London teams in 1927. Denis Cussen is standing on the extreme left*

# Hospitals Rugby

## Dublin Hospitals Cup

### 1920

|  | Result | For | Against | Date | Comment |
|---|---|---|---|---|---|
| Dental Hospital | Win | 11 | Nil | 13th Feb |  |
| St Vincent's Hospital | Loss | Nil | 27 |  |  |

### 1921

|  | Result | For | Against | Date | Comment |
|---|---|---|---|---|---|
| St Vincent's Hospital | Win | 8 | Nil | 17th Feb |  |
| Meath Hospital | Loss | Nil | Nil | 14th Feb | Meath won in extra time |

### 1922

*Cussen missed the competition through injury*

### 1923

|  | Result | For | Against | Date | Comment |
|---|---|---|---|---|---|
| Dental Hospital | Loss | 3 | 16 | 31st Jan |  |

### 1924

|  | Result | For | Against | Date | Comment |
|---|---|---|---|---|---|
| Dun's Hospital | Loss | 3 | 7 | 29th Jan |  |

### 1925

|  | Result | For | Against | Date | Comment |
|---|---|---|---|---|---|
| Dental Hospital | Loss | Nil | 3 | 29th Jan |  |

## London Hospitals Cup

### 1927

|  | Result | For | Against | Date | Comment |
|---|---|---|---|---|---|
| London Hospital | Win | 3 | Nil | 8th Feb |  |
| Guys Hospital | Loss | Nil | 13 | 24th Feb |  |

### 1928

|  | Result | For | Against | Date | Comment |
|---|---|---|---|---|---|

# Hospitals Rugby

| | Result | For | Against | Date | Comment |
|---|---|---|---|---|---|
| St Thomas' Hospital | Win | 3 | Nil | 1st Feb | |
| St Barts Hospital | Loss | Nil | 10 | 14th Feb | |

### 1929

| | Result | For | Against | Date | Comment |
|---|---|---|---|---|---|
| Charing Cross Hospital | Win | 71 | Nil | 7th Feb | Cussen scored three tries |
| Kings Hospital | Loss | 5 | 16 | 12th Mar | |

### Dublin v London Hospitals

| Playing for | Result | For | Against | Date | Comment |
|---|---|---|---|---|---|
| Dublin | Loss | 12 | 17 | Nov 1923 | Played in Dublin |
| Dublin | | | | Nov 1924 | Selected but didn't play |
| Dublin | Loss | 0 | 3 | Nov 1925 | Selected but didn't play |
| London | Win | 9 | 8 | Nov 1927 | Cussen scored a try |

*Denis Cussen's Hospitals Rugby record*

# Leinster Provincial Team

While Connacht was established as a branch of the IRFU in 1885 and Connacht had a player on the Irish team (South African born Henry Anderson as early as 1903), Connacht were not included in the interprovincial games played each year until the Inter Provincial Championship was started in 1946/47. Before then, Munster, Leinster and Ulster played each other each year in what were in effect, trials for the impending international season. Each year, each province would play a game against the other two, alternating home and away from year to year.

## 1920/21

On 1st November 1920, Denis' fellow medical student and rugby player, Kevin Barry was executed at Mountjoy for his part in an IRA attack. Cussen had crossed paths on the field with Barry on at least one occasion and possibly more. This was the height of the War of Independence. Trinity was predominantly protestant. Cussen was catholic but his family were not political. Nonetheless, he needed to be careful in a charged political environment.

Cussen's first taste of Trinity's first XV rugby came during the team's tour of the British Universities. As a result, he was out of Ireland when one of the most significant events in Irish history took place.

### Bloody Sunday

Sunday 21st November 1920, Bloody Sunday. That morning, IRA operatives killed fifteen British Intelligence Agents at addresses around Dublin. Then, during the afternoon, British Forces raided Croke Park during a football game. Shooting into the crowd, they killed fourteen civilians including a woman, two children and one of the players. Eighty more were injured.

# DEADLY HAIL

## Thousands of Football Spectators Under Fire

## TWELVE KILLED

### Indescribable Scenes of Panic at Croke Park

Scenes of horror, which will never be forgotten by those witnessing them, took place at Croke Park yesterday during the progress of a challenge match between teams representing Dublin and Tipperary.
Shortly after the start the spectators were startled by the sound of rifle shots, and a panic ensued—men, women, and children stampeding wildly in an effort to get out of the ground.

*The Evening Herald Headline*

It is perhaps significant that the Trinity team lost back-to-back games against Queens University and Oxford University in the aftermath of the attacks. Those games were both played away from Dublin. After playing Oxford on 9th December, the team returned to chaos.

Amid the chaos of the Bloody Sunday aftermath, Denis Cussen exploded onto the Leinster and Ireland national teams. Remarkably, the Trinity team kept playing. Denis scored a drop goal in Trinity's game against Blackrock on 11th December and he scored two tries a week later when Edinburgh University came to Dublin. Trinity would have been a potential target for any reprisals from the nationalists and security around these games was heightened as a result. The heightened security and threat didn't put Denis off his game.

## Leinster Trial Match

A trial match for the Leinster team was announced for 5th January. In it, a combined Dublin Universities team was named to take on a 'Rest of Leinster' side. Cussen was not selected for either side, however, he was a late replacement and played for Universities. The Irish Independent on Monday 3rd January reported:

> "This match between Universities of Dublin and Rest of Leinster will be played in the College Park on Wednesday, and the proceeds will be handed to the Fund for Dublin Associated Hospitals. A few changes have been made from the sides originally picked, T West (Wanderers) replacing W Collopy (Bective) on the Leinster side, while J Donovan, D Cussen and V Coughlan will take the places of Marais, Russell, and de Bruyn on the Universities team."

On 5th January he played in the Dublin Universities team that played the Rest of Leinster. The Rest of Leinster side easily beat the students 18 nil and there wasn't much said in the newspaper reports about Cussen's performance. The Irish Independent merely saying *"Sullivan was sound in the centre, though at times inclined to bore Cussen into touch; and O'Connor tackled and stopped well. Cussen got few chances on the wing, and Malan and Steward were handicapped by the inability of their forwards to get the ball".*

### THE LEINSTER FIFTEEN.

After the match in the College Park yesterday, the Leinster Selection Committee picked the following team to play Munster at Limerick on Saturday week, January 15:—
J M'Connell (Monkstown); H. Cormac (Clontarf); T. Wallis (Wanderers); D. Sullivan (Univ. Coll.); and D. Cussen Dublin Univ.); J. Clarke (Bective), and W Cunningham (Lansdowne). N. Purcell (Lansdowne) (capt.); J. Bermingham (Blackrock); A. Courtney (Univ. Coll ); W. P. Collis W-n-derers); R. J. Crichton (Dublin Univ.); W. P. Collopy (Bective); P. Dunn (Bective); J. A. Mather (Monkstown).

That night the Leinster team to play Munster the following week was named and Denis Cussen was included.

*The Leinster team announced for the Jan 1921 game v Munster*

There was unrest all over the country in the weeks after Bloody Sunday. Denis Cussen was supposed to make his Leinster debut at home in Limerick but after martial law was declared, the game was moved to the Mardyke in Cork instead.

# Leinster Provincial Team

## MARTIAL LAW AREAS

### Includes All Munster and Part of Leinster

Martial law has been extended to the whole of Munster, as well as to Wexford and Kilkenny.

It was applied on Dec. 10 to Cork, Kerry, Limerick, and Tipperary, inclusive of the Cork and Limerick Boroughs. Now by another proclamation it includes Clare, Waterford (city and county), Wexford, and Kilkenny.

The proclamation of martial law is signed by the Lord Lieutenant, but another proclamation by General Macready, Commanding-in-Chief the Forces in Ireland, notifies the declaration of martial law and the appointment of Military Governors. These are to be the generals, or other officers commanding the 6th Division and the 16th and 18th Infantry Brigades.

**ARMS TO BE SURRENDERED.**

*Martial Law declared 5th January 1921*

Because of the disruption around the country, there had been little if any rugby played in Munster in the months leading up to the inter provincials and so the Munster team that was assembled didn't have any chance against the Leinster team.

Leinster won the game 14-nil and Denis scored a try on his debut Leinster appearance.

*Denis (seated on the right) with the Leinster team beaten by Ulster in January 1921*

Having won and scored on his debut, Cussen turned out for his second game in Leinster colours against Ulster at Lansdowne Road on 21st

January. He isn't mentioned in the match reports but Ulster won the game 8-5. Across the two games Denis had done enough to make the Irish national team and never looked back.

The Leinster team that Denis made his debut with in 1921 was crammed with talent. Almost all of them won Ireland International caps. Henry Cormack on the wing won three Ireland caps. Thomas Wallis won five. Tony Courtney from Nenagh, a doctor like Denis won seven caps. Another doctor, Bob Collis won seven, Dick Collopy won thirteen. The team was captained by Noel Purcell. The Purcell family were originally from Limerick. Noel was an Irish champion swimmer. He competed in the 1920 Olympic Games in Antwerp for Great Britain and won a gold medal in the Water Polo event. He proudly wore a shamrock and the word Ireland stitched into his togs while competing. By the time the 1924 Olympics came around, Ireland sent its own team and Purcell captained the Irish Water Polo team, becoming the first person to represent two different nations in Olympic history. Purcell won four Ireland rugby caps and later became a referee and Irish selector.

## **1921/22**

A year on, and with international appearances to his name, Cussen was again selected for the Leinster team in 1921/22. Their opening game was in Belfast against Ulster who had beaten them the previous year. The team took the train to Belfast the day before with some new faces in the team. Denis' team mates from Trinity, Joseph Gillespie, William O'Donel and Reuban Owens all joined the team that year.

Ulster and Ireland captain Ernie Crawford had to withdraw from the game with a leg injury and Leinster were tipped to win but again, Ulster came out winners in a poor game. Without their captain and talisman, Ulster still managed to win the game 11-5.

A week later it was evident that Cussen was finding his feet in the Leinster team. He scored two tries as Leinster left it late but defeated Munster 15-8 at Lansdowne Road.

> *"The second of the Rugby Inter Provincials was played yesterday at Lansdowne Road before a good attendance, when Leinster were lucky to beat Munster by two goals (one dropped) and two tries to two goals (penalty). The Munster men had all the better of the first half, both*

backs and forwards, and though Bradley's try was doubtful, they were worth more than a five-point lead at half time.

Munster continued to have the best of it, especially forward, in the second half, and after attacking for a considerable time Bradley landed a penalty goal putting the southerners eight points up. Munster had the better of the game in a general way till the last quarter of an hour, when Crichton from a line out sent out to Collopy who gave to O'Donnell, and he later transferred to Wallis, who dropped a great goal from outside the Munster 25. After passing between Collopy and Egan the latter made a great opening before sending out a wide pass to Wallis, who snapped up to score a fine try. Good passing by the home backs resulted in Dallas kicking ahead, and Cussen following up beat three opponents before racing round behind the posts, for Wallis to convert. Before no side another bit of passing, in which Clark, Stewart, and O'Donnell took part, resulted in the latter sending Cussen in for another try.

Cormac was a distinct success at full for Leinster, and his club mate, Dallas, played well in the centre. Wallis was variable on the left wing. Cussen, in the last half, gave quite a good display, and his first try was a beauty."

## 1922/23

Cussen continued his presence in the Leinster team in the 1922/23 season. In 1923 Trinity fullback EC Davis was called up. Mark Sugden and Jammie Clinch, both Trinity team mates of Cussen, made their first Leinster appearance. Six Trinity men played on the Leinster team that year.

Their first game was played against Munster at the Mardyke in Cork on 13th January. Cussen scored a first half try which contributed to a narrow Leinster victory. They won 11-9. Cussen's try was described as follows in the match report.

> "Cunningham, cutting through splendidly, ran to O'Connell, when he passed to Sugden, the latter gave to O'Donel, and he to Cussen who crossed far out for a try, which Crichton failed to convert."

## Leinster Provincial Team

The Leinster team who so narrowly defeated Munster in a Rugby trial at Cork on Saturday last.

The match report also described a second half try which illustrates how the game has changed over the last one hundred years. Dribbling with the ball has completely disappeared from the game over the last one hundred years.

> *"Leinster for a time took command. Collopy, Maguire and Cunningham each had dashes for the line and only just failed. The visitors were awarded a free, but Crichton's attempt to place a penalty goal was wide. Following a cross-kick by Cussen, Hamilton dribbled away. Davies should have stopped him but fumbled badly and Hamilton dribbled on, covering the whole length of the field and scoring a try. Davy hit the crossbar with his kick from the touch-line".*

A week later Leinster came up against Ulster. Having lost heavily the previous year, Leinster knew they had a tough game ahead of them and so it proved.

Played at Lansdowne Road in front of a partisan home crowd, Leinster fell behind early and never recovered. They finished the first half down by 24-3. Tries from Jackson, Stephenson (2) and McClenaghan (2) for Ulster were offset by and unconverted try by Leinster's Maguire.

The match report makes it clear that Ulster were better all over the field. In the second half Leinster came into the game a little more but the game ended 16-29. Cussen had a quiet game and didn't get on the scoreboard.

Cussen (standing on the right) with the Leinster team beaten by Ulster in 1923

The Irish Independent's report included a sub-story about the number thirteen shirt. A few days beforehand, Wales refused to have a number 13 jersey.

> "Rugby players re not superstitious, as a rule but on Saturday the Welsh side declined to wear the No. 13 jersey. Voyce of the English team, did not object to the number on his jersey.
>
> In the final Irish trial match on Saturday No. 13 jersey on the Ulster side was worn by G.V Stephenson, who was more responsible for the victory than any other player, and Ulster won by a margin of 13 points."

## 1923/24

In the last week of May 1923 Denis Cussen injured his ankle during the athletics season. While he was running again within six weeks, the injury hampered him for eighteen months and so he played less rugby in 1924 in the lead up to the Olympic Games. He was selected for the Leinster team in January 1924 and played in both inter-provincials that year.

# Leinster Provincial Team

Leinster's opening game was against Munster at Lansdowne Road on 5th January 1924. Leinster won the game at a canter by 23-nil and Denis was on the scoreboard.

For those that would end up playing on the Irish team in the Five Nations this was the first of a series of games. A week later, the second interprovincial game was to be played. A week after that, the Ireland trial game was scheduled and that was quickly followed by the opening Five Nations game against France.

*Denis Cussen sitting on the left with the Leinster v Munster 1924*

It was a poor-quality game, played in miserable conditions and in front of a miserable crowd. The match report in the Irish Independent read *"Munster at no part of the game ever raised the slightest hope of redeeming themselves and shaped as a very moderate side"*. To their defence, they lost a man after ten minutes to injury and played the rest of the game a man short. In the first half Leinster didn't take advantage of their superior skill or numbers and only managed to score one try (by Collopy). That try wasn't converted and the first half ended 3-0 to Leinster.

> *"The first items of interest in the second half were a good dribble by Crichton and a fine run by Cussen. Play was near half-way when good passing by Clarke and Barrington saw Sugden giving the "dummy" twice to score behind the posts and Ballagh converted. In the last*

*twenty minutes the Leinster forwards seemed to wake up and added five tries. Clever passing by Collis and Collopy resulted in Collopy crossing, and next Sugden gave to Cussen, who trust over."*

Wingers Alfred Atkins and Jim Ganly, and lock Charles Hallaran added tries as Leinster routed their opponents.

A week later, on Saturday 12th January, Leinster travelled to Belfast. This was a historic game as it was the first to be played at Ravenhill. Prior to 1924, Ulster games were played at Balmoral.

In bitter cold, Leinster were beaten 14-6. It could have been more as Ulster played three-quarters of the game with one man less after GV Stephenson went off injured.

Leinster scored first after Robert Crichton charged down an Ernie Crawford kick. Mark Sugden picked up the loose ball and dove over the line to score. Crawford made amends when he kicked a penalty to bring the teams level. Tries to Crawford and McClenaghan gave Ulster a 11-3 lead at the break. Ulster pushed further ahead early in the second half when Gardiner scored. A brief rally in the closing stages for Leinster wasn't enough. Crichton scored to make it 14-6 and that was it.

After four attempts, Denis had four losses against Ulster. They were by far the most dominant province at that time.

## 1924/25

With the distraction of his attempt to qualify for the 1924 Olympic Games behind him, and with his ankle injury now fully healed, Cussen threw his full focus on rugby in the winter of 1924 and spring of 1925.

The first of the Inter Provincials was held a little earlier than usual, at the end of November 1924. Denis was selected for the Leinster team

## Leinster Provincial Team

that travelled to Limerick to play Munster at the Markets field. Munster had been poor for the previous few years but this year they put up a strong show and were narrowly beaten by Leinster 13-16. With the game being in Limerick, it is certain that Denis would have had a lot of family support in the crowd of 5000 spectators. As usual, due to the time of year that the games were played, the conditions were challenging and the field was soggy. For the forwards it was appealing but for a sprinter like Denis, it made life difficult.

### A FORWARD STRUGGLE.

#### Kennedy's Great Display for Leinster.

Leinster, 16 pts.; Munster, 13 pts.

The huge attendance which witnessed the meeting of Munster and Leinster in the first Inter-Provincial of the season at Limerick on Saturday was treated to a thrilling game. The adverse conditions of

Leinster had the best of the opening half and were ahead by 11 points at half time. Two penalties kicked by Leinster full back D Kennedy of Wanderers gave Leinster a strong start. Cork's John Jagoe, who played for Dolphin, intercepted and ran in a try for Munster but then Leinster scored twice before half time. Eugene Davy let Hogan away to run in a try and that was followed by Collopy scoring a try from a cross kick.

Munster rallied in the second half. McCormack scored a try for Munster. This was followed by another by Hanly who collected from a line out and scored. Munster were unlucky not to score again and Leinster held on to win 16-13. Denis Cussen is not mentioned in match reports so had a quiet game but conditions meant that it was really a forward's tussle.

# Leinster Provincial Team

*Cussen sitting third from the right with the Leinster team that defeated Munster in Limerick in December 1924*

Two weeks after the game in Limerick, Cussen and the Leinster team played Ulster at Lansdowne Road. In much better conditions than they had experienced in Limerick, Denis scored his one and only win over Ulster in six attempts and he was the man of the match with two tries.

In the first half Cussen played an important role both in attack and defence. At one point Hewitt from Ulster picked up a loose ball and made an impressive run. He looked certain to score but Cussen intercepted him and put in a huge clearing kick to touch. Then not long before the interval, a rush by the Leinster forwards brought play into the Ulster half and Terence Millen picked the ball from the scrum, passed to Cussen who dove over for a try. A second try by Atkins gave Leinster an 8-nil half time lead.

A brilliant solo try, scored by Ulster's Galloway in the second half, gave Ulster hope. He received a kick, ran half the length of the field, chipped the ball over the advancing Kennedy, gathered and ran over to score. Denis Cussen then put the game out of Ulster's reach. Mid way through the half, he picked up a ball that went astray and burst over to score his second try of the game. Leinster won the game 11-3.

## 1925/26

Leinster's first Inter Provincial game in December 1925 was against Munster. When the team was announced on 13th, six days ahead of the game at Lansdowne Road, Denis Cussen was named in a very strong team that featured eleven internationals.

Cussen was in exceptional form at the time. He scored for Trinity against Queens on 7th December. He scored again in their game against UCD on 10th December and on the day before they were due to play Munster, he scored for Trinity against Cambridge.

There is no indication as to why but when Leinster took on Munster, Cussen didn't play. With so many games in quick succession and his final exams also happening, he must have been exhausted.

Over December and January 1926, Denis was in transition in his personal life. He graduated from Trinity in December, went home to Newcastle West for Christmas and in January took up a role at St

Leinster Provincial Team

Mary's Hospital in London. Over this period his rugby life was very hectic. Playing for nine different teams on both sides of the Irish Sea over the course of three months he was a busy man. Without Cussen, Munster won the game 37-11.

*Evening Herald – 8th January 1926*

Denis Cussen's was back in the Leinster team a month later as they tool on in the second Inter-Provincial game at Ravenhill. Leinster lost 22-16 in a fast and exciting game. The newspaper report said that Ulster were deserving winners and the feature of the play was the all-round excellence of the Ulster backs who rose to totally unexpected heights. It went on to say that *"Leinster's international half-back combination failed to rise to the occasion and Orchard and Hall were never seriously troubled".*

Leinster got off to a great start when Atkins scored after ten minutes. He followed that up ten minutes later with a second but neither were converted. Ulster then came back into the game. Frank Hewitt 'left Cussen standing for a glorious try which Stephenson converted'. Before the break Hamilton scored a second for Ulster and they went into the break 8-6 up.

Two quick tries at the start of the second half killed off Leinster's resistance. Hewitt scored by leaping over the backs of two Leinster players and touching down, and Hamilton intercepted a Terence Millin pass to run in the second.

Leinster eventually worked a good movement in which Sugden, Davy Cussen, Hogan, Collis and Stuart all handled before Stuart got over for a score. Stuart, a great friend of Cussen, was only capped by Ireland on two occasions. He never scored in the national shirt but was quoted after this game as saying *"Would that this were for Ireland"*, echoing the last words of Patrick Sarsfield as he died on a battlefield in Huy. In the final minutes, Hewitt put Orchard over for a final Ulster try and they won the game 22-16.

## 1926/27

*Newspaper headlines 6th September 1926*

## Leinster Provincial Team

In September 1926, Denis was living in London. On 6th of that month, he would have picked up the newspaper to hear about one of the most tragic episodes in Limerick history. Forty-eight lives were lost the previous night, when a makeshift cinema went up in flames in the town of Drumcollogher, just a few miles from Denis' home town in Newcastle West. The tragedy was sparked when a candle being used by the projectionist was knocked over onto highly flammable nitrate film reels. Poor access led to a third of those present losing their lives in the scramble to get away from the flames. Given the proximity to Newcastle West, many local families were impacted personally.

Just four weeks after the tragedy, Leinster travelled to Limerick for their first Interprovincial game of the 1926/27 season. Leinster played Munster in Limerick on 4th December 1926. Denis Cussen was by then playing for St Mary's Hospital in London and didn't play in what must have been a very poignant game. Leinster won the game 18-6.

The following day the team was announced for the second Inter-Provincial, against Ulster a week later and Denis was named in the team for what would be his final game for Leinster on December 11th 1926.

Played at Lansdowne Road, this was Cussen's seventh time to take on Ulster. Unfortunately, he was unable to add to his solitary victory from two years earlier as Leinster were beaten 20-8.

7000 spectators turned out in relatively good conditions for rugby. Despite the successive losses, there was confidence in the Dublin press that Leinster could win.

> **LEINSTER v. ULSTER.**
>
> The following team will represent Leinster against Ulster at Lansdowne road next Saturday:—
> **Full-back**—D. Kennedy (Wanderers).
> **Three-quarters**—V. Harris (Lansdowne), T. J. Millen (Dublin University), J. B. Ganly (Monkstown), and D. J. Cussen (St. Mary's Hospital).
> **Half-backs**—M. Sugden (Edinburgh W.), and E. Davy (Lansdowne).
> **Forwards**—M. Brosnan (U.C.D.), A. Buchanan (Dublin Univ.), S. J. Cagney (London Irish), J. D. Clinch (Northern), J. Farrell (Bective Rangers), R. Flood (Dublin Univ.), W. J. Franks (Richmond), T. O. Pike (Lansdowne).
>
> \* \* \*
>
> DENIS CUSSEN, I understand, has been doing big things on the other side, and when the way is pioneered he is a match winner in himself. To be candid, however, I am banking on Sugden and Davy to balance the scales in favour of Leinster. The latter I consider a vastly improved player. Though others have been spoken of as likely to supersere Sugden, I am not prepared to believe it, at present anyhow.
>
> \* \* \*

Cussen's nerves were on show early when he knocked on after a pass from Terrence Millen. Through the half, the teams seemed level with Leinster maybe having slight superiority. Ulster were hampered when Rea had to leave the field injured. McVicker had to drop out of the pack to cover this position until her returned to the field. After fifteen minutes Leinster took the lead. Eugene Davy drew in two Ulster defenders before releasing to Jim Ganly to score. Cussen's old Trinity team mate, Pike kicked the conversion.

Ernie Crawford made two try saving tackles in the first half and that set Ulster up to be ahead at the break. First McCenaghan scored for Ulster after a lightning pass from Hall who had sidestepped Millen and then just before the break Ulster went ahead. Murray let Atkinson through at the Leinster 25-yard line, and the latter punted passed Cussen for a try which Stephenson converted. At half time Ulster were up 10-5.

Jim McVicker scored for Ulster at the start of the second half. Then Cussen scored after a *'glorious movement by Ganly and Cussen that let Ganly cut through and throw a long pass to Cussen to cross in the corner'*. Unfortunately, that wasn't enough as Caruth scored again for Ulster and they won the game 20-8.

## 1927/28

Denis Cussen played in the first two games of the Five Nations, against France on 1st January 1927 and against England on 12th February 1927. He didn't feature in the games against Wales or Scotland. By the time the inter-provincial games came around again in December, he was effectively retired and so didn't take part.

Denis Cussen had scored eight tries in his twelve games for Leinster. His position was taken by Jack 'Joxer' Arigho whose name came from his Swiss grandfather. Arigho played his club rugby with Lansdowne and went on to earn sixteen international caps and scored six tries.

## Leinster Provincial Team

### 1920/21

|  | Result | For | Against | Date | Comment |
|---|---|---|---|---|---|
| Munster | Win | 14 | Nil | 15th Jan | Cussen scored a first half try |
| Ulster | Loss | 5 | 8 | 21st Jan | Played. Didn't score |

### 1921/22

|  | Result | For | Against | Date | Comment |
|---|---|---|---|---|---|
| Ulster | Loss | 5 | 11 | 14th Jan | Played. Didn't score |
| Munster | Win | 15 | 8 | 20th Jan | Scored 2 tries |

### 1922/23

|  | Result | For | Against | Date | Comment |
|---|---|---|---|---|---|
| Munster | Win | 11 | 9 | 13th Jan | Cussen scored a try |
| Ulster | Loss | 16 | 29 | 20th Jan | Played. Didn't score. |

### 1923/24

|  | Result | For | Against | Date | Comment |
|---|---|---|---|---|---|
| Munster | Win | 23 | Nil | 4th Jan | Cussen scored a try |
| Ulster | Loss | 6 | 14 | 12th Jan | Played. Didn't score |

### 1924/25

|  | Result | For | Against | Date | Comment |
|---|---|---|---|---|---|
| Munster | Win | 16 | 13 | 30th Nov | Played. Didn't score. |
| Ulster | Win | 11 | 3 | 13th Dec | Cussen scored 2 tries |

### 1925/26

|  | Result | For | Against | Date | Comment |
|---|---|---|---|---|---|
| Munster | Win | 37 | 11 | 19th Dec | Cussen didn't play |

## Leinster Provincial Team

| | | | | | |
|---|---|---|---|---|---|
| Ulster | Loss | 16 | 22 | 10th Jan | Played. Didn't score |

| 1926/27 | | | | | |
|---|---|---|---|---|---|
| | **Result** | **For** | **Against** | **Date** | **Comment** |
| Munster | Win | 18 | 6 | 4th Dec | Cussen didn't play |
| Ulster | Loss | 8 | 20 | 10th Jan | Played and scored |

*Denis Cussen's Leinster Caps*

Leinster Provincial Team

# English Clubs

### Dublin University's Programme.

TRINITY this season will be without three of their International forwards. J. D. Clinch has obtained a commission in the Middlesex Regiment; R. Y. Crichton is not eligible, and will probably be seen out with Wanderers, while J. M. Stuart has taken up a scholastic position in London, and will assist Blackheath.

The brothers Cussen, Sugden, and Bingham all remain, while Buchanan and Dickson, both of whom assisted Wanderers, are expected up this term. T. J. Millin, who was "capped" against Wales last season, will captain the side.

The 'Varsity tour commences on November 19 against Oxford. Edinburgh University will be met on the 21st, and Glasgow on the 23rd. The Trinity-Cambridge match will take place at Dublin on Dec. 17, and earlier in the season (October 28) Liverpool University visit College Park.

In September 1925, as the rugby season was about to kick off and just a few months before Denis Cussen would graduate from Trinity Medical School, the Trinity team for the upcoming rugby season was announced. Denis was signed up and would be playing the season with Trinity. As the season would typically go beyond the calendar year, this left Denis with some logistics to cater for as he had accepted the role of Assistant House Surgeon at St Mary's College in Paddington, London and would be starting there after the Christmas break.

The success the Trinity team had that year further complicated things. Denis found himself in the incredible position of playing for seven different teams in the space of three months as he transitioned to life in London. In Ireland he was playing for Trinity, Leinster and the Irish team. On top of that he started playing for Blackheath and was selected to play for both the Middlesex County team and the Barbarians. He also began his St Mary's career playing with both their full team and their rugby sevens team. Between December 13th and April 24th, Denis crisscrossed the Irish sea and while turning out for nine different teams, played at least twenty-one games.

Denis Cussen graduated from Trinity Medical School in December 1925. He was selected to play for Ireland in the 1926 Five Nations Championship in the spring. His first game for Blackheath was in the middle of the Five Nations and so Denis commuted to Ireland for games both with the National team but also with Trinity who reached and won the Bateman Cup final in the early months of that year.

| Date | For | Against | Result | Competition |
|---|---|---|---|---|
| 2nd Dec | Qualified from Trinity Medical School | | | |
| 13th Dec | Leinster | v Munster | Won | Inter Provincial |
| 10th Jan | Leinster | v Ulster | Loss | Inter Provincial |
| 16th Jan | Trinity | v Instonians | Lost | |
| 20th Jan | Trinity | v Wanderers | Won | |
| 23rd Jan | Ireland | v France | Won | 5 Nations |
| 30th Jan | Ireland | | | Trial game for Ireland |
| 13th Feb | Ireland | v England | Won | 5 Nations |
| 20th Feb | Blackheath | v Cambridge | Lost | Debut for Blackheath |
| 27th Feb | Ireland | v Scotland | Lost | 5 Nations |
| 4th Mar | Barbarians | v East Midlands | Won | Edgar Mobbs Memorial. Named in team but withdrew |
| 6th Mar | Blackheath | v Oxford | Win | |
| 13th Mar | Ireland | v Wales | Lost | 5 Nations |
| 15th Mar | Trinity | v Bective (Cup) | Won | Leinster Senior Cup Cussen scored 2 tries |
| 25th Mar | Middlesex | v Somerset | Lost | |
| 27th Mar | Blackheath | v Newport | Won | Was named but didn't play |
| 2nd April | St Mary's | v Penzance | Won | St Marys Easter Tour of Cornwall |
| 5th April | Barbarians | v Swansea | Lost | |
| 12th Apr | Trinity | v UC Dublin | Won | Leinster Senior Cup Final Cussen scored a try |
| 17th Apr | Trinity | v Garryowen | Won | Bateman Cup Final Cussen scored 2 tries |
| 24th April | St Marys 7s | v Harlequins | Lost | Middlesex 7s. Lost in final. |

*Known games that Denis was involved in spring 1926*

# Blackheath

Denis Cussen's friend and team mate from both Trinity and Leinster, Ian Stuart, also moved to London at the start of 1926. They both agreed to play with Blackheath though it was a loose agreement rather than a formal signing.

Cussen's debut came a couple of weeks later on 20th February, in a surprising loss to Cambridge University. While the students had British and Irish Lion Rowe Harding in their ranks, Blackheath were the stronger team on paper. The newspaper reports suggested Cussen had little opportunity to impress.

> *"On the right of the three-quarter line that very effective attacker, Cussen, was little more than a spectator, despite the fact that his next-door neighbour was Francis (referring to T Francis International Player). It was not the fault of that neighbour that Cussen was starved. Indeed, Francis was very easily the start turn of the match, quite apart from the clever goal-kicking by which he tried to turn defeat into victory. More often than not when Francis was given the ball, he was at the time necessarily boring Cussen into touch."*

After his debut, Cussen made the dash to Edinburgh where a few days later he played for Ireland in the Five Nations against Scotland. Ireland won that game 0-3. From Edinburgh Cussen travelled to Bedford north of London for a game with the Barbarians and then he returned to London for his second game for Blackheath against Oxford on March 6th. In his absence Blackheath had won their game against Old Leysians.

On 6th March Cussen turned out at Oxford. The Oxford team wasn't particularly strong at the time and had no internationally capped players while Blackheath had number internationals spread across their team. Blackheath won easily 23-3.

Ireland had beaten France, England and Scotland in the Five Nations, on 13th March they were playing Wales with a grand-slam in their sights. Because of this, Denis Cussen missed the next Blackheath game against Bath. That weekend Blackheath and Wales won but Ireland secured a Five Nations victory despite losing to Wales.

Having missed the Bath game because of the International, Denis also missed the following Blackheath game against Birkenhead as he was back in Dublin playing in the Leinster Senior Cup with Trinity. Trinity won and Blackheath lost to Birkenhead that weekend.

Cussen was named in the Blackheath side for their March 27th game against Newport. Had he played, he would have faced Dr William Roche with whom he was friendly as they were both Limerick men. Cussen was called up by the Middlesex County team for the same weekend and so didn't turn out as Blackheath had their first win over Newport in twenty-one years.

Cussen then went on the St Mary's Hospital rugby tour of Wales over Easter and played for the Barbarians. From there he went back in Ireland playing with Trinity in the Bateman Cup. He didn't play again for Blackheath. In all he had made just two appearances for them.

*Cartoon depicting Blackheath's new high-profile players in 1926*

| Date | For | Against | Result | Competition |
|---|---|---|---|---|
| 20th Feb | Blackheath | v Cambridge | Lost | Debut for Blackheath |
| 27th Feb | Blackheath | v Old Leysians | Win | Didn't play. International duty. |
| 6th Mar | Blackheath | v Oxford | Win | Played and Won 23 – 3 at Oxford |
| 14th Mar | Blackheath | v Bath | Win | Didn't play. International duty. |
| 20th Mar | Blackheath | v Birkenhead | Loss | Didn't play. With Trinity |
| 27th Mar | Blackheath | v Newport | Won | Named but didn't play |
| 4th April | Blackheath | v Blackwell | Won | Didn't play |
| 5th April | Blackheath | V Bristol | Won | Didn't play |
| 10th April | Blackheath | V Cardiff | Loss | Didn't play |
| 17th April | Blackheath | V Leicester | Loss | Didn't play. At Bateman Cup |

# St Mary's Hospital

After only half a season and two matches with Blackheath, Denis Cussen transferred to the rugby team at St Mary's Hospital, where he was employed as a physician. Had he remained with Blackheath, he might well have faced the touring New Zealand Māori side, which narrowly defeated them 9-6 in November 1926.

Founded in 1851 and situated in Paddington, central London, St Mary's Hospital has long been one of the world's foremost medical institutions, renowned for ground-breaking innovations.

In the stratified society of 1920s Britain, professional advancement often hinged on personal endorsements. Denis Cussen was appointed casualty house surgeon in 1926, an opportunity almost certainly secured through the recommendation of Sir Arthur Porritt. Like Cussen, Porritt was an accomplished athlete, having represented New Zealand in the 1924 Olympics. As house surgeon at St Mary's that same year, Porritt worked closely with Cussen upon his arrival. Just down the corridor, Alexander Fleming was pioneering his research on penicillin, earning the Nobel Prize in 1945, during Cussen's tenure at the hospital. Several of Cussen's rugby teammates at St Mary's collaborated directly with Fleming in his laboratory.

English Clubs

As a leading teaching hospital, St Mary's vied with giants like Guy's for top talent. To attract the finest students, the faculty emphasised not only medical excellence but also the cultivation of the "whole man", producing well-rounded gentlemen who embodied the institution's values. Rugby played a central role in this ethos, deemed the ideal sport for aspiring physicians: it fostered fierce yet bounded competition, upholding principles of fair play and gentlemanly conduct. The team built lasting camaraderie and instilled deep loyalty to the hospital.

Rugby was introduced at St Mary's in the early 1860s, with the formal club established in 1866. Ever since, the institution has produced a remarkable array of international players and captains. Among them, "Tuppy" Owen-Smith, a South African cricket international, earned ten England rugby caps between 1934 and 1937; Tommy Kemp secured five. Nim Hall (17 caps), Edward Scott (5), Norman Bennet, Lew Cannell, Trevor Wintle, and Kevin Simms all represented England after honing their skills at St Mary's. Perhaps the most celebrated alumnus is JPR Williams, who amassed 55 caps for Wales and eight for the British and Irish Lions. David Rocyn-Jones played alongside Cussen for St Mary's before rising to President of the Welsh Rugby Union. Nim Campbell earned Scotland honours, while Irish international Jim Murphy O'Connor also traces his roots to the hospital's team.

St Mary's Hospital (Standing) White, Cotman, Marshall, Hinchcliffe, Wilson, Carnegie, Brown, Emmerson (Sitting) Davies, Ayres, Waters, Starkie, Child, Cussen, Barber, Jennings

Denis Cussen throwing into a line out in 1926.

Denis Cussen played for St Mary's Hospital between 1927 and 1931. This was the twilight of his rugby career. Between 1927 and 1929, Cussen was a regular on the team playing in all of their Hospitals Cup games and the majority of their club games. In 1930 and 1931 he was less involved and only turned out occasionally.

Outside of the St Mary's Hospital games, Denis also played in a few other exhibition games in 1927. On 27th February, he played for a Dominion Students team that took on Combined Universities (Oxford and Cambridge combined). In October he also played in an exhibition game at Harrow School. That game had been organised by his ex-Trinity and Ireland teammate IMB Stuart.

**Sir Arthur Espie Porritt**

Arthur Porritt was a friend, work colleague and competitor of Denis Cussen. Porritt was born in Wanganui, New Zealand in August 1900. He was educated at Wanganui Collegiate before moving to Otago University. Following his father into the medical profession, he was a

Rhodes scholar and received a scholarship to continue his education at Magadalen College, Oxford.

An athlete of note, he was the New Zealand Olympic Team's captain in Paris in 1924 where he won bronze in the 100m behind Harold Abrahams. He again represented New Zealand at the 1928 Olympic Games in Amsterdam where he competed with Denis Cussen in the 100m event. Cussen beat him on two occasions in the lead up to those games. Porritt's athletic career was then curtailed by an ankle injury. He later managed the New Zealand team at the Empire Games in London 1934 and the Olympics in Berlin in 1936. He was a member of the International Olympic Committee from 1936-67.

Porritt completed his medical education at St Mary's where he was a colleague of Cussen's. Having completed his education, he was appointed House Surgeon at St Mary's in 1928. Due to his ankle injury, he did not play rugby with St Mary's but he was a keen supporter of the team and was a regular on the touchline during games.

Porritt was appointed surgeon to the royal household in 1936 and served in that position until 1967, during the reigns of King George VI and Queen Elizabeth II.

In World War II, he saw active service with the Royal Army Medical Corps. He was a distinguished medic and served as President of the Royal College of Surgeons from 1960-1963 and President of the Royal Society of Medicine from 1966-1967.

Porritt was married twice. He first married Mary Frances Wynne Bond in July 1926. They later divorced and he married Kathleen Mary Peck in 1946.

He was created Baronet in 1963 becoming Baron Porritt of Wanganui and Hampstead. In 1967 he returned to New Zealand where he was Governor General between 1967 and 1972.

Following his governorship of New Zealand, he returned to England where he was made a life peer. Sir Arthur Porritt died in London in 1994.

## Middlesex County Championship

Having moved to London and started playing for Blackheath in 1926, Denis became eligible to play in the English County Championship.

In March 1926, during the busiest period of his rugby life, Denis was selected to play for Middlesex in a friendly game against Somerset. Lining out alongside some rugby luminaries such as England captain Wavell Wakefield and British and Irish Lions captain Ronald Cove Smith, Denis made his Middlesex debut against Somerset in Weston-Super-Mare on 26th March 1926.

> **Middlesex XV. v. Somerset.**
>
> The following XV will represent Middlesex against Somerset at Weston-super-Mare to-day:—
>
> D. N. Rocyn Jones (Old Leysians); W. H. Drogglever (Old Haileyburians), J. W. G. Hume (Old Millhillians), E. C. R. Hopkins (Wasps), and D. J. Cussen (Blackheath); E. F. Spong (Old Millhillians), and A. N. Other; W. W. Wakefield (Harlequins), R. Cove-Smith (Old Merchant Taylors), H. V. Brodie (Harlequins), S. J. Cagney (London Irish), R. H. Bettington (St. Bart.'s Hospital), A. C. McLeod (London Scottish), E. Craven (Sidney Sussex College), and J. F. Hampton (Royal Air Force.)

*Denis Cussen named in Middlesex side March 1926*

The match report was glowing in its praise for the game. *"If all rugby games were played in the same splendid spirit as the Somerset v Middlesex math at Weston-Super-Mare yesterday, there would be a greater demand for such contests than there is today. It was one of the finest sporting displays witnessed for a long time, and was made all the more delightful because both sides endeavoured, and to a large measure succeeded, to provide a high standard of play. Because of this the result became a secondary consideration and it is not too much to say that everyone who witnessed the game went away entirely satisfied".*

*Indeed, it was an exciting game. Somerset got off to an early lead when Gibbs scored a try in the first five minutes. For most of the first half, Somerset had the advantage and attacked relentlessly. Attacks by Middlesex were fleeting and easily rebuffed. However, in the last ten minutes of the first half, Middlesex ran in three tries, one scored by Cussen and put eleven points on the scoreboard. The other two tries were scored by Cagney and Spong. Middlesex went into the break with an 11-5 lead."*

Middlesex extended their lead early in the second half when Rocyn-Jones kicked a penalty. A second Gibbs try brought the score back to 14-10 but Middlesex hit back when Hopkins scored. He however was injured in scoring and had to leave the field. Going into the final parts of the game Middlesex were ahead 17-10 but down a man.

In the last ten minutes a drop goal and a try sored by the appropriately named RB Quick made it 17-17. The conversion of Quick's try agonisingly hit the post for Somerset. With just a few minutes left on the clock, Gibbs scored his third try of the game and Somerset won 20-17.

In October 1926, Denis was again selected to play for Middlesex. This time in the opening round of the County Championship. Middlesex were drawn to play Sussex in the first round and the game was played at Worthington on Wednesday 20th October.

This was the first time Sussex had taken part in the County Championships. The sport was pretty immature in that county which only had four clubs at that point. They were however captained by Ernie Hammett who was an England international. He won eight caps and was on the British and Irish Lions tour of Argentina in 1927.

Playing alongside Denis for Middlesex was Sir James William Lennox Napier (4th Baron Napier). From a military family, he had been injured three times during WW1 and was held as a prisoner of war for a time. Before the war he had been educated at Rugby School so was a rugby player since his youth. He was later appointed an OBE in 1944.

Another player playing with Middlesex was William Charles 'Wick' Powell. A powerful scrum-half, Powell was capped by Wales twenty-seven times and captained them on two occasions.

The Middlesex team was Sir JWL Napier (Richmond), CEW Macintosh (London Scottish), NM Clarke-Lens (Upper Clapton), ECR Hopkins (Harlequins), RG Stanley (London Hospital), WC Powell (London Welsh), H Ford (Blackheath), JD Collier (Rosslyn Park), JM Hampton (Royal Air Force), E Macdonald (London Hospital), W Morgan (London Irish), F Shepherd (H.A.C), WAV Thomas (London Welsh) and JF Turck (Upper Clapton).

Middlesex went ahead almost immediately when Powell kicked a penalty. Almost immediately after that, Denis Cussen scored his first try for Middlesex.

Sussex's experienced captain kept them in the game. Almost all of their play came through Ernie Hammett. He scored a try in the first half to keep them in the game but Powell, Macintosh and Morgan scored tries for Middlesex before half time.

Sussex put up a fight in the second half and scored twice through Matthews and Lee but the stronger, more experienced Middlesex team closed out the game when Powell and Macintosh each scored tries.

Middlesex won the game 25-13. Because rugby wasn't established in Sussex, many of the home fans didn't know the game but the newspaper suggested that *'this fine display of rugby would bring them back to watch again'*.

Despite having scored on his County Championship debut, when the team was announced for Middlesex's second round game against Eastern Counties, Denis wasn't in the team. It isn't clear if he was injured or dropped. Middlesex won the game easily by 49-5.

In the third round, Middlesex were drawn against Kent. Again, Cussen was absent when Middlesex lost 26-18 at Rectory Field on 2nd December. Middlesex were out of the County Championship.

Denis Cussen's County Championship career was over. He had played for Middlesex twice and scored on each occasion.

# English Clubs

| Middlesex County Team | | | | | |
|---|---|---|---|---|---|
| | Result | For | Against | Date | Comment |
| Somerset | Loss | 17 | 20 | 25th Mar 1926 | Cussen scored a try |
| Sussex | Win | 25 | 13 | 20th Oct 1926 | Cussen scored a try |

*Denis Cussen's Middlesex County record*

STOPPING HIM GOOD AND TRUE: A STRONG TACKLE.

*This incident is from the recent Hospitals Cup match between London and St. Mary's, won by the latter. D. J. Cussen, the Irish International and St. Mary's wing three-quarter, is being tackled.*

# Rugby Sevens

Just a week after winning the Bateman Cup with Trinity, Denis Cussen was played in another historic game. On Sunday 25th April, the first ever Rugby 7s tournament played in the south of England and at the home of English rugby, Twickenham, took place. This was the first Middlesex Sevens tournament that is still played annually today.

Rugby Sevens can be dated back to 1883 when a Scottish rugby club in the town of Melrose ran into financial difficulty. It was decided to host a fundraising sports day at the end of that season. Two local butchers, Edward 'Ned' Haig and David Sanderson, came up with the novel idea of playing a tournament of shortened games with just seven players, three forwards, two half-backs and two backs. The extra space on the field would make it faster and more of a spectacular spectacle. The idea was adopted, and the first Rugby Sevens tournament took place in Melrose in April 1883. Sanderson captained the winning team and scored the winning try in the final that day. The tournament was a success and the format became a regular fixture in the border regions of Scotland.

It took twenty-one years for the first Rugby Sevens tournament to be held outside of Scotland. In 1921, tournaments took place in South Shields in the north of England, Buenos Aires in Argentina and in April 1921 the first Rugby Sevens tournament played in Ireland took place in Belfast. Denis' brother Bertie played in that competition. It would take a few more years before Rugby Sevens was played in southern England and at the home of English rugby, Twickenham.

In 1926, Dr Russell-Cargill who was a member of London Scottish RFC and an administrator for the Middlesex County rugby team, announced that a Rugby Sevens competition would be held to raise funds for Middlesex Hospital. Forty-nine teams applied to take part and preliminary rounds had to be played to whittle down that number to sixteen who would take part on the day. The participants were London Hospital, St George Hospital, St Mary's Hospital, Kings College Hospital, Richmond, Wasps, Harlequins, London Welsh, London Scottish, London Irish, Blackheath, Rosslyn Park, Saracens, Old Boys, Old Blues, Old Merchant Taylors, Old Haberdashians and Old Haileyburians.

The competition was held at Twickenham and a crowd of 15,000 spectators turned out to enjoy the new sport. The event raised $1,621 for the hospital restoration fund. With his season playing for Blackheath just finished, and perhaps as an indication of his changing allegiance, Denis turned out for St Mary's Hospital and not Blackheath.

St Mary's beat Saracens, Wasps, Old Boys, and Old Merchant Taylors on their way to the final where they met Harlequins. Denis Cussen scored in the semi-final win over Old Merchant Taylors but couldn't get over the line in the final. Harlequins beat St Mary's 26-3.

The Harlequins team on that historic day was Wavell Wakefield, William Browne, James Chick, Joseph Worton, Vivian Davies. Richard Hamilton-Wickes and John Gibbs.

The St Mary's Hospital team for the tournament included Denis Cussen, Stuart Craddock who was working with Ian Fleming in the penicillin lab at St Mary's, Rupert Hadley Scott, Ernest Thomas Winstanley Starkie, Thomas Lamb Scott, William Gourley Harvey and David Rocyn-Jones.

The game of rugby sevens was so new and entertaining that a newspaper report wrote under a headline of "Seven-A-Side Rugby Lessons of the new game".

*"to criticise seven-a-side rugby from the rugby point of view is impossible, since one differs from the other as chalk does from cheese. But it is highly spectacular and when played by experienced teams, as on the border, the tactics employed must be well worth watching."*

# SEVEN-A-SIDE RUGBY.

## HARLEQUINS SECURE A NEW CUP.

### By DARK BLUE.

A big success attended the efforts of the Middlesex County Rugby Union's committee to provide Londoners with a novel form of entertainment in the shape of a seven-a-side tournament, the first ever held in the south of England.

A crowd of about 15,000 spectators attended, and they were kept amused and interested for over four hours while a number of teams fought out the various rounds on the fine ground at Twickenham. Several matches were also decided at Orleans Park and Teddington, the results of which were announced by loud-speaker, but the semi-finals and final were played at headquarters.

In the end the Harlequins defeated St. Mary's Hospital with ease, and thus became the first holders of the Kinloss Arber cup. The Harlequins were by far the strongest side on paper. They had W. W. Wakefield, W. F. Browne, and J. S. Chick forward, and J. R. B. Worton V. G. Davies, R. H. Hamilton-Wickes, and J. C. Gibbs behind—six old internationals and the R.A.F. and Hampshire captain.

## The Evening Mail Cup

The first sevens rugby competition played in Ireland was on 30th April 1921, a full five years before it was played at in Southern England and Twickenham. That competition was won by Queens University RFC.

From 1926 an annual seven a side competition was played for between Leinster clubs. Traditionally played as an end of season fundraiser, the cup was sponsored by the Evening Mail Company and the tournament was consequently known as the Evening Mail Cup.

The first Evening Mail Cup was won by Dublin University Football Club. As it was just after Denis had moved to London, he was not on the team. His brother Bertie and other DUFC players who had won the Bateman Cup that year were on the team. The winning team was made up of future polar explorer Edward Bingham, John Cherry who was the son of Ireland's Chief Justice, Maxwell Scott McIntosh from Clontarf the son of a Methodist doctor, one of the four Pike brothers, Robert, Ireland scrumhalf Mark Sugden, medical student James Herbert Wallace and Bertie Cussen.

The IRFU have recently abandoned the sevens game, a sad and retrograde step, considering Denis Cussen was one of the pioneers of the format in England and his brother Bertie was also a pioneer back home in Ireland.

# Ireland International

## 1921

Having established himself in the Leinster team in the 1920/21 season, Denis Cussen was in the shop window for international honours. In January 1921 he played for Leinster against Munster at the Mardyke in Cork in what was a trial for the international team.

INTER-PROVINCIAL RUGBY TRIAL IN CORK.
LEINSTER V. MUNSTER.

*Denis Cussen (standing 4th from left) with the Leinster team*

The newspaper reports say that *"the weather was not very good for the game; a light rain having fallen since early morning. This cleared somewhat before the match commenced, but rain fell during the second period. The ground was in fair condition, but a little heavy. The attendance was very large".*

# Ireland International

On the opposition side were established internationals like Tipperaryman, Paddy Stokes who played for Garryowen and won twelve international caps, and fellow medical student and Limerickman WJ Roche (UCC) who would later go on to play for the British and Irish Lions on their 1924 tour to South Africa.

> *"The teams were far more evenly matched than the score would seem to indicate. There was little to choose between the forwards on either side, and though Leinster got possession more frequently, Munster beat their opponents on the loose. In the back division, however, Leinster were far superior and it was this superiority that won them the game".*

> *"Munster attacked strongly but were beaten back and towards the close of the first half another movement saw Cussen score for Leinster."*

The game finished 14-nil to Leinster and Denis Cussen was prominent in the match reports, with one saying *"D Cussen is rapidly developing into a fine wing three-quarter. He has everything in his favour – pace, steadiness, and cleverness".*

Off the back of his strong performance in that game, Cussen was invited to play in the final trial match held on January 29th at Lansdowne Road. Cussen had not done enough to be selected in the 'probables' team and so turned out for the 'possibles'. That didn't prevent him from having a starring role in the game. In the first half the probables were far superior *'and it was only the sterling defence of Cussen, Sullivan and Moss that foiled the many attacks in which Cunningham, Foster, Stephenson and Cormac were noticeable'.*

At half time, Cussen was asked to switch sides and so he played for the probables in the second half. The newspaper report said

> *"Quite one of the features of the game was the display given by Cussen; Playing on the possibles side in the first half, he was changed to the probables side in the second half, and during both sessions performed brilliantly and can be said to have played himself on to the Irish team. He registered two very clever scores for the probables, while the combination between himself, Stephenson and foster was a big factor in the scoring of five tries in the second half."*

The probables team won well (27-5) and Cussen scored. He had taken his opportunity. That evening, he was named in the Irish team to play against England two weeks later. The Sunday Independent calling out the bravery of the selectors.

> "The selectors are to be congratulated on their work. They could not have done much better. Cussen's choice is unique in that he was playing for Trinity 2nd XV this season and only got his place after Christmas but T Lyle who played on the first Irish team that defeated England in 1887 was on Trinity 2nd that season"

*Denis Cussen scoring a try in the 1921 Irish Trial Game*

So good was Cussen's performance in that trial, that the Irish Life magazine printed a full-page cartoon about him. It was printed on February 4th 1921.

Another endorsement for Cussen's selection came in the Irish Independent on Monday 31st January. Under the headline **Cussen's Meteoric Rise,** it said:

> "The big surprise of this selection of D Cussen, the Dublin University champion boxer and Irish international jumper. He played himself onto the team in Saturdays mat match, scoring one grand try after beating

Ireland International

*four of the opposition in a swerving run. Cussen and Purcell (Lansdowne) are double internationalists, the latter having played with the British water polo team at the Olympic Games, where they won the World's Championship."*

The Irish Life cartoon 4th February 1921

Having played the trial match on January 29th and making the Irish team, there was no rest for Cussen who, just three days later on

Wednesday 2nd February, turned out for Dublin University against University College. Trinity (Dublin University) won the game 13-nil. Cussen was again on the score sheet.

## England v Ireland
## Twickenham
## 12th February 1921
## England 15 – Ireland 0

Denis Cussen, aged twenty, made is international rugby debut at Twickenham on 12th February 1921. Also making their debuts that day were Henry Cormack, Thomas Mayne, Tom McClelland, JJ Bermingham, Charles Hallaran and Noel Purcell.

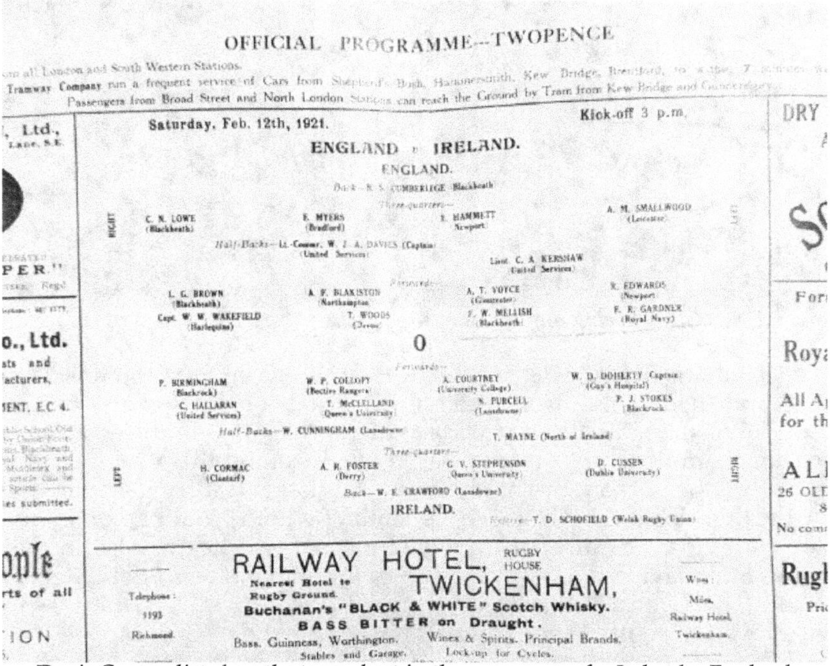
OFFICIAL PROGRAMME--TWOPENCE

Passengers from Broad Street and North London Stations can reach the Ground by Tram from Kew Bridge and Gunnersbury.

Saturday, Feb. 12th, 1921. Kick-off 3 p.m.

ENGLAND v IRELAND.

ENGLAND.

Back—R. S. CUMBERLEGE (Blackheath)

Three-quarters—

C. N. LOWE (Blackheath) E. MYERS (Bradford) E. HAMMETT (Newport) A. M. SMALLWOOD (Leicester)

Half-Backs—Lt.-Commr. W. J. A. DAVIES (Captain) (United Services) Lieut. C. A. KERSHAW (United Services)

Forwards—

L. G. BROWN (Blackheath) A. F. BLAKISTON (Northampton) A. T. VOYCE (Gloucester) R. EDWARDS (Newport)

Capt. W. W. WAKEFIELD (Harlequins) T. WOODS (Devon) F. W. MELLISH (Blackheath) F. R. GARDNER (Royal Navy)

0

Forwards—

P. BIRMINGHAM (Blackrock) W. P. COLLOPY (Bective Rangers) A. COURTNEY (University College) W. D. DOHERTY (Captain) (Guy's Hospital)

C. HALLARAN (United Services) T. McCLELLAND (Queen's University) N. PURCELL (Lansdowne) F. J. STOKES (Blackrock)

Half-Backs—W. CUNNINGHAM (Lansdowne) T. MAYNE (North of Ireland)

Three-quarters—

H. CORMAC (Clontarf) A. R. FOSTER (Derry) G. V. STEPHENSON (Queen's University) D. CUSSEN (Dublin University)

Back—W. E. CRAWFORD (Lansdowne)

IRELAND.

Referee—T. D. SCHOFIELD (Welsh Rugby Union)



*Denis Cussen listed on the team sheet in the programme for Ireland v England*

In front of a record attendance there were formalities ahead of kick off when the Irish team were introduced to King George V who was accompanied by the Duke of York (later King George VI). Having been introduced, the teams accompanied the King to the end of the stand where he unveiled a memorial tablet dedicate to all rugby men that fell in the war. These formalities delayed kick-off by ten minutes.

*Denis Cussen being introduced to King George V at Twickenham in 1921*

Twickenham ground was opened in 1910. Between then and this game England had only been beaten there on one occasion, by the Springboks. England had already beaten Wales 18-3 in the first round of the championship. Ireland had a bye meaning this was their first game of the season and it showed. England, featuring names like Arthur Blackiston and Tom Voyce, both of whom would go on to play for the Lions in South Africa, were a far superior team. Also in their ranks and playing the last of his games for England was Frank Mellish. Mellish had won a military cross during WW1. After the championship he moved to South Africa and became a Springbok.

Ireland were behind 3-nil at half time. Arthur Blackiston scored the first half try for England. Cussen got one opportunity in the first half but was dragged to the floor by Wavell Wakefield. The fight that Ireland

Ireland International

showed in the first half fell away as the game progressed and England pulled away. Brown and Lowe scored two more tries; both were converted by Cumberledge. Lowe then added a drop goal and the game finished 15-nil to England. Having won the wooden spoon the previous year, Ireland were again going to struggle this season.

*An original page from Mary Cussen's scrapbooks*

*Photo shows Denis Cussen and Capt. Hinton of the IRFU laying a wreath at the Cenotaph in London ahead of the Ireland v England game in 1921*

# Ireland International

On 17th February, just five days after his international debut, Denis Cussen was back on the field. He played, alongside his brother Jack, for Baggot St Hospital against St Vincent's Hospital in the Hospitals Cup. Denis scored a drop goal as Baggot Street beat the defending champions 8-nil.

A week later, the Baggot Street team were back in action against Meath Hospital. The game ended nil all at full time and after extra time Meath Hospital ran out winners 8-0. The newspaper reports call out two major defensive tackles from Cussen which were crucial in making the game go to extra time.

**Ireland v Scotland**
**Lansdowne Road, Dublin**
**26th February 1921**
**Ireland 9 – Scotland 8**

Denis Cussen's second international appearance was a more successful outing. He scored his first international try in Ireland 9-8 win over Scotland at Lansdowne Road.

*The St John's Ambulance Corp's Pipers leading the Scotland team out 1921*

Scotland came to Dublin confident of victory. They had beaten Wales in their previous game and Ireland had lost to England. This was the 39th time Ireland and Scotland had played and a record crowd of an estimated 20,000 turned out. The newspapers reported that *"Though previous matches between Ireland and Scotland have produced better and more brilliant play, it is doubtful if a more exciting struggle has ever taken place than that of Saturday. There were some intensely thrilling moments throughout the game and consequently, it was most interesting to watch while the issue was in doubt till the final whistle. The crowed reached record dimensions, there being scarcely and inch of standing room available".*

Denis Cussen (seated 2nd right) with the Ireland team that played Scotland in 1921

Following the usual formalities, the game kicked off to great expectation but Ireland were sluggish in the first half.

> *"Our backs failed to take the chances provided, especially in the first half, when Stephenson on three different occasions ignored Cussen, his failure to pass on the first occasion resulting in the Scots coming away to open the score. In the second half he was less guilty in this respect, with the result that after letting Cussen off on the right wing, and getting a return pass from the old Blackrock boy, the Queen's man completed a grand bit of play by scoring a try".*

> *"Cussen got two chances in the match scoring a try from the first and then sending in Stephenson off the second, while his fielding and kicking were perfect."*

After eighteen minutes and with Ireland behind on the scoreboard, Denis Cussen scored his first try for Ireland.

> *"McClelland picked up at the centre and passed to Cunningham, who sent along to Cormac. The Clontarf man cross kicked, and Purcell fielded and passed to Cunningham who put Cussen over, and Crawford made a fine attempt to convert".*

Scotland led by a goal and a try (8) to Denis Cussen's try for Ireland (3) at half time. To make matters more difficult, Ireland lost left winger Henry Cormac to injury for ten minutes of the second half.

> *"Play was ongoing for twenty-one minutes of the second half when Maybe got his backs going, and passing between Foster and Stephenson saw Cussen dashing along the touch line to repass to Stephenson, who raced over".*

Ireland scored again after twenty-seven minutes of the second half when Bill Cunningham scored. Ireland had to hang on as Scotland threw everything at them in the final thirteen minutes and, only for a wayward pass, could have scored in the final minute. Ireland won by three tries (9 points) to a goal and a try (8 points). This was Ireland's third successive home victory over Scotland.

### MONDAY, FEBRUARY 28, 1921.

# RUGBY INTERNATIONAL
## Ireland Defeats Scotland After Great Tussle
## ONE POINT VICTORY
## Record Crowd Thrilled by Exciting Finish

# Ireland International

*Denis Cussen featured in a second Irish Life cartoon after the Scotland game in 1921*

## Ireland v Wales
**Balmoral, Belfast**
**12th March 1921**
**Ireland 0 – Wales 6**

The current home of rugby in Belfast, Ravenhill, was not opened until 1924. Prior to that, Irish rugby internationals played in Belfast were played at the Agricultural Showgrounds in Balmoral. This was the venue for Denis Cussen's third international appearance. He must have gone into the game on a high, having scored in the previous game against Scotland. Unfortunately, his season had already peaked and Ireland's two remaining games, against Wales and France, would prove to be disappointing.

Going into the game, Ireland had played Wales on thirty previous occasions and had won only nine. Of those, seven were played in Ireland. Wales were also struggling in the competition but came into the game on the back of a win over France a fortnight earlier. The game was widely viewed as a playoff to avoid the wooden spoon.

Cussen again took his place on the wing at Balmoral. 15,000 spectators turned out in appalling conditions hoping to see Ireland win back-to-back games. It wasn't to be. Ireland were beaten 6-nil. A first half penalty, kicked by Cardiff winger Codger Johnson gave Wales a 0-3 half time lead. In the second half an unconverted try by Melbourne Thomas, gave Wales the win.

In a match report in the Athletic News, the reporter referred to this game as one of the dullest he'd ever attended. By all accounts, Wales deserved their victory. Ireland were hampered by the late withdrawal of scrumhalf Thomas Mayne who was replaced by Harry Jack who won his second cap, the other being seven years earlier. Ireland lost the toss and played into a stiff breeze in the first half. Wales dominated up front and won the game in the scrums. Cussen didn't get much opportunity going forward but made a few important defensive interventions.

The loss, Ireland's fourth successive loss to Wales, left Ireland rooted to the bottom of the Five Nations table and needing a victory in their final game in Paris to avoid a wooden spoon.

**France v Ireland
Stade Colombes, Paris
9th April 1921
France 20 – Ireland 10**

The Irish War of Independence was in full flight in the run up to Ireland's final game of the season. In the two weeks between the Wales

## Ireland International

and France games the Irish Republican Army had carried out ambushes at Clonbanin and Crossbarry in Cork, Clifden in Galway and Headford in Kerry, killing at least twenty British troops. In response the Black and Tans also undertook major actions such as burning fourteen houses down in response to the attack at Clifden.

Amidst rising unrest at home, Ireland travelled to Paris for their final game of the 1921 Five Nations. The game was played at Stade Colombes which would a few years later in 1924, host the Olympic Games rugby tournament.

*Stade Colombes Paris where Ireland played France in 1921*

Following Ireland's defeat to Wales and England, the game was a dead rubber with no bearing on the outlook for who would win the championship. England had already won a grand slam having beaten France in their previous game two weeks earlier. It was a must win for Ireland though.

For Denis Cussen, it was a big week. He had won his first Leinster Senior Cup with Dublin University a few days before this final international game of the season. Trinity (Dublin University) had won their first-round game in the cup before Ireland travelled to Belfast to play Wales. Since then, Cussen had scored two tries in the second-round game against Bective and another two tries against the 2nd Welsh Regiment in the semi-final. The final was played on 4th April and Trinity beat University College Dublin.

France were favourites going into the game and came away with a 20-10 win however, the result flattered the French. Ireland scored first with a try from Paddy Stokes but France hit back almost immediately to level the scores. The sides were level at half time.

In the second half, France played with a slight breeze at their backs but again it was Ireland who scored first. Hooker Bill Collopy scored for Ireland but again France hit back almost immediately. As the game progressed, Ireland fell away and France scored two tries in the final twenty minutes to run out winners. Cussen wasn't prominent either positively or negatively in the match reports.

Ireland finished the championship with a second wooden spoon in a row. Six Irish players, four in the pack including captain George (WD) Doherty played their final international game in Paris that day.

| Pos | Team | Played | W | D | L | PF | PA | PD | Pts |
|---|---|---|---|---|---|---|---|---|---|
| 1 | England | 4 | 4 | 0 | 0 | 61 | 9 | 52 | 8 |
| 2 | France | 4 | 2 | 0 | 2 | 33 | 32 | 1 | 4 |
| 2 | Wales | 4 | 2 | 0 | 2 | 29 | 36 | -7 | 4 |
| 4 | Scotland | 4 | 1 | 0 | 3 | 22 | 38 | -16 | 2 |
| 4 | Ireland | 4 | 1 | 0 | 3 | 19 | 49 | -30 | 2 |

*1921 Five Nations table*

## 1922

In 1920, the British Government passed the Government of Ireland Act (1920). That act was intended to create two devolved governments on the Island of Ireland, one for the northern counties, the other in Dublin. The Irish War of Independence ended in a truce in July 1921 and led to the Anglo-Irish Treaty which changed the plan and instead created the Irish Free State. What this would mean for the Irish Rugby team was hotly debated over the autumn and winter of 1921. Would there now be two team? Where would Ireland games be played? What anthem would be played? In the end, the decision was made to in effect ignore partition. The IRFU would develop Ravenhill as a new ground in Belfast and would alternate games between Dublin and Belfast. It would take a long time for things to settle going into the 1922 Five Nations there were no changes.

Having established himself in the Irish team in 1921 and with a Leinster Senior Cup win with Dublin University to his name, Cussen would

# Ireland International

have been confident of his place in the Irish team going into the 1922 international season.

On 4th January 1922, the first of the Irish trials took place at Lansdowne Road. Newspaper reports suggest that *'few reputations were enhanced'* on the day however, Denis Cussen made his presence known when he *'wound up a nice movement by racing over in the corner'*.

Three days after the trial game, Dáil Éireann voted 64 to 57 to accept the Anglo-Irish Treaty. Following the Treaty's ratification, in accordance with article 17 of the Treaty, Britain formally recognised the Provisional Government and the Irish Free State was established.

A second trial game was played at the end of January. Denis Cussen turned out on the 'probables' side who won the game 37-nil. Major Southwell Fitzgerald, writing in the Daily Mail said:

> "Cussen was rightly selected as he is coming into his own after having played with the trinity team who would break the heart of any wing three-quarter".

**Denis Cussen (seated 2nd left) with the Probables team Ireland trial 1922**
*Back row: Hallaran, McVicker, Wallis, Thompson, Wheeler, Magrath, Egan, Owens, Stewart*
*Front row: Murphy, Cussen, Stephenson, Collopy (Captain), Mayne, Bradley*

Cussen scored two tries in the game and set up three more. He was duly selected for the Irish team to play England in the opening round of the championship. The Daily Mail reported on February 1st:

*"In the three-quarter line chosen for Ireland we have T.G Wallis and Denis Cussen. The former, on account of his unorthodoxy in attack, is always dangerous when he has the ball, while Denis Cussen, now that he gets the ball, can make his way more quickly than anyone in Ireland over the goal line".*

The selection included six new caps as Ireland attempted to break their wooden spoon streak. One of the new caps was Sam McVicker from County Antrim who was the first of three brothers who would play for Ireland, the others being Jim and Hugh.

**Ireland v England**
**Lansdowne Road**
**11th February 1922**
**Ireland 3 – England 12**

The weeks leading up to Ireland's first game of the Five Nations, at home to England, were momentous. It was a very tense time as the Provisional Government took control of the new Irish Free State in January and the formal handover of Dublin Castle by the British on 16th January. On February 10th, the day before the game, the Free State (agreement) Act was tabled in Westminster which would legislate for the change in the status of Ireland. On the day of the game there was a gun battle at Clones railway station in County Monaghan between IRA volunteers and members of the Ulster Special Constabulary who were travelling to Belfast at the time. There were five people killed in the incident.

Amidst all this change socially in Ireland, Ireland took on England at Lansdowne Road. A crowd of 17,000 turned out to see if Ireland, with changes from the team that finished the previous year's championship, could change the trend of underperformance in international rugby. Sullivan (UCD), Wheeler and McVicker (Queens), Owens and Thompson (Trinity), Bradley (Dolphin) and Halloran (Portsmouth) all came into the team. Davidson, Mayne, Bermingham, Courtney, Doherty, Purcell and Stokes stepped aside.

Ireland International

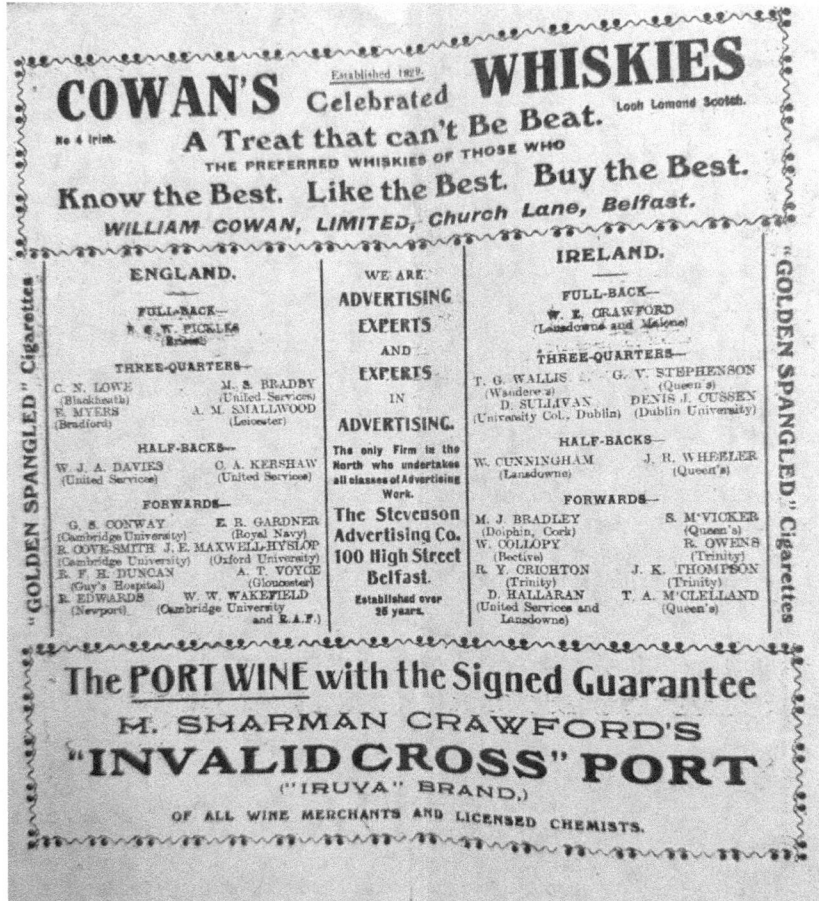

*Team sheet as printed in the match programme*

The game was played in relatively good conditions with just a slightly soft pitch, the result of the thawing overnight frost. Ahead of the game the band of the Dublin Metropolitan Police and pipers from Trinity College entertained the expectant crowd. This was to be the most entertainment that the home crowd were to have.

Ireland struggled, perhaps because of all the new caps, and were defeated 3-12.

The game was reported as:

*'Disappointing and disheartening as reasons had been forthcoming for believing that the time had arrived for a turn in the tide of Ireland's fortunes in Rugby internationals. Last season the team had improved in every match, and in the last – that against France – played a really good game. Eight powerful and clever English forward and a wonderfully skilful scrum half dashed to the ground all these hopes and expectations after thirty minutes' play. Ireland were beaten by four tries to one and deserved to be beaten by a far larger score. It was a hollow beating, and left no room for excuses of any kind. The troubled state of the country, so useful for explaining away other happenings, does not hold here, for there never were any troubles in our rugby football world, except the trouble of finding a team capable of beating England and the other countries.*

The 1922 Ireland v England match programme

*There was little consolation to be had from the match, except the knowledge that, just as the English side won the day by straight, clean play, the Irish side went under also playing the game to the best of their ability and in the true spirit of the Rugby code. It only remains for us to accept the defeat with the best grace possible, congratulate Captain Davies, Kershaw, and the thirteen other Englishmen on their play, and live on in the hope that someday in the near future Ireland will be able to place as fine a team in the field. That she will do so may not be so improbable as at the moment appears. We have not to stretch our memories back so far as the day when an Irish forward crossed the English line "festooned with Saxons" to remember seeing English teams just as badly beaten as was the Irish side in this match.".*

## Ireland International

Denis Cussen didn't get much of an opportunity going forward in the game but the match reports indicate that he played an important role in defence, making some try saving tackles and helping to keep the score down. The Irish Independent reported:

> *"Cussen was even worse off on the right wing as he only got about three transfers, but fairly came out of his shell as a defender, going down to the rushes pluckily and tackling in great style, while once he went after Wakefield when the big Air Force man was clean away, and hauled him down".*

Towards the end of the game one of Cussen's tackles on William Wavell Wakefield resulted in him leaving the field injured. He had strained his left thigh and as a result missed the rest of the championship. Wakefield would become 1st Baron Sir William Wavell Wakefield of Kendal and was knighted in 1944. He captained England to two grand slam titles in 1923 and 1924. He didn't get past Denis Cussen that day though.

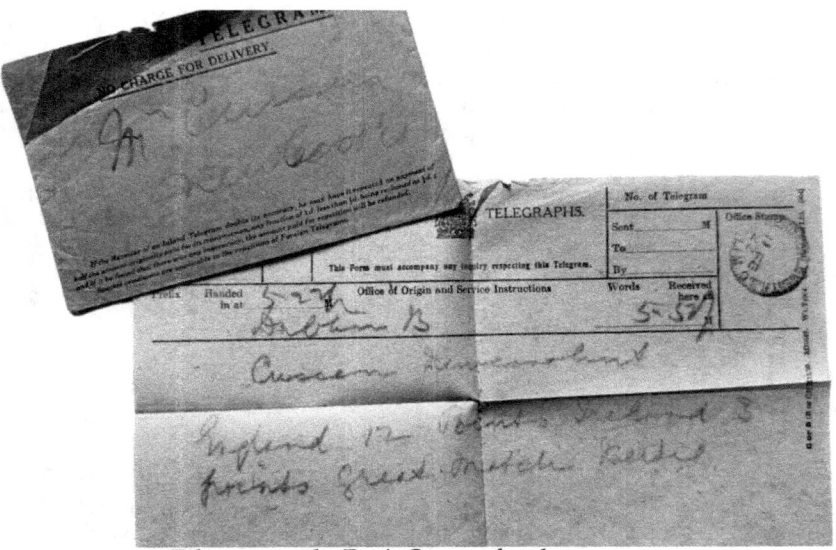

*Telegram sent by Denis Cussen after the game*
*"England 12 points. Ireland 3 points. Great match indeed".*

Without Cussen for the remaining three games, Ireland's season was poor. They were beaten 6-3 by Scotland away at Inverleigh, Edinburgh,

11-5 by Wales in Swansea but beat France at home in the final game. That win, put Ireland just ahead of France who shared the wooden spoon. Both had just two points and had the same points difference (-13). Henry Stephenson, who took Cussen's place while he was injured, failed to score in the three remaining games.

In those three games, Henry 'Harry' Stephenson played alongside his brother George. When George Stephenson retired in 1930, he had forty-two caps which was a world record at the time. That record stood until Jack Kyle overtook him in 1957. George also held the Irish try-scoring record (14) for over sixty years. That record wasn't broken until 1991 when disgraced former player Brendan Mullin overtook him. Stephenson also held the points scoring record for Ireland. This wasn't bettered until Tom Kiernan reached ninety points in 1968.

As the tournament progressed, momentous events were happening around Dublin and Ireland. Many Irish Republican Army officers were against the treaty and in March held a convention at which they agreed to officially repudiate the authority of the Dáil to accept the treaty. Civil War was brewing. Then on April 14th, six days after Ireland played France at Lansdowne Road in Ireland's final game of the championship, Anti-Treaty IRA militants stormed and occupied the Four Courts in the centre of Dublin. They occupied the buildings, hoping to trigger a military confrontation, for two months.

| Pos | Team | Played | W | D | L | PF | PA | PD | Pts |
|---|---|---|---|---|---|---|---|---|---|
| 1 | Wales | 4 | 3 | 1 | 0 | 59 | 23 | 36 | 7 |
| 2 | England | 4 | 2 | 1 | 1 | 40 | 47 | -7 | 5 |
| 3 | Scotland | 4 | 1 | 2 | 1 | 23 | 26 | -3 | 4 |
| 4 | Ireland | 4 | 1 | 0 | 3 | 19 | 32 | -13 | 2 |
| 4 | France | 4 | 0 | 2 | 2 | 20 | 33 | -13 | 2 |

*1922 Five Nations table*

## 1923

Since the last Five Nations, the Irish Civil War had broken out. At the end of June, two months after the Anti-Treaty forces took the Four Courts, the Irish National Army stormed the building. The following day there was a massive explosion at the building and Ernie O'Malley surrendered.

## Ireland International

One of the most significant weeks in Irish history took place in August. On 12th August, Arthur Griffith who had been part of the delegation that negotiated the treaty with Britain and was the President of the Dáil, died suddenly in Dublin. His funeral on 16th August brought Dublin to a standstill. On 17th Dublin Castle was formally handed over to the National Army with the withdrawal of the last British troops. Then, on 22nd August 1922 Michael Collins was shot and killed in an ambush at Béal na Blath.

On 6th December 1922, twelve months after the signing of the Treaty, the Irish Free State officially comes into existence. The treaty gave the six counties of the north, the option to 'opt-out' and on 7th December the Northern Ireland Parliament voted to do so. On 8th December, Northern Ireland re-joined the United Kingdom. From a rugby perspective, there would be no change. Rugby would maintain an all-Ireland team.

One of the most prominent rugby writers at the time was Major, the Hon, Southwell Fitzgerald. Fitzgerald was retired from the 7th Royal Fusiliers and lived in Rathmines. He died suddenly on 17th November 1922. His final article was published in the Daily Mail the day before his death. In it he was looking forward to the 1923 rugby season and reviewing the playing of an early trial game. He said *"the three-quarter line is now an active, strong quartet, of whom Mark Sugden and Denis Cussen should represent Ireland this year."* He was proven correct. When the final trial was played on 27th January 1923, Denis Cussen now fully recovered from his thigh injury, was selected in the 'probables' team. The probables won the game 28-16. Cussen scored one try in the game and *"the Trinity man was always looking out for work and did his share of defence well"*. He was duly selected for the team for the first game of the championship away to England two weeks later.

**England v Ireland**
**Leicester**
**10th February 1923**
**England 23 – Ireland 5**

Ireland International

*The Ireland team that played England at Leicester Feb 1923*
Back row: McClenehan, Hall, Gardiner, Mahony, Cunningham, Gray, Jackson, Trift (linesman)
Front row: Collopy, McClelland, Stephenson, Thompson (captain), Halloran, Cussen, Crawford, Bradley

*Four Accountants, a Student of Divinity and a Boxer!*
Irish Times ahead of the Ireland v England game 1923

*Official Programme.*          Price 1d.

# ENGLAND v. IRELAND

Saturday, February 10th, 1923.

KICK OFF 3 P.M.

## LEICESTER FOOTBALL GROUND.

**ENGLAND**
(WHITE)

*Back—*
F. GILBERT
(Devonport Services)

*Three-quarters—*
(1) C. N. LOWE   (2) E. MYERS   (3) L. J. CORBETT   (4) A. M. SMALLWOOD
R.W. (Blackheath)   R.C. (Bradford)   L.C. (Bristol)   L.W. (Leicester)

*Half-Backs—*
(5) W. J. A. DAVIES (Captain)    (6) C. A. KERSHAW (Scrum)
(Navy)                                     (Navy)

*Forwards—*
(7) G. S. CONWAY    (9) R. COVE-SMITH    (8) F. W. SANDERS
(Rugby)          (Old Merchant Taylors)        (Plymouth Albion)

(10) E. R. GARDNER    (11) W. G. E. LUDDINGTON    (12) H. L. PRICE
(Devonport Services)      (Devonport Services)       (Leicester)

(13) A. T. VOYCE      (14) W. W. WAKEFIELD
(Gloucester)          (Cambridge)

Referee  T. H. VILE, Esq.
(Newport)

*Forwards—*
J. K. S. THOMPSON (Captain)     T. McCLELLAND
(Dublin University)                (Queen's University)

R. D. GRAY      C. F. HALLORAN      J. MAHONY
(Old Wesley)      (United Services)      (Cork Constitution)

M. J. BRADLEY     R. COLLOPY     D. CUNNINGHAM
(Dolphin)       (Bective Rangers)      (North of Ireland)

*Half-Backs—*
J. B. GARDINER (Scrum)      W. HALL
(North of Ireland)              (Instonians)

*Three-quarters—*
R. D. McCLENAGHAN   F. JACKSON   G. V. STEPHENSON   D. J. CUSSEN
L.W. (Instonians)   L.C. (North of Ireland)   R.C. (Queen's University)   R.W. (Dublin University)

*Back—*
W. E. CRAWFORD
(Lansdowne)

**IRELAND**
(GREEN)

FORTY MINUTES EACH WAY.

*Ireland and England Teams listed in the match programme*

The 1923 championship was the fourth since it restarted after the war. Ireland had won just two of their twelve games in that time and had

# Ireland International

'won' three back-to-back wooden spoons. They needed something to change. Alas, the opening game away at Leicester against England who had the opposite record since the competition restarted with two championship wins in three years, gave Ireland little hope.

This was the first time in seventeen years that England had played an international game at Leicester. A large portion of the 30,000 spectators who turned out were Irish and cheering for the men in green. The day before the game it rained heavily and overnight a heavy frost covered the area, however the pitch was covered in straw so when the game came around, it was in excellent condition and suited an open game.

> *"The Irish team experienced a most humiliating defeat at Leicester on Saturday, when England piled up 23 points against them, and though Ireland got a try, which was converted, and reduced the winning margin to 18 points, the scoring of the Saxons was the heaviest ever recorded since these contests were instituted in 1875".*

> *"On Saturday it was obvious from the start that the Irish pack was outweighed, and the general impression at Leicester was that they were on the young and light side. It is seventeen years since Ireland met and beat England at Leicester by 2 goals and 2 tries to 2 tries. That side contains the names of many men who made Irish Rugby history, compared to whom our present representatives are mere pigmies".*

> *"In the first half the English side had altogether the better of matters, and the occasions were rare when the Irish representatives were out of their own 25. There was a period in the second moiety, however, when Ireland rallied so boldly and with such determination that they looked like coming out of the match with more credit in the matter of points than they actually did. For fully fifteen minutes in the second half our forwards put great dash into their play, dash that was quite reminiscent of famous Irish packs of the past. They were unable to keep it up, however, and in the closing stages of the game England had maters all her own way".*

Ireland's second half surge led to their only try and Denis Cussen played a hand in scoring it.

> *"Gardiner, dodging round the scrum, made ground before passing to Cussen, and the later thew inside to McClelland who forced his way over for a try".*

Ireland International

Apart from the try, there was little for Ireland to celebrate though Denis Cussen did come close on other occasions and acquitted himself well in the circumstances. *"Cussen made full use of any chances he got, and never failed to bring down his man"*.

*England v Ireland at Leicester 1923*

Ireland lost 23-5 against an England side that would go on to win the first of two back-to-back grand slams. For England Kershaw and Davies were superstars of their time. They ran rings around the Irish to the extent that a journalist was quoted as saying of Davies, *"If you can't tackle him, at least you could 'muss' his hair"*.

**Ireland v Scotland
Lansdowne Road
24th February 1923
Ireland 3 – Scotland 13**

With Ireland now on a run of eleven defeats in thirteen games, their next game was at home against Scotland. Despite the string of losses, 18,000 people packed into Lansdowne Road in the hope that Ireland would turn the corner. Ahead of the game the band of the Dublin Metropolitan Police played to entertain the crowd. In gloomy and wet conditions, the teams took to the field accompanied by the referee, the unfortunately named Mr Vile. Englishman Vile *'turned out in white shirt and knickers'*.

With four changes to the side that lost in Leicester, Ireland again fell short. Ireland started well and had the upper hand for the first twenty minutes, and scored first but fell away. The newspaper reports make it clear that the issue was up front where the Ireland forwards *'lacked vim'*. Ireland lost the game by 3 points to 13.

*"The two Irishmen who distinguished themselves most in yesterday's game were Cussen and Crawford, both backs".*

*"Ireland's only try was the first of the match. It was a dashing effort by Cussen, the Irish champion sprinter, who bowled over two Scots on the line as he crossed at the corner. He never got as near to the line again in the match, but he did one thing which was better than scoring almost. Gracie, the Scottish hero of their Welsh match, had hoodwinked a few Irish players, and was cutting across the centre. Then Cussen darted in, took him with a waist hold, and stood him literally on his head. The crowd was immensely pleased, particularly as Gracie showed no ill-effects of his acrobatic turn".*

Opposing Cussen in this game and scoring a try was Eric Liddell. Liddell played seven times for Scotland between 1922 and 1923. The Scotsman reported after their victory over Ireland:

*"It was entirely due to a clever move by Liddell that the Scots owed their lead. It was again due to Liddell that Scotland went further ahead.*

*Never again should it be (held) against him that he is 'only a runner'. The Edinburgh University man improved on any previous display, and he showed that he was now come to appreciate the value of his speed."*

Ireland International

Cussen would also come up against Liddell on the running track where Liddell was better known. Like Cussen, as the 1924 Olympic Games loomed in Paris, Liddell had to choose between his rugby and athletics and chose to focus on the opportunity to got to the Olympics.

A devout Christian and son of missionaries, Liddell declined to compete in the 100-yards at the Paris Olympics because the heats were to be held on a Sunday. Instead, he focused on and ran in the 400-yards. In that race he set a new world record and won Olympic gold. He also won a bronze medal in the 200 yards. His dilemma about whether or not to compete in the 100-yards became the Hollywood movie, Chariots of Fire.

DOWN AGAIN

Eighteen Thousand Witness Ireland's Defeat

CUSSEN'S BRILLIANT DAY

Scotland beat Ireland by 2 goals and 1 try (13 points) to 1 try (3 points) at Lansdowne road, yesterday, before 18,000 spectators. This is our second defeat this season, as we had lost at Leicester to England.

After the game, the Irish selectors announced the team for the following game, home to Wales. They made two changes, both in the forwards. Denis Cussen was again selected as wing-three-quarters and would win his eight cap.

Ireland International

*Cussen featured in an Irish Independent cartoon after Ireland v Scotland in 1923*

**Ireland v Wales
Lansdowne Road
10th March 1923
Ireland 5 – Wales 4**

Desperate for a win, Ireland took on Wales at Lansdowne Road in their third game of the 1923 season. By the time the game came around, Ireland had no points from two games and Wales had played three, losing to England and Scotland before beating France at home the week before the Ireland game. Cussen's try and all-round display against Scotland gave him confidence going into the game and the crowd felt that this was a game Ireland could win.

# Ireland International

*Cussen seated on the right with the Irish team ahead of the game v Wales in 1923*

Buoyed by the fact that Wales struggled to field a team of forwards of any experience, Ireland took their chance and managed to squeeze out a win finally. Northern Union (Rugby League) had poached most of the talented Welsh forwards and the eight that were fielded against Ireland were lacking in both weight and experience. The Irish forwards who struggled in their first two games, were finally able to get the better of an opposition pack. Ireland beat Wales 5-4 thanks to another Denis Cussen try.

All of the points were scored in the first half. After seventeen minutes Denis Cussen scored Ireland's try.

> *"The Irish line got away in a grand passing bout; W Cunningham, Hall, Gardiner, Stephenson, all handled before Cussen received. He made a great dash, but was tackled. Hall, however, dribbled up to the line, where Cussen, flashing up, regained possession to score a try at the corner, which Crawford, from a very difficult position, converted with a grand kick".*

After half an hour Wales struck back with a drop goal scored by Albert Jenkins. Cussen had other chances in the game and was very prominent in defence but there were no other scores in the game. Cussen's try had given Ireland a victory at last.

*Freeman's Journal headline 12th March 1923*

**France v Ireland
Colombes, Paris
14th April 1923
France 14 – Ireland 8**

Ireland's fourth and final game of the championship was away in Paris. One newspaper report opened with *'Brilliant sunshine with a pleasantly cool breeze favoured the last rugby international of the season, but the attendance at the Colombes ground was scarcely as large as was expected, not more than 20,000 people being present'*. That said it all with regards to the performances of Ireland and France in the 1923 five nations championship. France had lost all of their games and Ireland had a solitary win to their name going into this game.

Having gotten the better of a poor Welsh pack in the previous game, Ireland were back against a powerful forward pack and it showed. *'The Irish forwards had started somewhat slackly, but after France had scored, they improved, and brought off some fine rushes'*. Ireland managed a try in the first half, scored by Arthur Douglas who was making his Ireland debut on the opposite wing to Denis Cussen. At the interval France led 6-5.
In the second half, *'France began strongly and, as before, their forwards secured the ball from nearly every scrummage. The Irish forwards put little or*

*no dash in their play, but the backs tackled well'*. France pulled away and won the game.

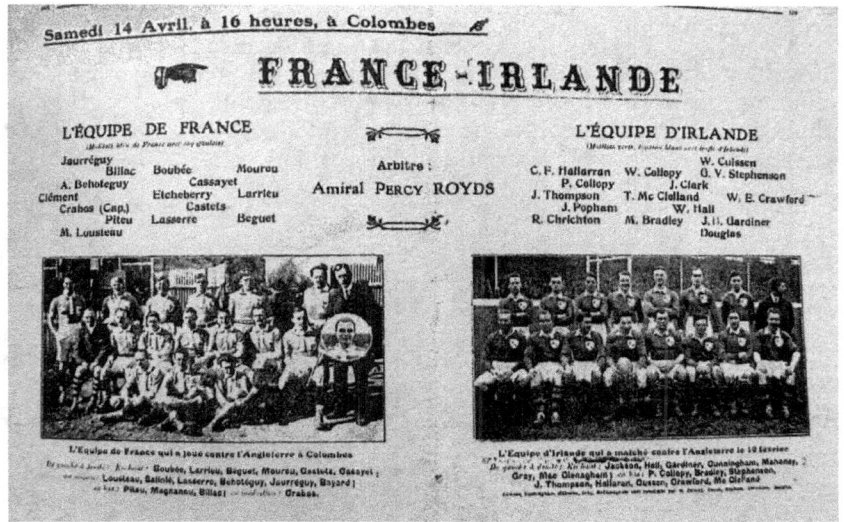

Team sheet from the match programme

Ireland, France and Scotland shared the wooden spoon in the 1923 five nations.

| Pos | Team | Played | W | D | L | PF | PA | PD | Pts |
|---|---|---|---|---|---|---|---|---|---|
| 1 | England | 4 | 4 | 0 | 0 | 50 | 17 | 33 | 8 |
| 2 | Scotland | 4 | 3 | 0 | 1 | 46 | 22 | 24 | 6 |
| 3 | Wales | 4 | 1 | 0 | 3 | 31 | 31 | 0 | 2 |
| 3 | France | 4 | 1 | 0 | 3 | 28 | 52 | -24 | 2 |
| 3 | Ireland | 4 | 1 | 0 | 3 | 21 | 54 | -33 | 2 |

1923 Five Nations table

## 1924

1924 was a big year. The Olympic Games were held in Paris, the Tailteann Games were held at Croke Park and the British and Irish Lions toured South Africa. Denis Cussen had injured his ankle in May 1923, just before the Irish Athletics Championships. While he was only out of competition for around six weeks, he didn't fully recover from the injury for over a year. His performances on the rugby field in the winter of 1923/24 were lacking just a fraction of pace and so he didn't make the Irish rugby team in 1924.

In his absence, England won a grand slam in the Five Nations. During this season Carston Catcheside scored tries for England against all of the other teams becoming the first person do achieve this. With HGV Stephenson playing in Denis' place, Ireland won two games and lost two games, finishing in the middle of the table.

## 1925

By late 1924, Denis Cussen had fully recovered his pace and was showing his old form on the rugby field. Going into the Irish trials in January 1925, he was selected on the 'probables' team but they were beaten 21-13 by the possibles. In the second trial game, played in Dublin, Cussen scored a try as the probables narrowly won 27-26. A third trial game was played on 31st January. This time Denis was selected on the 'possibles' side and again didn't make the Irish team.

In 1925 Scotland's Johnnie Wallace matched Catcheside's feat as Scotland won a grand slam. Their game against Scotland was Ireland's only loss of the season as they came second in the championship.

## 1926

Denis Cussen graduated from Trinity in December 1925. Now a qualified doctor he was able to return home to Newcastle West for a family Christmas. There is a note in Mary Cussen's scrapbook saying *"All home for xmas but Kitty. Bert had a rib broken and Denis a blood vessel in forearm"*.

Coming into the 1926 five nations championship, Denis Cussen hadn't played for Ireland for three years. His last game had been against France in the 1923 championship.

England had won the grand slam in 1924 and Scotland had equalled them in 1925, winning their first ever grand slam. Ireland hadn't won a championship since their shared win with England in 1912. In the 1925 championship Ireland had finished joint second with an impressive away win in Paris and an away draw with England. Optimism had returned to the rugby public who were desperate for an Irish championship win. That would come in 1926 and Denis Cussen would play a key role.

Strangely, the annual trial game of probables v possibles for the Irish team was played after the first game in 1926. A team was selected to play France by the selectors based on club and provincial performances. The Daily Mail published an article on 13th January in which they criticised the team selected to represent Ireland. Cussen, recalled to the team, wasn't spared criticism and had a point to prove.

> *"I greatly fear the Cussen-Stephenson wing, which on previous occasions was anything but satisfactory. Those who attended a certain international at Lansdowne Road have unhappy recollections of Stephenson's disposition to cut through almost every time, and Cussen might as well have been on the touch-line. Indeed, he spent most of his time in its vicinity waiting in vain for a sight of the ball".*

**Ireland v France**
**Ravenhill**
**23rd January 1926**
**Ireland 11 – France 0**

Denis Cussen earned his tenth cap in the opening game of the 1926 five nations at Ravenhill, Belfast. A good French side, whose pack *'won practically every scrum in the game'*, made Ireland work hard for their 11-nil victory. Ireland's points coming from a goal, a penalty and try.
Cussen didn't score but came close having *'passed the full-back and looked all over a scorer only to be hauled down by the French defender Revillon'*. It was an important victory for Ireland and for Denis Cussen as he went about re-establishing himself in the Irish team.

Communications were limited in the 1920s. Denis took the time to send a telegram back to his family in Newcastle West, announcing Ireland's victory with *"Ireland 11 Points. France Nil"*. The telegram was kept by Mary Cussen. It is an amazing artifact from a championship winning year for Irish rugby.

Ireland International

*Ireland v France match programme January 1926*

*Denis Cussen featured on a Will's Cigarette collectable card during the 1926 season.*

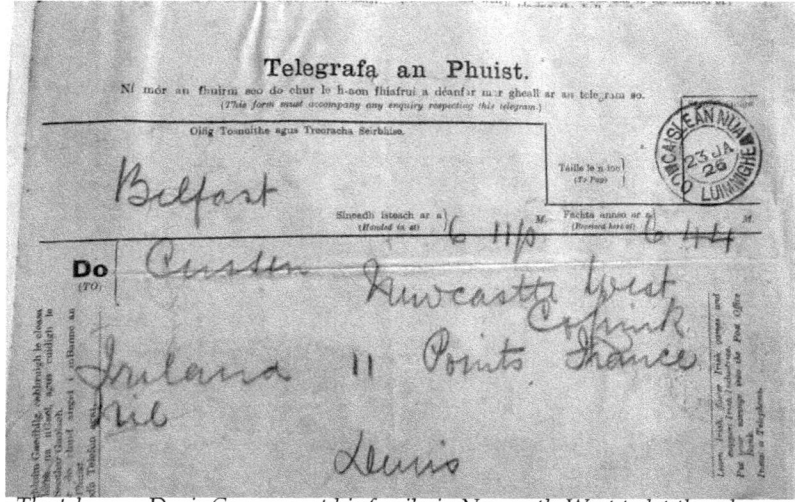

*The telegram Denis Cussen sent his family in Newcastle West to let them know that Ireland had beaten France in the five nations in 1926*

# Ireland International

The final trial game, played after the first game of the season, took place at Lansdowne Road on Saturday 30th January, two weeks before the second game of the championship. Denis Cussen had justified his place with his performance against the French and turned out for the 'probables' who won the trial game by three goals and four tries to two tries.

Denis Cussen (centre) with the 'probables' team in 1926

8,000 turned out to watch the game despite heavy rains the previous night. Cussen had two glorious chances in the first half. On one occasion he made a dive for the try line and touched the ball down but he hit the flag on the way over so no try was awarded. On another occasion, he had a clear run for the line but was tackled at the last minute by possibles defender Jim Ganly. He was also close to scoring in the second half but again was taken out by a tackle. He had done enough though and was selected for the team to play England two weeks later.

**Ireland v England**
**Lansdowne Road**
**13th February 1926**
**Ireland 19 – England 15**

Having gotten the season off to a great start with a solid win over France in Belfast, Ireland took on England in the second game. Ireland hadn't beaten England in fifteen years. An article in the Irish Times ahead of the game said, *"we who follow the fortunes of Ireland have not much to encourage the belief that our team will be triumphant"*. Triumph, they did. This game, played at Lansdowne Road, would be one of the highlights of Denis Cussen's career.

Ireland International

*Denis Cussen (left) takes to the field against England 1926. Ernie Crawford (right)*

Ireland International

*Denis Cussen shakes Tim Healy (Governor General of Ireland) ahead of the England game.*

*Match tickets from Ireland v England 1926*

*Match Programme from Ireland v England 1926*

# Ireland International

Team sheet Ireland v England 1926

Ireland went behind to an early try and the crowd would have been forgiven for thinking another defeat was coming but Ireland dug deep. Denis Cussen was instrumental in Ireland's first try. He broke through the English defence and created an opening for George Stephenson to score. The conversion was missed. Periton scored a second English try under the posts and the conversion made the score 3-10. Cussen went close with another break for the line only to be *'smothered by a wonderful Catcheside tackle'*. A penalty to Ireland brought the score to 6-10 before a third Cussen break almost made it over the line, only for him to drop the ball a yard short. Ireland went into the interval behind by four points but Cussen was playing a blinder of a game.

In the second half Ireland had the better of things up front. *'The forwards did not relax under their disappointments, as they had done in other times. They possibly remembered Twickenham last year. Bearing down on the English line again, the worked a scrimmage near the touchline. Sugden and Cussen did the rest. The scrim worker, with little room, fooled the English backs and gave it to Cussen, who struggled over. Few had hopes of the kick being converted, but from the minute Stephenson got his boot to the ball there was never any doubt'.*

Ireland were ahead by a point.

***Ireland v England 1926***
Back: Bradley, Farrell, Buchanan, McVicker, Llewellyn (referee), Payne, Sugden, Cagney
Middle: T Hewitt, Stephenson, Crawford (Capt), Hallaran, F Hewitt
Frond: Davy, Clinch, Cussen

Shortly afterwards, *'a long kick by Davy sent play into the luck corner, where Sugden and Cussen had operated so successfully some time earlier. One would have thought the English would not be caught in the same manner twice. They were. Sugden slipped away again on the blind side, parted to Cussen a bit earlier this time. Cussen now had to do more; he had to carry two Englishmen with him over the line, emulating the deed of the famous player, whoever he was who crossed the line festooned with Saxons'.* The conversion, taken from almost exactly the same spot as the earlier one was kicked successfully by Stephenson this time. 16-10.

Ireland International

*Cussen in full flight, waiting for a pass from Eugene Davy 1926*

England hit back in the closing stages with an unconverted try, bringing the score to 16-15. With the crowd roaring Ireland on, there was sufficient time remaining for Denis Cussen to dribble along cleverly, pick up, and direct a pass off his foot to the Hewitts, a way out by themselves on the other side of the field. Frank got to it and went over for the winning try. The conversion was again missed by Stephenson and the game finished 19-15.

Ireland had beaten England for the first time in fifteen years. Ireland had scored four tries. Cussen had scored two and set up the other two.

> *"Having passed through troubled times extending over many years, when the gam almost ceased to be played, and even then, only under extreme difficulties, Irish Rugby football retrieved its former high position, when, on Saturday our team triumphed over England in one of the most exciting matches ever played. We are not being uncomplimentary to the Englishmen when we state that it is they of all the other countries we dearly like to beat."*

> *"Denis Cussen at last reached the heights that most of us always believed he had the essentials for; of his many fine achievements I liked best that rasping punt across the field to the Hewitts which gave us the final score".*

> *"The pent-up longing for such an event was let loose with a vengeance, and the crowd of ordinarily common-sense individuals who we*

characterise as "the Lansdowne Road crowd", allowed themselves for a few moments to become almost uncanny in their display of jubilation".

The Irish field in an article on 20th February had this to say:

*"The three men about whom I felt any way uneasy were Cussen, Clinch and Bradley. I was afraid of Cussen's collaring, of Clinch's fitness, and of Bradley's ability to hook. I can only say now that, after Stephenson, they were the three greatest successes of the match. Cussen has often played brilliant games as far as attack was concerned, but he always seemed to lack confidence in defence, not certainly for want of courage. On Saturday he was a footballer in every sense of the word".*

Now with two wins and this morale boosting win over England, Ireland began to consider the possibility that they would win a championship. Next up was Scotland away.

**Scotland v Ireland
Murrayfield, Edinburgh
27th February 1926
Scotland 0 – Ireland 3**

Ahead of the game there was newspaper speculation that Denis Cussen would be moving to England now that he had qualified as a doctor.

## Ireland International

Speculation was that he might sign for Blackheath FC. The game itself was almost as dramatic as the previous game against England.

> *"It was a remarkable match, remarkable for the pace maintained on the frightfully heavy ground, and for its keenness. From the first thrilling attack by Scotland in the opening minutes to the climax, the spectators were kept on the top-toe of expectation. Almost every minute something looked like happening. One minute the Scots were struggling desperately to thwart those terrible Irish rushes, and the next the Irishmen were being sorely tried in preventing their rivals from crossing their lines. At times it seemed impossible that scoring could be stopped but always were the defenders the masters".*

Five minutes from the end of the game and with the score locked at nil all, there was a long break as Scotland's out-half Waddell and Ireland's Browne were treated as they both lay prone in the middle of the field after a collision. Both players had to be carried from the field injured. Browne, bleeding from the head, was able to return to play but Waddell was unable to return for the final passages of play.

> *"On the resumption Ireland renewed their attack, first on one wing and then on the other. Suddenly Clinch tore loose with the ball. Tackled, he passed to Davy. In turn the ball went to Stephenson and to Gage, and the Irish left win hurled himself over the line while half in the grasp of Drysdale. Pandemonium broke out among the Irish supporters, to be renewed tenfold when, after Stephenson had failed to convert, "Time" was whistled by the referee"*

Another huge win for Ireland. Scotland, the grand slam winners the previous season had been beaten. Ireland now had three wins and just Wales stood between them and a grand slam of their own.

After the game, it was confirmed that Denis Cussen would be moving to London to take up a role at St Mary's Hospital and that he would be playing his rugby with Blackheath.

Ireland International

*Post-game function - Scotland v Ireland game in 1926*

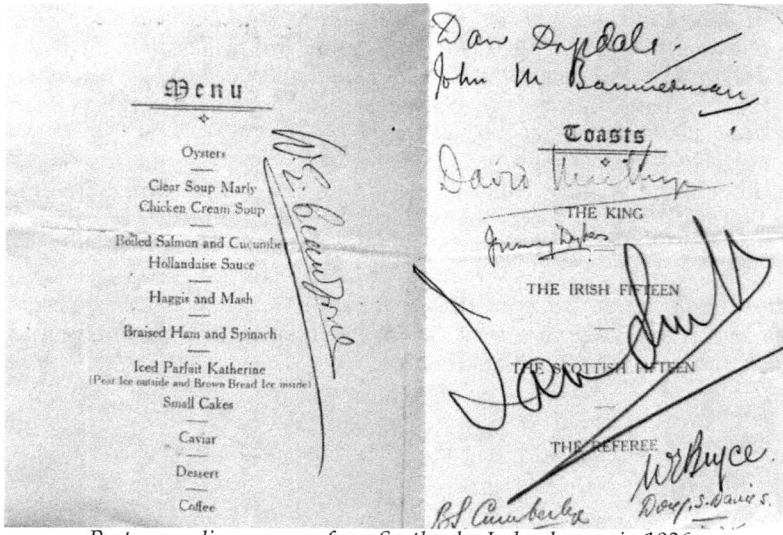

*Post-game dinner menu from Scotland v Ireland game in 1926.*
*Signatures including British and Irish Lion Dan Drysdale*

# Wales v Ireland
Swansea
13th March 1926
Wales 11 – Ireland 8

Two weeks after the dramatic win at Murrayfield, Ireland travelled to Swansea for their final game of the 1926 five nations. Wales had won one, drawn one and lost one game. Ireland had a first ever grand slam in their sights. 50,000 supporters turned out at the St Helens ground for the much-anticipated game. An estimated 5,000 of those were thought to have travelled from Ireland in anticipation. All indications were that Ireland would win at a canter but unfortunately, that wasn't to be the case.

*Denis Cussen (seated third from right) and the Irish team beaten by Wales in 1926*

Wales started unexpectedly well but an early penalty gave Stephenson the chance to put Ireland ahead. A converted try, scored by Rees, put Wales in front on the scoreboard before Hanrahan for Ireland scored a try to put them ahead by three points at the break (5-8). It should have been more. Cussen scored a perfectly good try that was unfairly disallowed.

*"Cussen played the part of onlooker for the greater part of the game, and his principal role was keeping Harding out, which he did fairly effectively. He had one dash for the line early on, which he crossed with two Welshmen hanging on to him. Why the score was disallowed will, I suppose, remain a mystery, as it was as fair a try as has ever been obtained. It was said that the referee's vision was obscured by the forwards, and he gave the benefit of the doubt to the defending side. That may be so, and his vision must have been obscured on numerous other occasions – notably when a Welsh forward deliberately truck one of the Irish three-quarters (Cussen) in the mouth".*

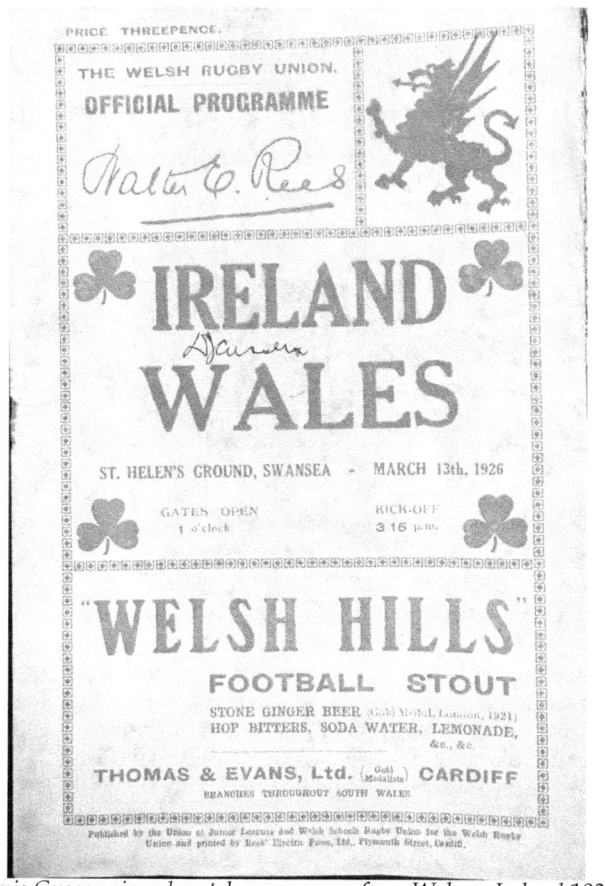

*Denis Cussen signed match programme from Wales v Ireland 1926*

Wales came back strongly and dominated the first thirty minute of the second half. Again, it was the Irish forwards who were short of their competitor's capabilities. *"One can have nothing but admiration for such a sterling pack, but greater admiration still must be felt for the heroic defenders, who, plunging themselves down with reckless abandon, repelled invasion after invasion".* The Irish defence couldn't hold though. Tries by Herrera and 1924 Lions captain Rowe Harding put Wales ahead going into the final ten minutes. Ireland rallied and after the referee, Mr BS Cumberledge, got injured and had to be replaced, Ireland drove hard at the Welsh line but were unable to breech it.

*Denis Cussen going over for his disallowed try against Wales.*

Wales won by a placed goal and two tries (11 points) to a placed goal and a penalty goal (8 points). Ireland's chance at a first ever grand slam was gone but they had won the five nations championship (shared with Scotland) for the sixth time and for the first time since 1912. Denis Cussen had undoubtedly been one of the stars of the Irish team, if not the championship.

| Pos | Team | Played | W | D | L | PF | PA | PD | Pts |
|---|---|---|---|---|---|---|---|---|---|
| 1 | Scotland | 4 | 3 | 0 | 1 | 45 | 23 | 22 | 6 |
| 1 | Ireland | 4 | 3 | 0 | 1 | 41 | 26 | 15 | 6 |
| 3 | Wales | 4 | 2 | 1 | 1 | 26 | 24 | 2 | 5 |
| 4 | England | 4 | 1 | 1 | 2 | 38 | 39 | -1 | 3 |
| 5 | France | 4 | 0 | 0 | 4 | 11 | 49 | -38 | 0 |

*1926 Five Nations table*

## 1927

After the 1926 five nations, Denis Cussen moved to live in London. He continued to play for Dublin University for the first few months of the year, winning the Bateman Cup in April, beating Garryowen. He then focused on playing his rugby with Blackheath.

*Cussen (number 2) slings out a long pass when tackled by Stephenson during the Ulster v Leinster trial game – Dec 1926*

In December 1926, Cussen returned to Ireland for the annual international trials. As had been the case the previous year, the final Interpro games were used as an initial trial with the formal trial game being played after the first game of the championship. Having been a standout the previous year, there was little doubt Cussen would be selected and that was the case when the team was announced for the first game of the year against France. The game was played in Paris on New Year's Day 1927.

**France v Ireland**
**Paris**
**1st January 1927**
**France 3 – Ireland 8**

Ireland travelled to Paris on 1st January 1927 as reigning Five Nations champions. France had won the wooden spoon the previous year and so Ireland were confident of victory. The game would be remembered for something other than the rugby that was played that day.

Both teams arrived at the ground five minutes after the advertised starting time, leaving 30,000 spectators waiting. Ireland managed a narrow win, scoring eight points to France's three. Denis Cussen had a poor game. *"Cussen failed to elude Jaureguy, whom he failed also to*

# RUGBY GAME IN PARIS BREAKS UP IN BATTLE

PARIS, Jan. 1.—(AP)—The unsportsmanlike conduct today of rugby fans at a match between France and Ireland in Colombes stadium, attended by 30,000 spectators, is likely to result in Ireland asking the International Rugby Union to exile France.

After the Irish team had defeated the French players, 8 to 3, a crowd of fans invaded the field to get at the referee, R. L. Scott of Scotland, who was saved from a severe manhandling only after police had interfered. The crowd howled and jeered at Scott but no blows were delivered, due to the activity of the police in holding off the mob. A force of 190 reserves was summoned from Paris to take Scott out of the stadium by a back gate.

During play, the match degenerated into a regular Donnybrook Fair, the players mixing freely and getting out of the referee's control.

intercept in his dash for the line. Cussen's cross kick would, but for Stephenson's intervention, have been disastrous for Ireland, yet it came off against England last season".

France got over the Irish line on three occasions but two tries were disallowed due to infringements. Besson scored the one, unconverted French try. For Ireland the scores came from a penalty by Stephenson and a try for Davy which was converted by Stephenson. The game, however, will be remembered for the scenes at full time rather than the quality of the rugby. French fans, unhappy at the loss, stormed the field to attack the referee who had to be protected by dozens of police. Many of the Irish players were also caught up in the melé and also had to be shepherded from the field. A similar thing had happened a couple of years earlier and the IRFU issued a statement afterwards stating that Ireland would withdraw from future competitions if their players safety wasn't ensured.

*France v Ireland made headlines around the world in 1927*

Ireland International

*The Irish team that played France in 1927*

After the Ireland game in Paris, there was a full month before Ireland's second game in London. In the interim Scotland had won two games (against France and Wales). They would again be the main competition for the championship that year.

An unconvincing performance by Ireland broadly in Paris, and Denis Cussen's perceived poor form, relegated him from 'probables' to 'possibles' when the Ireland international trial game was played at Lansdowne Road on 29th January 1927.

Cussen began on the possibles side with Jim Ganly his opposition on the probables. Ganly scored twice in the first half of the game. *"It would be unfair to blame Cussen for either of the two tries obtained by Ganly in the opening half of the game on Saturday. He was not concerned even indirectly with the mistake which paved the way for Ganly's first score, and the way for the second was cleverly pioneered by Frank Hewitt, leaving the Monkstown man a clear run in".*

Despite his oppositions apparent success, the selectors had seen enough to restore Cussen to the probables side for the second half.

# Ireland International

*Cussen, seated 2nd right, with the 'possibles' team – Ireland trial January 1927*

"When Sugden and Cussen, were both transferred to the probables side there was a decided improvement in the wing man's play. They operated the blind side business a few times, and against a defence less conversant with its mode of attack, a couple of scores would have resulted. I am convinced the Cussen owes his retention to the return of Sugden, the selectors having in mind how the pair hoodwinked the English defence twelve months ago. Cussen is capable *of brilliant things at times, and we can only hope that at Twickenham he will achieve his best".*

*Cussen playing for the possibles in the 1927 trial game, January 1927*

**England v Ireland
Twickenham, London
12th February 1927
England 8 – Ireland 6**

Denis Cussen's final game for the Ireland team came on 12th February 1927 against England. The game was played at Twickenham, just a few miles from where he was then living.

Despite it being underwhelming, Ireland had had a good start with their win away in Paris. England too had had a good start. The beat Wales 11-9 at home. Both teams were playing their second game of the championship.

For the game, England made five changes from their opening round win over Wales. Three of those were to their pack; Law, Eyres and

Ireland International

Davies came in to bolster their forward line but ironically, all three were dropped after the game and never played for England again.

*Cussen, seated 2nd left, ahead of his final cap against England, February 1927*

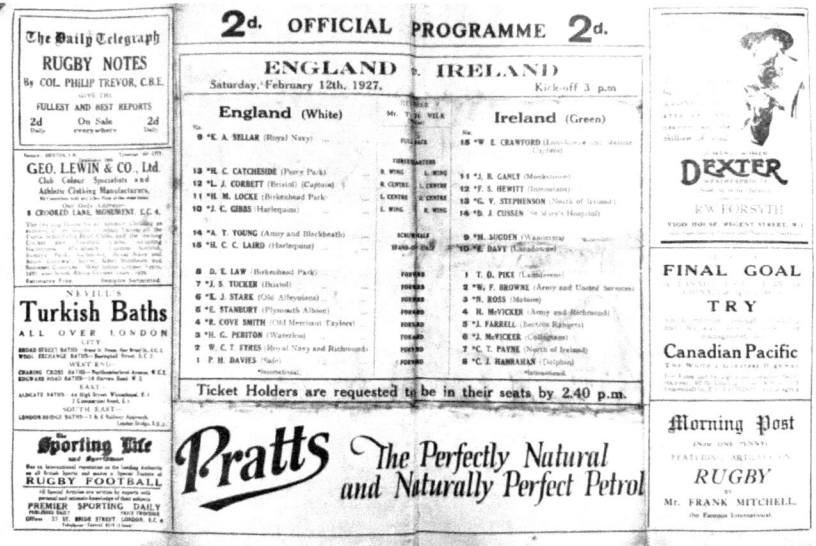
*Teams listed in the official match programme*

# Ireland International

The game was in doubt the day before the game due to thick fog which had enveloped London and its suburbs. It cleared on the day and the playing surface had been under a blanked of straw all week to ensure it wasn't frozen over.

Taking to the field that day with the Irish team, Cussen was the third longest serving of the players. Only Ernie Crawford and GV Stephenson had earned their first cap before him. Cussen had seen a lot of change around him in the Irish team. He was still just twenty-six years old which was the average age of the team that day. He was one of just two Munster born players (the other being Theodore Pike from Thurles. Rugby was still dominated by Ulster and Leinster with seven and eight representatives each. Cussen's career had lasted longer than the other six players alongside whom he had made his debut in 1921. Already gone were Henry Cormack, Thomas Mayne, Tom McClelland, JJ Bermingham, Charles Hallaran and Noel Purcell.

While Cussen was signing off, Theodore Pike and Hugh McVicker were making their debuts. Pike was the brother of Andrew and Robert Pike who Cussen had played with Trinity. A flanker, Pike went on to be capped seven times for Ireland. He toured Argentina with the British and Irish Lions in 1927. He later entered the diplomatic core, became Governor of British Somaliland and was knighted in 1956. Hugh McVicker, from Ballymoney in Antrim, was a second row who played five times for Ireland. He died in Peshawar, Pakistan four years later while serving with the British Army.

It had taken Ireland thirteen attempts to beat England. They finally did so at home at Lansdowne Road in 1887. Their first win against England in England didn't come until their win at Rectory Field in 1894. This was the forty-fourth game between the two teams. Ireland had won thirteen. There had been three draws but Ireland had never won at Twickenham. Having won the championship the previous year, expectations were high that Ireland would finally win there. At least ten thousand Irish rugby fans packed into Twickenham for the game with an estimated two thousand having travelled across by ferry for the game. The newspaper reports commented on the Irish that swarmed to London. *"London today was an encampment of green-garbed invaders. The girls were as prominent as their brothers and sweethearts"*. By the time kick-off came, there were an estimated forty-five thousand spectators in the stadium.

Ireland were playing with a weakened team. Clinch, Bradley, Cagney and Gage were all injured and missed the game. The team also travelled late to London, arriving the day before the game when they would usually have travelled on the Thursday to give them time to recover from the journey.

Ireland kicked off and had the better of the opening passages of play but neither side managed to score in the opening twenty minutes. Ireland then opened the scoring when GV Stephenson kicked a penalty which looked like it would fall short but instead, bounced on the cross bar and went over to give Ireland the lead. For the rest of the first half, it was end-to-end stuff, with both sides attacking.

> *"Young was prominent, but Davy caught him and got possession. The Irish out-half cut through and passed out to Cussen, who made a great burst along the win, but was taken by Sellars. After some forward scrambling England attacked again, but Crawford was again in the limelight. Browne was always prominent both in the loose and in the tight. Ireland were still having the advantage in the scrums, and just before the interval the men in green were nearly over, Ganly being taken the line."*

Ireland went into half time with a three to nil advantage. The second half opened mush as the first half ended.

> *"Following a line out, Young passed to Locke, but Cussen brought the latter down. A scrum near the Irish goal line saw Young passing to Corbett, and the latter gave to Catcheside. The wing man had a great dash but was Ganly tackled his man, and kicked to touch."*

Young finally got over the Ireland line and his try was converted by Corbett. England were ahead 5-3. As the half progressed, Ireland managed to get a try. The newspaper reported that it was impossible to know which Irish forward scored it but it turned out to be McVicker on his debut. The try was unconverted so going into the closing stages Ireland had a one-point lead at 5-6. Corbett got a late score for England which was not converted giving them an 8-6 lead. In the final minutes, Ireland battered the English line but couldn't get over for a winner.

Unfortunately for Denis and the Irish team, Ireland fell short and again failed to win at Twickenham despite a thrilling encounter. *"After one of the most strenuous and most exciting football battles ever witnessed at Twickenham, Ireland went down before England yesterday in the struggle for the International Rugby Championship. The margin that separated the teams at the finish was only two points"*

The game against England proved to be Denis Cussen's final one in an Irish jersey. Two weeks later Ireland played Scotland in Dublin and won 6-0. Jim Ganly took over on Cussen's wing and scored one of the tries. Ahead of the game, the Evening Herald ran a piece in which they wrote, *"Cussen's great qualities should not be forgotten. His pace and thrust for the line must live in the memories of those who have seen him in action".*

Two weeks after Scotland, Ireland played Wales in Dublin and again won, this time 19-9. Again, Jim Ganly was on the scoreboard. Ireland finished the championship as joint winners with Scotland.

*Denis Cussen featured on 1927 Will's Cigarette cards*

Ireland International

| Pos | Team | Played | W | D | L | PF | PA | PD | Pts |
|---|---|---|---|---|---|---|---|---|---|
| 1 | Scotland | 4 | 3 | 0 | 1 | 49 | 25 | 24 | 6 |
| 1 | Ireland | 4 | 3 | 0 | 1 | 39 | 20 | 19 | 6 |
| 3 | England | 4 | 2 | 0 | 2 | 32 | 39 | -7 | 4 |
| 4 | Wales | 4 | 1 | 0 | 3 | 43 | 42 | 1 | 2 |
| 4 | France | 4 | 1 | 0 | 4 | 19 | 56 | -37 | 2 |

*1927 Five Nations table*

| Date | Against | Venue | Result | Comment |
|---|---|---|---|---|
| 12th February 1921 | England | Twickenham | 15-0 Loss | |
| 26th February 1921 | Scotland | Lansdowne | 9-8 Win | Scored a try |
| 12th March 1921 | Wales | Balmoral, Belfast | 0-6 Loss | |
| 9th April 1921 | France | Colombes, Paris | 20-10 Loss | |
| 1st February 1922 | England | Lansdowne | 3-13 Loss | |
| 10th February 1923 | England | Leicester | 23-5 Loss | |
| 24th February 1923 | Scotland | Lansdowne | 3-13 Loss | Scored a try |
| 10th March 1923 | Wales | Lansdowne | 5-4 Win | Scored a try |
| 14th March 1923 | France | Colombes, Paris | 14-8 Loss | |
| 23rd January 1926 | France | Belfast | 11-0 Win | |
| 13th February 1926 | England | Lansdowne | 19-15 Win | Scored two tries |
| 27th February 1926 | Scotland | Edinburgh | 0-3 Win | |
| 13th March 1926 | Wales | Swansea | 11-8 Loss | Disallowed try |
| 1st January 1927 | France | Paris | 3-8 Los | |
| 12th February 1927 | England | Twickenham | 8-6 Loss | |

*Denis Cussen's 15 International Caps*

During his career, Denis Cussen played alongside some legends of the Irish game.

## Ernie Crawford (1891-1959)

William Ernest "Ernie" Crawford was born in Belfast on 17 November 1891. He had a remarkable career.

Crawford was the son of Henry Crawford, a drapery salesman and Katie (nee Sadlier). The family were Methodist and Ernie was educated at the Methodist College in Belfast and then later at Belfast Mercantile College. He then trained as a chartered accountant. While studying, Crawford played rugby union for Malone in Belfast and soccer for Cliftonville and showed strong athletic capability.

In a sign of the complexity of society at the time, Crawford signed the Ulster Covenant in 1912, pledging to defend Ireland from Home Rule.

**Covenant:—**  PLACE OF SIGNING,

BEING CONVINCED in our consciences that Home Rule would be disastrous to the material well-being of Ulster as well as of the whole of Ireland, subversive of our civil and religious freedom, destructive of our citizenship, and perilous to the unity of the Empire, we, whose names are underwritten, men of Ulster, loyal subjects of His Gracious Majesty King George V., humbly relying on the God whom our fathers in days of stress and trial confidently trusted, do hereby pledge ourselves in solemn Covenant, throughout this our time of threatened calamity, to stand by one another in defending, for ourselves and our children, our cherished position of equal citizenship in the United Kingdom, and in using all means which may be found necessary to defeat the present conspiracy to set up a Home Rule Parliament in Ireland. And in the event of such a Parliament being forced upon us, we further solemnly and mutually pledge ourselves to refuse to recognise its authority. In sure confidence that God will defend the right, we hereto subscribe our names.
     And further, we individually declare that we have not already signed this Covenant.

*William Ernest Crawford      Avigna Windsor Park Belfast.*

Crawford qualified as an accountant in 1914, just as the first world war began and so he enlisted in the 6th Royal Inniskilling Dragoons and was sent to France. He was injured severely in the arm during a battle at Arras in May 1917 and was forced to spend the remainder of the war in an administrative role.

Crawford left the army in 1919, moved to Dublin and took up a role as an accountant for the Rathmines and Rathgar urban council.

Despite his injured arm which lost him the strength in three fingers, he returned to his sporting activities and played rugby with Lansdowne with whom he was club captain in 1921/22 and 1922/23. He also played soccer with Bohemians, though because of his focus on rugby, he played mostly for their second team.

Crawford made his Ireland rugby debut at Lansdowne Road in 1920 against England. That season Ireland lost all four games. An outstanding fullback, Crawford made thirty appearances for Ireland between 1920 and 1927. During his career he kicked six conversions and two penalties. He captained the team from 1924 until 1927. His final game came against Wales in March 1927.

Like Cussen, Crawford was also successful in another sport. Having played in the Irish trial, Crawford was selected to play for the Irish Olympic Soccer team in 1924. He travelled with the team to Paris but didn't play during the tournament.

After retiring from playing, Crawford became a selector for the Irish team and was part of the management team when Ireland won the grand slam in 1948. He also served as president of the IRFU in 1957.

Crawford is regarded as one of the best fullbacks ever to play the game. He was honoured by the French government for his contribution to the game and was even featured on a Tongan stamp.

Crawford returned to Belfast where he became the City Treasurer. He died in January 1959. He was 67.

## James 'Jammie' Clinch (1901-1981)

Another rugby icon from Cussen's playing days was James 'Jammie' Clinch. Clinch was born in Dublin in 1901, the son of Dr Andrew Clinch who himself made ten appearances for Ireland and toured with the British and Irish Lions in 1896.

Like Cussen, despite being a catholic, Jammie Clinch studied medicine at Trinity, though he never graduated. While at Trinity he played with

Cussen on the DUFC rugby team that won the Leinster Senior Cup in 1920 and 1921, the latter with Cussen. He later moved to Wanderers and so missed the 1925/26 Bateman Cup success.

*James 'Jammie' Clinch (left) and Denis Cussen (right)*

An exceptional flanker, Clinch represented Leinster on twenty occasions between 1920 and 1932, the majority of those with Cussen also in the team.

Clinch won the first of thirty Ireland caps against Wales in 1923. Like his father, Clinch was selected for the British and Irish Lions and toured with them to South Africa in 1924. He also played for the Barbarians. Clinch's final Irish cap came in 1931.

Clinch completed his medical studies at the Royal College of Surgeons before moving to Wales where he worked as a general practitioner. Late in life, Clinch returned to Ireland and he died in Dublin in 1981.

# Mark Sugden (1902-1990)

*Mark Sugden (sitting front), Denis Cussen (sitting left)*

Mark Sugden was born in Staffordshire, England in 1902. His father was a protestant silk manufacturer. The family moved to Dublin, where his father set up a business on Adelaide Road, when Sugden was four years old.

Sugden spent his teenage years back in England where he was educated but he then returned to Ireland to study at Trinity College.

Sugden broke into the DUFC first XV in the 1923/24 season. He played initially at centre but later moved to scrumhalf when Bertie Cussen joined the team and proved to be a better centre. That switch was the making of Sugden. Alongside the Cussen brothers, he won the Leinster Senior Cup in 1925 and the Bateman Cup in 1926.

Sugden was capped 28 times by Ireland between 1924 and 1931. He scored three tries in the Ireland shirt. He is reputed to have invented 'the dummy'. His caps for Ireland came at scrumhalf, a position in which he is viewed as one of the greatest ever and a position he might never have played were it not for Bertie Cussen forcing his move there at Trinity.

Sugden also played cricket for Ireland between 1924 and 1930. That team also featured Samuel Beckett, the renowned playwright. Having retired from rugby and cricket, Sugden moved to Scotland where he was a teacher for a few years. He then moved to Dartmouth where he taught at the Britannia Royal Naval College.

Sugden retired from teaching in 1984. In 1987, he and his Ireland out-half partner, Eugene Davy, were the inaugural entrants in the Irish

Rugby Writers Hall of Fame. Sugden died in Dartmouth in January 1990.

## George Vaughan (GV) Stephenson (1901-1970)

George Vaughan Stephenson was born in Dromore, County Down. His father, George Snr, was from Cork and was the local Church of Ireland clergyman. His mother, Gertie, was born in South Africa.

George (known as GV) was the younger of two rugby playing brothers. Harry, a year older, also played for Ireland.

The Stephenson brothers were educated at Clanrye preparatory college in Belfast. George went on to study Medicine at Queens University. His brother Harry entered the army.
Both had significant rugby careers. Henry competed at wing three-quarter with Denis Cussen and won fourteen caps in total. George (GV) was also a back and played mostly at centre.

While studying at Queens, Stephenson won the Ulster Senior Cup twice (1924 and 1925). He went on to play for Ulster for almost ten years and was called up by Ireland for his first cap in April 1920. He went on to win a record breaking forty-two caps for Ireland between 1920 and 1930. That record would stand until Jackie Kyle won his forty-third twenty-seven years later. Stephenson also held the Irish try scoring record with fourteen. That record stood until Brendan Mullin broke the record in 1991.

Like Cussen, Stephenson moved to London to pursue his medical career. He played for London Irish and St Thomas Hospital before retiring. Stephenson lived in London for the rest of his life. He died in 1970.

Ireland International

# Rugby Centenary Match 1923

**England and Wales XV v Ireland and Scotland XV**
**Rugby School**
**1st November 1923**
**England and Wales 21 – Ireland and Scotland 16**

It is widely accepted that the game of rugby was *'invented'* by William Webb Ellis when he picked up the ball and ran with it during a school football match in 1823. To celebrate the centenary of that event, a Centenary Match was played on 1st November 1923. The game was played at Rugby School in England where Webb Ellis' infringement happened.

The Centenary Match featured a combined England and Wales XV playing a combined Ireland and Scotland XV. Some legends of the game, international captains and British and Irish Lions players turned out on each side.

Denis Cussen was one of seven Irishmen invited to play on the Ireland and Scotland team. He was one of only two from the Irish Free State and the only Munsterman selected. Joining him were Irish captain Ernie Crawford from Belfast (Lansdowne) who was capped thirty times by Ireland, George Stephenson (Queens) from Dromore, County Down got thirty-two caps, Dubliner Bill Cellopy (Bective) nineteen Irish caps, Tom McClelland (Queens) from Ballymena earned sixteen caps, Robert Crichton (Dublin Uni) from Downpatrick earned fifteen caps and John Buchanan (Stewartonians) from Belfast won three Irish caps.

The contingent of Irishmen were joined by eight Scots. Archibald Gracie (Harlequins), born in Columbo, Sri Lanka earned thirteen Scottish caps and was awarded the military cross during WW1. Henry Stevenson (Portsmouth), played fifteen times for Scotland and international cricketer.

Scrumhalf William Bryce (Selkirk) was born in England but was capped eleven times by Scotland and earned the same number of caps at Field Hockey. Jimmy Dykes (West of Scotland), played twenty times for Scotland and five times for the Barbarians. John Bannerman (Baron Bannerman of Kildonan OBE) (Glasgow), was capped thirty-seven times by Scotland and became President of the Scottish Rugby Union in 1954. Ludovic Stuart (Glasgow), played eight times for Scotland and six times for the Barbarians. Number eight Doug Davies (Hawick) played for Scotland and toured with the British and Irish Lions in 1924. Flanker Jock Lawrie (Melrose) made eleven appearances for Scotland.

England and Wales were represented by eight Welsh and seven Englishmen.

From Wales were Mel Baker (Newport) with three Welsh caps and who had toured with the British and Irish Lions in 1910. Tom Johnson (Cardiff) played for Wales twelve times and captained them on one occasion. Wales centre Arthur Cornish (Cardiff) was capped ten times. Another Welshman Rowe Harding (Swansea) was capped by Wales seventeen times and toured South Africa with the British and Irish Lions in 1924. Lock Tom Roberts (Newport) played nine times for Wales. Ambrose Baker (Neath) was capped by Wales five times before switching codes and playing twice for the national rugby league team. Stephen Morris (Cross Keys) was a flanker capped by Wales on nineteen occasions and Gwilym Michael (Swansea) was capped three times by Wales.

From England were Harold Locke (Birkenhead Park) who was capped twelve times. Cecil Kershaw was born in Bangladesh and played scrumhalf for England on sixteen occasions. He was also three-time British fencing champion and competed at two Olympic Games. Dave Davies was capped at out-half by England on twenty-two occasions.

He and Cecil Kershaw played together for England on fourteen occasions and never lost when they played together.

Wavell Wakefield (Leicester) was the elder brother of Roger Wakefield who had toured with the British and Irish Lions in 1927. Wavell was capped thirty-one times by England and captained the team thirteen times. As captain, he led England to back-to-back grand slam titles. He was knighted in 1944 and became Baron Wakefield of Kendal in 1963. Flanker Tom Voyce (Gloucestershire) was capped twenty-nine times by England and toured South Africa with the British and Irish Lions in 1924. Geoffrey Conway (Oxford) though born in Wales was capped by England on eighteen occasions. William Luddington (Devonport) was capped by England on thirteen occasions. He later joined the Royal Navy and was killed during the second world war when his ship, HMS Illustrious, was attacked.

*The Ireland & Scotland Team 1923*
Back: Dykes (S), Crichton (I), McClelland (I), Buchanan (I), Stuart (S), Davies (S)
Middle: Collopy (I), Crawford (I), Gracie (S), Bryce (S), Cussen (I), Lawrie (S), Bannerman (S)
Front: Stephenson (I), Stevenson (S)

The game was played on November 1st back at the Rugby school on the same pitch as William Webb Ellis had picked up the ball. Each player who was selected was hosted by a local family. Denis Cussen was hosted by Charles Paget Hastings at his home at 'Mayfields' on

# Rugby Centenary Match 1923

Horton Crescent, just a few yards up the road from the school. Hastings worked at the school as an 'assistant mister'

Ticket for the game were understandably scarce. Those invited were either guests of the school headmaster or the English Rugby Union. Two thousand attendees were there to witness the game with about a third of those being schoolboys from the school.

> *"Played under ideal conditions before a fine company of spectators, the rugby centenary match on the playing fields of Rugby School yesterday ended in a victory for England and Wales, who defeated Scotland and Ireland by two placed goals, two dropped goal and a try (21 points) to two placed goals and two tries (16 points).*
>
> *As might have been expected, the attendance included numerous famous players of years ago, not to mention many well known in modern rugby, and provided the keenest enthusiasm. Fast and tremendously keen, the match was open enough to satisfy the most exacting, and the fact that so much scoring took place rendered the play particularly interesting and enjoyable to watch"*

Cussen didn't get on the score sheet during the game but acquitted himself well. The Irish Independent reporting that *"Cussen got little to do, but made no mistakes and did well in defence"*.

*Rowe-Harding's jersey from the Centenary Match in 1923*

# Rugby Centenary Match 1923

*Players and their hosts at Rugby*

# Rugby Centenary Match 1923

*Denis Cussen (seated 2nd right) with the players of the historic centenary game 1923*

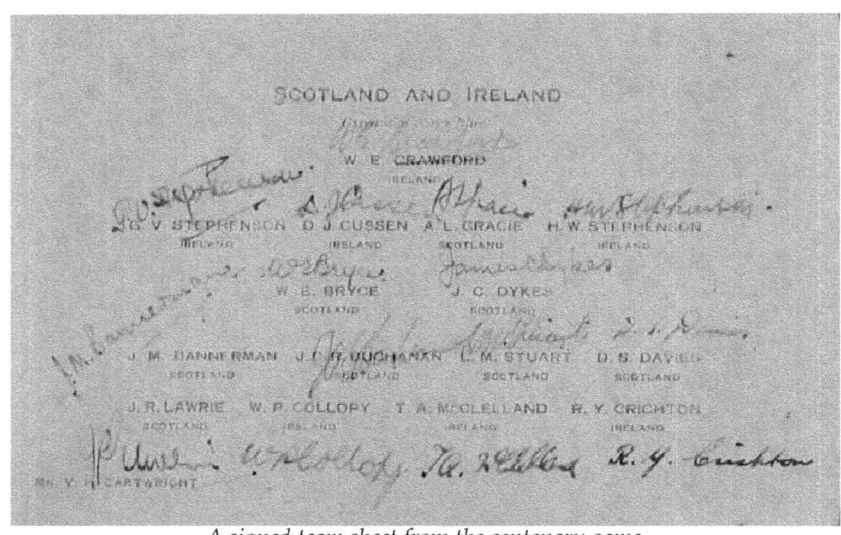

*A signed team sheet from the centenary game*

After the game, a formal black-tie dinner was held at the Great Central Hotel back in London.

The Jersey worn by Denis Cussen in the Rugby Centenary Game

# Barbarians

The Barbarians Football Club was formed in 1890 by William Percy Carpmael. One of the oldest rugby clubs in the world, the Barbarians are an invitational team who boast previous players that read like a who's who of the game; Bill Beaumont, Zinzan Brooke, David Campese, Dan Drysdale, Nick Farr Jones, Gavin Hastings, Jason Leonard, Jonah Lomu, Michael Lynagh, Victor Matfield, Richie McCaw, JPR Williams and Sonny Bill Williams have all worn the famous black and white shirt. From Ireland names such as Ernie Crawford, Ronnie Dawson, Mick Galwey, Jack Kyle, Willie John McBride, Brian O'Driscoll, Tony O'Reilly, Tom Reid and Tony Ward are Barbarians.

*The Ėspanade Hotel, Penarth – 'Home' of the Barbarians*

Originally the Baa-baas was based on the concept of putting together an invitational side to 'tour' Wales. Traditionally, they played four games each Easter against Penarth, Cardiff, Swansea and Newport. Later games against East Midlands and Leicester were added. It wasn't

Barbarians

until the 1950s that the Barbarians toured internationally and they have since gone on to become one of the rugby world's most recognised teams.

Basing themselves at the Éspanade Hotel in Penarth, the Barbarians Easter tour involved playing Penarth on Good Friday, Cardiff on Saturday, the team would play golf on Easter Sunday before playing Swansea on Easter Monday and rounding out the tour with a game against Newport at Rodney Parade on the Tuesday.

In 1926, Denis Cussen, by now playing for Blackheath, was invited to play for the Barbarians. It was a tremendous honour. Each year around thirty players were invited to play for the team. Each player would usually get two games over the weekend. Of the thirty-one players selected in 1926, thirteen of them were internationals. The following year, thirty-two players were selected of which twenty-five were internationals.

## 1926

At the start of March 1926, Denis Cussen was named in the Barbarians' team to play in the Edgar Mobbs Memorial Match against East Midlands. Mobbs was an English and Barbarians rugby player who had been killed in action at Passchendaele during the battle of Ypres in July 1915. From 1921, the annual game between the Barbarians and the East Midlands was named in his honour.

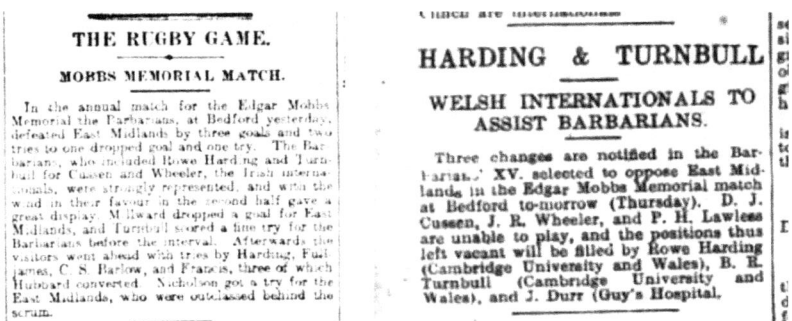

*Announcement of Denis in Barbarians team and subsequent withdrawal*

In 1926, the Edgar Mobbs Memorial match was played at Bedford on Thursday 4th March. This would have been Denis' first appearance for the famous team however, the day before the game he was forced to withdraw and was replaced.

The reason for his withdrawal was most likely due to his schedule. At the start of 1926, Denis was living in London and commuting to Ireland for Five Nations and Trinity games. He had played in Ireland's Five Nations game against Scotland four days earlier and played for Blackheath against Oxford two days after the Barbarians game.

A month later, with the tenth anniversary of the Easter Rising happening in Dublin, Denis travelled to the Éspanade Hotel in Penarth which served as the de-facto home of the Barbarians for decades. Here the team would get together, train and socialise ahead of their games. The social aspect of the Barbarians was important and golf was a key component of that. The year before Denis was invited to play for them, the Barbarians commissioned a large silver challenge cup which they presented to the Glamorganshire Golf Club in recognition of the support the club had given the Barbarians since their inception. That cup was awarded each year subsequently to the player in the squad who won the annual Easter Sunday golf tournament.

The games were held on successive days over the Easter week. The first game of 1926 was against Penarth on Friday 2nd April. Cussen didn't play in that game. The Barbarians won 33-17. He also sat out the loss to Cardiff the following day at Cardiff Arms Park.

Denis made his Barbarians debut against Swansea at St Helens Ground on Easter Monday, 5th April 1926. Captained by Scotsman David McMyn who went on the British and Irish Lions tour of Argentina in 1927, the team for the game included Ernie Crawford, Jammie Clinch and Mark Sugden from the Irish team. Also on the team was another Scotsman, Robert Kelly, who also toured with the Lions in 1927 and Henry Rew from England who was later killed while serving with the Tank Corp in Egypt in 1940.

Playing for Swansea was Dai Parker who won ten test caps for Wales and toured with the Lions in 1930. David Jenkins and Roy Jones also had international caps for Wales.

> *"This game at St Helen's on Monday was in pleasing contract to Saturday's match. The ball was thrown about freely, and although Swansea had the better of matters the Barbarians were always dangerous when near the Swansea line".*

Swansea came out on top in the game winning 17-11. Denis didn't get on the score sheet. The Barbarians tries were scored by Whitfield, Durr and Fellows-Smith.

The following day Denis again played for the Barbarians, this time against Newport. Amongst the Newport line-up was fellow Limerickman and doctor William Roche. Roche from Limerick City was a doctor living in Newport. He was previously capped by Munster and Ireland and had toured South Africa with the British and Irish Lions in 1924. He played for a number of years in Newport becoming the team captain in 1927. He is now a member of the Newport RFC Hall of Fame.

```
NEWPORT ATHLETIC GROUNDS.
    RUGBY FOOTBALL MATCHES.
       LONDON WELSH,
  SATURDAY, APRIL 3, AT 3.30 P.M.
           PONTYPOOL,
      EASTER MONDAY MORNING,
         At 11 o'clock.
         BARBARIANS
              v.
              NEWPORT.
    EASTER TUESDAY, AT 3.30 P.M.
       USUAL ADMISSION CHARGES.
```

The Barbarians won the game by six points to five. The six points came from a try by E Coley (England) and a penalty goal kicked by captain for the day Bettington.

This was the BaaBaas first victory over Newport in twenty-two years, only their second ever and the newspaper reports suggest it was well earned. The strength of the Barbarians in the scrum and strong running from the backs were called out in the various match reports.

The Barbarians finished their 1926 tour with two wins and two losses.

# 1927

When the initial squad was announced for the 1927 Barbarians tour, Denis wasn't among the twenty-five internationals named. Ten Scottish, six English, and eight Irishmen and one Welshman were initially named. The tour, coming at Easter, was just after the completion of the five nations competition and so it was common for players to have to drop out with injuries at the last minute. That was the case in 1927 and Denis was invited to join the team a few days before Easter.

> **BARBARIANS' TEAM.**
>
> **FAMOUS PLAYERS DROP OUT; OTHERS BROUGHT IN.**
>
> Some changes in the Barbarians' side to tour during the Easter holidays have been made. J. M. Bannerman, H. C. Catcheside, F. S. Hewitt, Ian Smith, K. A. Sellar, and W. H. Sobey drop out, and D. J. Cussen (St. Mary's Hospital), R. F. Kelly (Watsonians), M. Sugden (Wanderers), and W. G. Morgan (Cambridge University) are brought in.

*Denis (front extreme right) with the Barbarians squad of 1927*

The importance of the Barbarians Easter tour to the financial health of Welsh rugby is evident from a newspaper report just ahead of the games.

> *"This year they are bringing practically an international side, and those fortunate Welsh clubs favoured with fixtures are anticipating "bumper" gates. Penarth play them on Good Friday and I am convinced that if this was not an annual fixture the Welsh Football Union would have banned playing on that day many years ago. Penarth look to the*

*gate of Good Friday tiding them over the season. Some years ago, I inspected Penarth's statement of accounts, which showed a steady loss week by week until the visit of the Barbarians. The latter proved such an attraction that a heavy deficit was wiped out and the treasurer found himself with a nice sum in hand – quite an unusual experience for him."*

The Easter games started with a win over Penarth on 15th April. A record six thousand spectators packed into the Athletic Field as Denis lined out alongside Irish teammates Ernie Crawford and Mark Sugden. The Barbarians won the game by eight points to three. Denis Cussen performed strongly but failed to score.

*"There were some disappointing features of the game, for the Barbarians could never get into their stride through the stern defence of Penarth. Jack Bassett was chiefly responsible for holding up their attack and it is safe to say that if he had tackled and kicked in Welsh trial matches as he did on Good Friday, he would have been first choice for the international side this season. Four times he brought Cussen to earth when it seemed the Irish cap was well placed for a score"*

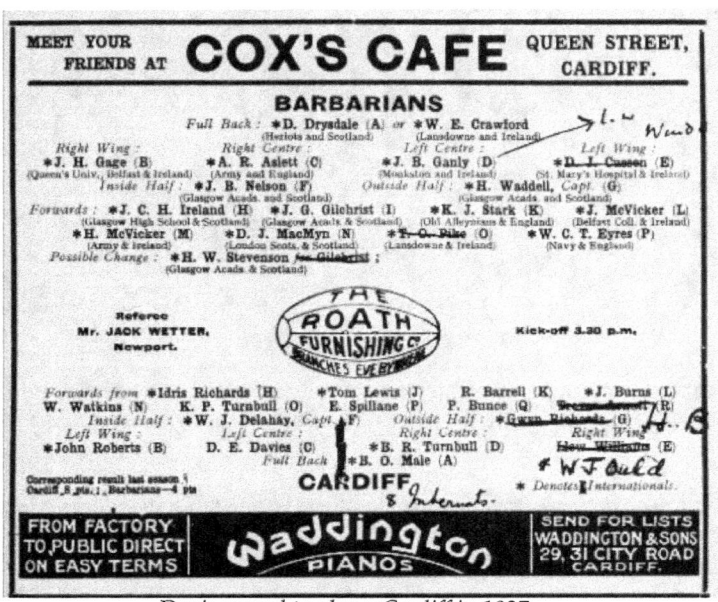

Denis named to play v Cardiff in 1927

Barbarians

The above team sheet for the third game of the series, against Cardiff, shows that Denis was named to play but was replaced late in the day, presumably due to injury.

In Denis' three games with the Barbarians, he won two and lost one.

| | Result | For | Against | Date | Comment |
|---|---|---|---|---|---|
| **Barbarians Easter Tour 1926** | | | | | |
| East Midlands | Win | 21 | 7 | 4th Mar | Cussen named but didn't play |
| Penarth | Win | 33 | 19 | 2nd Apr | Cussen didn't play |
| Cardiff | Loss | 4 | 8 | 3rd Apr | Cussen didn't play |
| Swansea | Loss | 11 | 17 | 5th Apr | Cussen played. Didn't score |
| Newport | Win | 6 | 5 | 6th Apr | Cussen played. Didn't score |
| Leicester | Loss | 8 | 13 | 28th Dec | Not selected |
| **Barbarians Easter Tour 1927** | | | | | |
| East Midlands | Win | 24 | 11 | 3rd Mar | Not selected |
| Penarth | Win | 8 | 3 | 15th Apr | Cussen played. Didn't score |
| Cardiff | Loss | 8 | 16 | 16th Apr | Cussen named but didn't play |
| Swansea | Win | 27 | 9 | 18th Apr | Cussen didn't play |
| Newport | Loss | 8 | 9 | 19th Apr | Cussen didn't play |
| Leicester | Loss | 13 | 16 | 27th Dec | Not selected |

*Barbarians results 1926 and 1927*

Barbarians

# National Athletics

Field sports and athletics have been pastimes have been played for centuries in Ireland, however, it wasn't until the 1880s that structure and organisation was put in place at a national level. The Gaelic Association for the Preservation and Cultivation of National Pastimes (GAA) was founded at Hayes Hotel in Thurles on November 1st 1884. They claimed jurisdiction over Gaelic games, athletics and cycling for the entire island of Ireland.

At the third recorded meeting of the association on January 17th 1885, also held in Thurles, rules were set out for the association. One of them was *"That after 17th March 1885, any athlete competing at meetings under other laws than those of the Gaelic Athletic Association shall be ineligible to compete at meetings held under the GAA"*. For a rugby player like Denis Cussen, this was problematic. He was effectively banned from any GAA events regardless of discipline.

Just a month after the GAA was founded, on February 21st, the Irish Amateur Athletics Association was founded. The IAAA was a sub-organisation of the Amateur Athletics Association which was the recognised administrator of athletics in Great Britain and Ireland. The IAAA also claimed jurisdiction over athletics for the entire island of Ireland.

While both organisations operated on the island in parallel for a number of years, there was a difference between them. As the IAAA was affiliated with the AAA in England, and the AAA was the recognised administrator of athletics for all of the United Kingdom and Ireland, any athlete who wanted to compete internationally, had to go via the IAAA route. Up until the establishment of the Irish Free State, Irish athletes would compete under the flag of Great Britain. The opportunity to represent Ireland was only within the AAA realm, in the annual home nations tri country competition against Scotland and England.

Denis as a rugby player and as an aspiring Olympian competed in the IAAA events and is notably absent from the GAA records for the time.

## 1920

Denis Cussen's first foray into national and international athletics competition was in 1920. The IAAA National Championships were held on 24th May that year. It is unclear if Denis Cussen took part but it is certain that he wasn't a medal winner. The 100-yards was won by MJ Stafford in 10 3/5 Seconds, Stafford also won the 220-yards and Cussen's other favoured competition, the long jump, was won by Sergeant Major Miller.

Despite either not taking place or not medalling, Cussen was selected to represent Ireland two weeks later when the Irish team to compete against England and Scotland at Crewe was announced. He is named alongside Miller for the long jump, with Stafford selected for the sprint races.

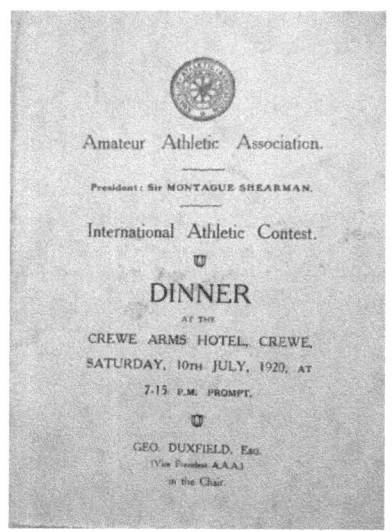

The Irish Athletics team began competing internationally as far back as 1876. That year, and the following, Ireland sent a team to compete against England. From 1895 until 1913, Ireland competed against Scotland annually and from 1914, Ireland, Scotland and England held an annual three-party international competition.

At the 1920 competition itself, held on 10th July at Crewe, Cussen managed to win a silver medal by jumping 21 feet and 7 inches. He was beaten by Scot W Hunter who beat him by four inches. The Irish Champion, Sergeant Major Miller didn't place.

At this athletics meeting, Cussen would also have had his first glimpse of sprinter Harold Abrahams and his first experience was a winning one. Abrahams, depicted in the movie Chariots of Fire, would win the sprint gold medal at the 1924 Olympics in Paris. In 1920, Abrahams won the 220-yards competition, but in the Long Jump, Cussen outjumped him into second place.

Ireland did not have their own team at the 1920 Olympic Games in Antwerp. Harold Abrahams represented Great Britain in the 100m, 200m and the long jump. If he had competed and matched his performance from Crewe, Cussen's distance of 21 feet and 7 inches (6.55m) would have placed him tenth at the games. Harold Abrahams came twentieth.

## 1921

*Denis Cussen (extreme right) at the start of the 100-yards final 1921*

Cussen cemented his reputation as an athlete of serious international capability at the I.A.A.A National Championships, held at Lansdowne Road on 16th May 1921.

> *"The feature of the open events was the triple success of DJ Cussen, the Irish international Rugby three-quarter, who defeated the older, Stafford in the 100-yards and 220-yards, and also annexed the long jump. In the 100-yards he won easily by four yards in a fine time of 10.2 seconds for a grass track, and the*

merit of his win in the furlong was enhanced by the fact that he was led by Stafford three yards in the straight."

In the 100-yards (President's Cup) Cussen easily beat the defending champion, MJ Stafford. The same pair battled it out in the 220-yards. Stafford was ahead by three yards as they came around the bend into the final straight but Cussen wore him down and overhauled him, winning by a yard in 24.2 seconds.

In the long jump, Cussen cleared 20 feet 11 inches almost two feet further than TC Gough in second. Gough only managed 19 feet and 2 inches. Cussen was the Irish 100-yards, 220-yards and Long Jump Champion.

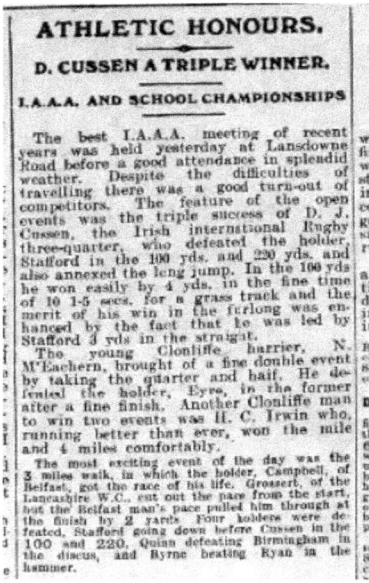

This qualified him for the international competition against Scotland and England. In 1921 that was held at Windsor Park, Belfast on July 11th.

In the 100-yards race, Cussen was up against Eric Liddell the Scottish Rugby International and future world record holder in the 400m. Cussen competed well but was beaten in to fourth place behind Liddell (gold), WA Hill from England and DI Black also from England.

Despite being the Irish Champion at the 220-yards, Cussen did not compete in that event in Belfast. That race was won by Hill with Eric Liddell taking third place.

In the long jump, Cussen placed second with a leap of 6.52m. The winner JL Dunn from Scotland beat him by 20cm.

*IAAA Celebration Dinner 1921*

## 1922

The 1922 I.A.A.A National Championships were held on Whit Monday, 5th June at Lansdowne Road.

Cussen retained his 100-yards title. He clocked a time of 10.6 seconds and beat RR Woods by a foot in the final. Woods won the 220-yards race. It isn't clear if Cussen took part.

Cussen also retained his long jump title with a jump of 22 feet and 1 inch, two feet further than J Connor who came second.

As Irish 100-yards champion and long jump champion, Cussen again qualified for the international series. In 1922 this was held at Hampden Park in Glasgow on Saturday 7th July.

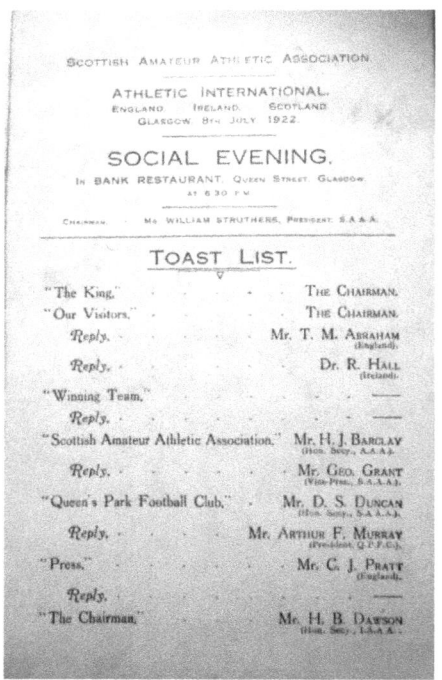

Englishman LC Royle won the sprint double of 100-yards and 200 yards with Scotsman Eric Liddell winning silver in both. Cussen again finished in fourth place in the 100-yards.

In the long jump competition, Denis Cussen again took second place. His jump of 6.62 metres (21 feet 8.7 inches) was better than the previous year but not enough as WH Childs from England outjumped him by eighteen centimetres.

## The Irish Free State

The founding of the Irish Free State in 1922 let to a shift in the administration of all sports in Ireland. Some of the implications are still visible today with rugby being an 'all island' team but in association football there are two Ireland teams.

The Anglo-Irish Treaty was signed on 6th December 1921. This gave all of the island of Ireland a form of independence. It also gave the counties of the north the option to opt out. The Irish Free State came into existence officially on 6th December 1922, one year after the treaty. The six counties of the north exercised their right to opt out and remain part of the United Kingdom. The first few months of the Free State saw all kinds of new bodies spring up. One of those was the National Athletics and Cycling Association.

With Denis Cussen as its last National 100 yard, the IAAA ceased to exist on July 18th 1922 and the GAA seeded the administration of athletics and cycling to the new organisation – the National Athletics and Cycling Association. For a period, there was a question as to whether the IAAA chapter in the north would join. There was concern that the NACA had banned members of the military and police forces from membership. Ultimately, that rule was dropped and the northern counties also joined the NACA.

## 1923

Under NACA, the same annual national championships continued to be held but with a slightly broader remit. NACA continued in existence until 2000 when Athletics Ireland and Cycling Ireland came into being.

The 1923 NACA National Championships were held on 30th June and 1st July at Croke Park. Unfortunately, Cussen had injured his ankle in May and was unable to take part in the inaugural NACA National Championships. In his absence Robert Rowan Woods won the 100-yards and Harry Conway won the long jump.

## 1924

NACA applied for and was granted membership of the International Amateur Athletics Association. They were admitted on 11th January 1924, giving them governance rights over all of the island and not just the Free State. With the Olympic Games being held in Paris that summer, it meant that any athlete who wanted to represent Ireland had to do so via NACA.

The Irish Olympic Council was established in 1922 during the provisional administration before the Irish Free State was even formed and was admitted to the International Olympic Committee once independence was achieved. Like NACA, the Irish Olympic Council saw itself as representing the entire Ireland of Ireland.

With funding in the new fledgeling state tight, Ireland first step into the Olympics was a tentative one. In team sports Ireland entered Water Polo and Football. Irish athletes also competed in thirteen athletics disciplines, seven boxing divisions and eight tennis events. Ireland was also represented in the Olympic art competition, with Jack Butler Yeats winning silver and Oliver St John Gogarty winning bronze in the literature competition.

The lack of funding meant that Ireland could only afford to enter one athlete per event at the 1924 Olympics. To represent Ireland, you had to come first in National Championships which were held at Croke Park on 8th June 1924. These would be National Championship, the Olympic trial and the Tailteann Games trial, all rolled into one.

### Inter-University Athletic Championships

A week before the championships, Denis Cussen competed in the Inter-University Athletic Championships at College Park. The Inter-University Athletics Championships were an annual event in which the University who won the most medals carried away the JP O'Sullivan Cup.

Denis, still not fully recovered from the ankle injury he had suffered a year earlier, competed for Trinity in the 100-yards, the shotput and, alongside his brother Bertie, in the long jump. Bertie also competed in the hurdles event.

In the 100-yards Denis won his heat. The Irish Independent reporting that he *"won easily in 10.45 seconds"*. In the second heat Robert Rowan Woods beat Harry Conway in a time of 10.25 seconds.

Cussen, Conway and Woods fought it out in the final but Cussen could only come in third *"by three-quarters of a yard after a great race"*. Conway won with Woods in second place.

Along with his brother Bertie, Denis came up against Harry Conway again in the long jump. Denis came second with a jump of 20ft 11 ¾ inches, two inches shorter than UCD's Conway. Bertie came in third, though unfortunately his jump distance wasn't recorded in newspaper reports.

Denis' last event was the 16lb shot. Again, he fell just short. He came second with a throw of 35 ft 9 inches, missing gold by just three inches.

Inter-Club Athletic Contests at College Park.—Finsh of the 100 yards final—D. Cussen (D. U.), on extreme right, was first, and R. R. Woods, second.
"Irish Independent" Photo.
*Irish Independent – Mon 30th June 1924*

## National Championships 1924

In the National Championships held at Croke Park on July 8th, Cussen would again compete with Woods and Conway. Joining them was WJ (Bill) Lowe. Born in Belfast but living in Manchester, Lowe was the dark horse.

With an opportunity to represent Ireland at the Olympic Games at stake, Cussen, Woods, Conway and Lowe took part in the 100-yards. In the first heat Robert Rowan Woods came first in a time of 10.45 seconds. Bill Lowe won the second heat by two yards in a time of 10.35 seconds. Cussen won the third heat but only clocked at time of 11 seconds. Conway won the fourth heat. The final heat was won by P Gummer, an Irishman living in London.

The winners of each of the heats lined up in the final. Five runners with just one Olympic place. In the end it was Lowe who won in a time of 10.35 seconds. He was going to the Olympics in Paris. Gummer came second a yard behind and Woods took the bronze medal. Cussen could only manage fourth place.

In the Running Long Jump competition, Denis and his brother Bertie also competed but again, they were beaten. Harry Conway won well.

Denis Cussen would miss the 1924 Olympics but he had qualified for the Tailteann Games.

# 1924 Tailteann Games, Dublin

The Tailteann Games were an ancient Irish sports festival that was deeply rooted in Irish culture and mythology. Held at Tara as far back as 632 BC, they had died out over time, with the last recorded instance running in 1168, the year before the Normans arrived in Ireland.

After the Anglo-Irish Treaty was ratified by Dáil Eireann in January 1922, plans got underway to establish an Ireland which, although still not fully independent, had strong cultural independence.

Corkman and Easter 1916 veteran, JJ Walsh was appointed to the cabinet position of Postmaster General in the first Cumann na nGaedheal government and it was he who was the driving force that led to the reestablishment of the Tailteann Games in 1924.

Walsh envisioned a games, modelled on the Olympics, that would be open to anyone with Irish blood and that would celebrate Irish sports, athleticism and culture. He set about putting the games together and found support in the Gaelic Athletic Association. Michael Cusack and Michael Davin had hoped to revive the Tailteann Games as part of the establishment of the GAA in 1884. They foresaw *"a national festival not only of athletics but also of music and poetry involving the Celtic Race throughout the world."*

Walsh was issued with £10,000 by the new government to improve the facilities at Croke Park which was the host the opening and closing ceremony for the games.

The games were to be held between 6th and 13th August 1922. As late as 8th June 1922, Walsh spoke in the Dáil saying the games would go ahead and would be twice as large as the Greek Olympics. Then, on 28th June, six weeks before the Opening Ceremony, anti-treaty forces occupied the Four Courts and the Civil War started. The games had to be postponed.

# 1924 Tailteann Games

*Poster for the original 1922 Tailteann Games*

When the Tailteann Games were eventually held in August of 1924, they were a mammoth event, even larger than the Paris Olympic Games which had just been held. Dublin was turned into a carnival of sports and culture. Events included, a horse show, a boating regatta, art competition, music competition, hurling and shinty, football, swimming, gymnastic displays, chess, tennis, golf, arts and crafts, tug-of-war, billiards, handball, clay pigeon shooting, motorcycle racing, dancing, diving, rodeo, literary award, boxing and cycling. The notable absences were Rugby, Soccer and Hockey which fell under the GAA's foreign games ban.

The Irish government were making a bold statement about what the new Ireland could do. To ensure that Ireland got as much exposure as possible, it was decided to loosen the requirement for the competitors to have Irish blood. A big effort was made to attract the Olympic athletes who had just competed in Paris to come and take part. In the end hundreds of them came to Dublin to compete. 6,500 athletes, representing Ireland, England, Scotland, Wales, Australia, USA, Canada, New Zealand and South Africa, converged on Dublin for the event.

**DE VALERA STILL OPPOSES JOINING TAILTEANN GAMES**

DUBLIN, Aug 1—Eamon de Valera, in a statement made public today, says his decision, reached several months ago, not to participate in Tailteann games remains unchanged and that it is binding on all Republicans.

The attitude of the Republicans, the statement adds, will be one of protest through noncooperation.

# 1924 Tailteann Games

## DAIL EIREANN
(Government of the Republic of Ireland)

### TO THE PEOPLE OF IRELAND AND TO EVERY MEMBER OF THE IRISH RACE:

# AONACH TAILTEANN

In the year 1921 Dail Eireann, the Government of the Republic of Ireland, in the confident belief that the Unity and Freedom of Ireland had been achieved, and that the Truce called for by Great Britain would result in the recognition of the Sovereign Independence of the Irish Nation, decreed that Aonach Tailteann, which in times past was the symbol of Irish Unity and Independence, and was last held by the Ard Righ, Roderick O'Connor, in the Twelfth Century, should be re-established, and that the inaugural Aonach should be held in the year 1922. But the Delegates sent to London in 1922, to negotiate a peace with Great Britain, yielding to the British threats of renewed and more terrible war, signed, without authority and in breach of previous undertakings, a so-called Treaty which purported to abolish the Republic of Ireland, to surrender the Sovereignty of this Nation and to partition our country. This unauthorised and unconstitutional action of those Delegates divided our people, and brought intense suffering and distress on the Nation and the inaugural Aonach, designed to be a great Republican festival, was of necessity postponed.

Now, in the midst of our renewed effort for Irish Unity and Independence, when the Republic is struggling for existence and President de Valera with the Minister of Finance and 1,200 soldiers of the Republic are held captive in military prisons, under the most inhuman conditions, for their refusal to give allegiance to a foreign King, and deny the Sovereignty of the Nation, certain persons, devoted to the British interest, having a member of the so-called Free State Government at their head, and encouraged by financial assistance from this so-called Free State Government, are endeavouring and preparing to hold games and festivals at Dublin in August, 1924, under the name of Aonach Tailteann, and thereby seek to delude our people abroad as to the national position.

The Government of the Republic, therefore, calls upon all citizens of the Republic not to give any aid or encouragement to or directly or indirectly promote or participate in the games or festivals, proposed to be held at Dublin in August, 1924, and falsely described as Aonach Tailteann, and the Government of the Republic also calls upon all members of the Irish Race throughout the world to refuse aid or encouragement and to refrain from participation in those games and festivals.

DUBLIN.
*April 8th, 1924*

pádraig ó ruitléir,
Acting President

*De Valera's call to boycott the Tailteann Games.*

Despite calls from Eamon De Valera for Irish republicans to boycott the games, the went ahead to great fanfare. Through July, Ireland was awash with 'qualifying trials' for the various sports, newspapers carried articles explaining some of the sports not generally known in Ireland and big names began to arrive in the country. Famed Westmeath Tenor Count John McCormack returned home to take part in judging the musical events.

# 1924 Tailteann Games

The opening ceremony, held at Croke Park on 2nd August, attracted not just a huge crowd of spectators, but also international news crews. The opening ceremony was an elaborate affair with all of the athletes parading in front of the crowds and dignitaries who were headed by JJ Walsh.

*Athletes parade around Croke Park*

*Athletes parade around Croke Park*

# 1924 Tailteann Games

*Actors in Celtic costume with Irish Wolfhounds lead the parade of athletes*

*International News Crews cover the opening ceremony*

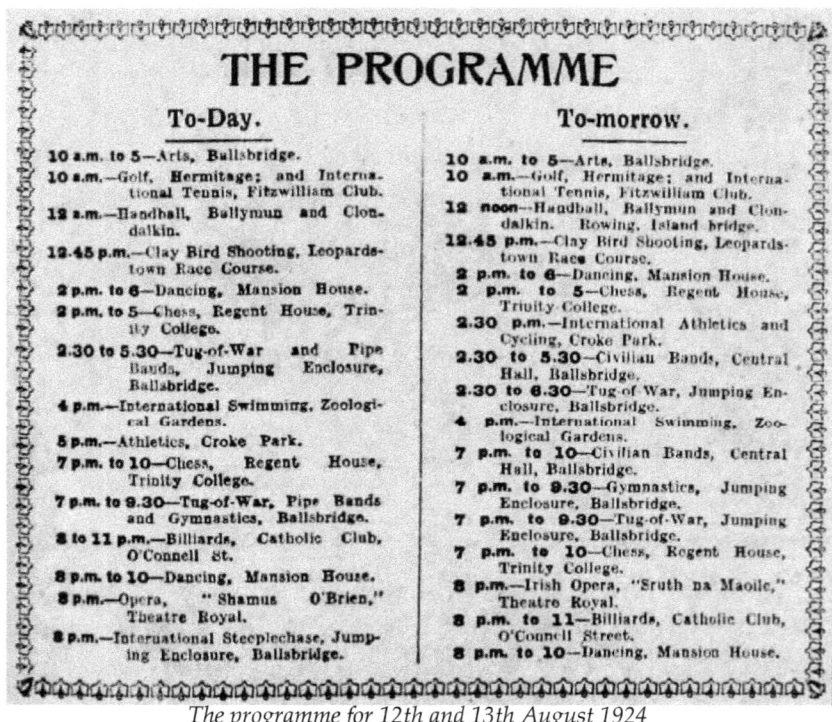

*The programme for 12th and 13th August 1924*

The 1924 Tailteann Games 100m field was a seriously strong one. Denis Cussen had qualified by making the final at the National Championships. Lining up against him was three-time Olympic medallist Jackson Stoltz. He had just won gold in the 200m and silver in the 100m at the Paris Olympics. He had also previously won gold in the 1920 Antwerp games. He was a superstar globally and it was a real coup to have him at the games.

New Zealand's Arthur Porritt, the bronze medallist in the 100m in Paris was in the field. Porritt would become a long-time friend and colleague at Cussen at St Mary's Hospital.

Cyril Coaffee from Canada. London born Coaffee had been captain of the Canadian team in the 1924 Olympic games and had made the semi-final of the 100m. Two years earlier, he had equalled the world record for the 100-yards at the Canadian National Championships.

## 1924 Tailteann Games

Neither Eric Liddell nor Harold Abrahams opted to come to Ireland for the Tailteann Games. Had they done so, it would have been one of the strongest ever line-ups for a 100m race.

The 100m event was held on Wednesday 13th August. With a field of twenty athletes, lots were drawn and the runners divided across four heats. Denis Cussen ran in the first heat against Coaffee (Canada), D Crowley (England) and J Reynolds (England). To qualify for the final, Cussen would have to win the heat or be the fasted loser. A difficult task.

In front of an expectant crowd of 20,000, Cussen came a respectable third place. Canadian Coaffee come first and Crowley second. The time was fast compared to what Cussen was achieving at that stage in his career. Coaffee crossed the line in 10.8 seconds, a foot ahead of Crowley.

The second heat was won by Olympic silver medallist Jackson Scholtz (USA). Cussen's local rival Harry Conway came third in that heat.

The third heat was won by McKechenneay (Canada). The Olympic bronze medallist Arthur Porritt from New Zealand came second.

*McKechenneay, Scholz and Hester training ahead of the games*

Edwin "Slip" Carr from Australia won the 4th heat. Carr had equalled the world record for the 100m in 1923. Injury had hampered his performance in the Olympics where he went out in the semi-final. Like Denis Cussen, he was also a rugby international having played for the

Wallabies on four occasions in 1921. His grandfather was from Roscommon.

The final was contested by the winner of each heat plus the fastest looser who was Hester (Canada) from the 4th heat. Denis Cussen watched on as Carr (Australia), Scholz (USA), Coaffee (Canada), Crowley (England), McKechanneay (Canada) and Hester (Canada) raced for glory at Croke Park. Carr won gold, just inches ahead of Scholz and Coaffee.

> *"The final of the hundred metres was thrilling. Scholz (USA), Carr (Australia) and Coaffee (Canada) in the foremost flight of world's sprinters, were concerned in a race where the pace of 10 yards per second was exceeded in Ireland for the first time. That track was rain laden, too, and knocked yards off the pace off the sprinters trained to cinder tracks. The tome for 100metres (10.2 seconds) was remarkable under the conditions.*
>
> *The sprinters were uneasy under Denis Power's pistol and Sholtz was left a yard with Carr well away. The Australian's long legs and stride helped him on the heavy sod, and Scholz seemed out of it at half way. The American crack found a torrent of pace, and finished with one of his lightning bursts. When he threw his right shoulder on the worsted, he seemed to me to have won, and a dead-head was the worst h could get. Coaffee of Canada ran a magnificent race at a smooth pace right through. Sholtz will reverse the verdict in the 200 metres".*
>
> *"Carr had a slight advantage on Scholz at the start, but he did not lose an inch until a few yards from the tape, when Scholz made his characteristic final effort, to be beaten by inches. Carr reached the semi-final of the event in the Olympic Games. The time of 10.8 seconds is 1/5 second behind the Olympic record, and 2/5 behind the world's best time held by Paddock (USA)."*

The same three competitors would also win the medals in the 200m which was contested the following day. Scholz took gold, Carr silver and Coaffee bronze in that event.

The 1924 Tailteann games continued for two weeks and was viewed as a great success. Competitors such as Johnny Weissmuller, who was a triple Olympic gold medallist swimmer, competed and won in the swimming competition which was held in the pond at the Phoenix

Park. He would find further fame playing Tarzan in a series of Hollywood films.

American Harold Osborn, a double high jump and decathlon winner at the Olympics won at Croke Park despite spirited competition from local Larry Stanley. Stanley had captained the 1919 All Ireland winning Kildare team.

**TAILTEANN GAMES**
AND
**America v. Ireland (Hurling),
Munster v. Ulster (Football),**
AT
**CROKE PARK, DUBLIN,**
SUNDAY NEXT, 3rd AUGUST, 1924.

*An advert for an International Hurling game played at the Tailteann Games*

The biggest events in terms of spectator numbers were the motorcycle races held in the Phoenix Park and air display put on by the newly formed Air Corp. These two attracted 40,000 and 20,000 spectators respectively. The Air Corp put on a display where they simulated attacking a castle erected on the grounds of the Phoenix Park. Fireworks and explosions simulated real bombs as plaster-of-paris objects were dropped from the passing aeroplanes.

## 1925

The 1925 NACA National Championships were held on Saturday 27th and Sunday 28th June at Croke Park.

In the 100-yards, Denis Cussen's brother Bertie competed in the first heat and came a narrow second place behind defending champion Bill Lowe who won in 10.4 seconds. Bertie was just a yard behind him in second. Denis won the second heat from Muirceartach Gregan in the same time as the first heat, 10.4 seconds.

Four competitors lined up in the final. The two Cussen brothers, Muirceartach Gregan and Bill Lowe.

In an explosive race, Denis Cussen blasted the field. He won by four yards and ran ten seconds flat. Second place went to Gregan. Bronze went to Shaw and Bertie came in fourth. Denis' time equalled the National Record which had stood since 1901 when Denis Murray set it. It had been equalled once previously by Fredrick Shaw in 1913.

Denis Murray was a Cork athlete who had represented Great Britain in the 1908 Olympic Games in London. This was before the Free State when Ireland was part of Great Britain. By taking the 100-yards and 220-yards double at the Irish AAA Championships for six successive years (1901-06), Murray completely dominated Irish sprinting in the early years of the 20th century. Murray had set his record while competing in the Amateur Athletics Association's National Championships at Huddersfield on 6th July 1901. Despite setting a record for an Irish athlete, Murray only finished third in that race.

Frederick Shaw, like Cussen, was a graduate of Trinity's medical school. He was a first cousin of George Bernard Shaw. Shaw had set his 10 second record at Celtic Park in Belfast on 19th July 1913. At the outbreak of WW1, he enlisted in the army and became a major in the Royal Army Medical Corp. He was awarded the Military Cross in January 1917 for distinguished service in battle. As well as being a record sprinter, Shaw was also a first-class cricketer and represented Ireland on a number of occasions. Shaw died at the young age of 43 in Iraq. He was working at Chief Medical Officer for Iraq Petroleum at the time.

Note that some references are made to Nathanial Cartmell also being the holder of the Irish record at 10 second flat. Cartmell was an American sprinter. References to him relate to him running that time in Ireland, as opposed to being an Irishman running the record. Cartmell competed in Ireland a number of times and ran 100-yards in 10 second in July 1909 during an invitational race at the Oval Ground in Belfast. Cartmell, who lost two fingers in a childhood accident with an axe, was a four-time Olympic medallist. At the 1904 Olympics he won silver in both the 100m and 200m. Four years later, he won gold in the 4x100m relay and bronze in the 200m at the 1908 Olympics. The 4x100m relay is notable as the USA team featured John Taylor who became the first African American to win Olympic gold.

# 1924 Tailteann Games

*Hurdler Dan Quinlan (left), Bertie Cussen (front), Denis Cussen (right) 1925*

Despite setting the record for the 100-yards, Denis Cussen did not compete in the 220-yards race which was won by Sean Lavan. He also didn't compete in the long jump which was won by J Connor from Belfast who cleared 22ft 10 ½ inches.

As was the practice at the time, the Irish winners went on to compete for Ireland in a triangular competition against England and Scotland. In 1925, that competition was held in Ireland for the first time and took place on 11th July at Croke Park. 10,000 spectators turned out to watch the events.

In the 100-yards, Cussen was beaten into third place by LJ Goody and HW Brooker, both from England. The Irish Independent gave a possible explanation for his defeat.

> "The brothers Cussen formed the wings of a sextette, RJ being on the outside with Goody on his left. After the break they got away to a perfect start. At about 60 yards Cussen was slightly in front, but he staggered as the result of putting his foot in a hole. Goody won from his compatriot by half a yard, with Cussen three yards off. Time, 10 Seconds."

1924 Tailteann Games

*The teams and officials who participated in the international competition between England, Ireland and Scotland in 1925 at Croke Park. Cussen is standing centre of the picture, eight from the right. Bertie is standing on the extreme right*

## 1926

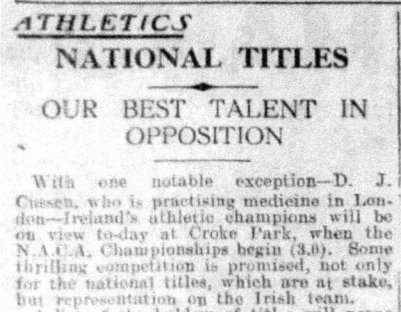

By now practicing medicine in London, Denis Cussen sat out the 1926 athletics season. The NACA National Championships held at Croke Park on 26th June. Cussen relinquished his 100-yards title to Sean Lavan. Bertie came in third behind J Eustace. The winning time was outside of Denis' ten second record.

*"From a perfect start the three raced together to the half-way mark, after which Lavan had a slight advantage, but Eustace held his pace splendidly to throw himself on the tape abreast with Lavan. Cussen was two yards off. Time 10.2 Seconds."*

Bertie extended the series of Cussen national titles when he won the long jump competition with a leap of 22ft 7¾ inches.

Bertie went on to compete in the triangular series which was held at Hampden Park. In the 100-yards, Bertie Cussen came in a credible fourth place behind Crawford from Scotland and Englishmen Gill and Green. He also claimed a silver medal in the long jump. He came in second with a jump of 6.82m, just thirteen centimetres behind GA Clarke from England.

## 1927

Again in 1927, Denis Cussen sat out the National Championships. In his absence Sean Lavan had a clean sweep of the championships winning gold in the 100-yards, 220-yards, 440 yards and the 120 yards hurdles. Bertie Cussen retained his long jump title, winning well with a jump of 6.81m.

In the triangular series held at Manchester, Bertie failed to make the medals in the long jump and Sean Lavan had to settle for second in the 220-yards and gold in the 440 yards.

1924 Tailteann Games

# 1928 Ireland's Fastest Man

1928 was Olympic year. Denis Cussen was living in London and was no longer playing rugby with the Irish national team. He was still very keen to represent Ireland though and when it was announced that the Irish National Championships would take place in Dublin on 23rd and 24th June, he made plans to be there. As had been the case in 1924, the National Championships would again serve as the trials for the Tailteann and Olympic Games.

In the lead up to the Irish trials Cussen took part in some races in London. In May he came third, behind R Leigh-Wood and Arthur Porritt, in the London Athletics Club Championships.

He then competed in the St Mary's Hospital sports event in the first week of June. The Evening Herald carried an article on 7th June which said:

*"Denis Cussen, the former Irish sprint champion, and joint holder of the Irish record of 10 seconds for 100-yards, competed at the St Mary's Hospital sports in London recently, when he showed he is as good as ever by doing 10 seconds for the hundred.*

*Cussen in addition to equalling the Irish record, defeated the New Zealander, AE Porritt, who was third in the Olympic 100 metres at Paris, and who is a probable competitor at the forthcoming Olympiad in Amsterdam.*

*Cussen also showed a return to his former prowess in the long jump by clearing 22ft 9in without a board take-off. This is 1 ½ inches better than Anglim's jump in the Decathlon last Saturday, which was the best effort of the Irish season so far. Cussen holds the Irish Inter-Varsity record of 22ft 10 in and his latest effort comes as a pleasant surprise.*

*If Cussen can spare the time for training he might prove capable of even greater things, and the above performances must certainly advance his claims to recognition by the NACA for the Olympic trials. Cussen has been out of athletics in Ireland for about two or three years, and on his last appearance in the 100-yards championship was the victim of cruel luck, as when leading halfway up he stuck his toe in a hole and cracked up."*

A week later, at Stamford Bridge, Cussen entered in the United Hospitals sports event. He again beat Arthur Porritt to win the 100-yards. He also won silver medals in the shot put and the long jump.

## FINE SPRINT BY CUSSEN

### Even Time at the United Hospitals Sports—Stallard Wins Mile

The fifty-seventh annual athletic meeting of the United Hospitals Athletic Club was held at Stamford Bridge yesterday, largely in a downpour of rain, which naturally was against competitors returning fast times.

The first event, however—the 100 yards Challenge Cup final—was favoured with brilliant sunshine, and the winner, D. J. Cussen (St. Mary's), equalled the time of 10 seconds set up by W. A. Steward (London), 15 years years ago. W. Hertzog (Guy's), the holder, secured third place, a foot away from A. E. Porritt (St. Mary's).

Porritt won the 220 yards Challenge Cup in 24 1-5s by a foot from W. W. Craner (London), with C. W. Harrison (Guy's) two yards behind, third.

*Daily Mirror – 15th June 1928*

Entries for the Irish Championships closed on 16th June and there was great excitement at the prospect of Cussen's return. His recent victories over Arthur Porritt at the St Marys and then United Hospitals games, and the fact that he was running 10 seconds flat raised the prospect of a great competition for the Irish title and the possibility that the national record of ten seconds flat could fall.

### D. CUSSEN FOR DUBLIN

D. J. Cussen, the old Irish Rugby international, will travel from London to compete in the Irish athletic championships on the 23rd and 24th instant at Dublin. Recently Cussen has accomplished the notable feat of beating A. E. Porritt, the famous New Zealand sprinter, on two occasions, his time in each case being 10s. dead.

## ATHLETICS
### OLYMPIC HOPES

#### D. CUSSEN TO COMPETE IN CHAMPIONSHIPS

Last night the entries for the Athletic Championships closed. An exceptionally large number have sent in their names, and very keen competition is expected in all events, in view of the fact that Ireland's representatives for the Olympic and Tailteann Games will be selected at the conclusion of the competition.

All our prominent athletes, including Lavan, Eustace, Coughlan, Moynihan, O'Connor, Shanahan, O'Dwyer, Moore, Dr. O'Callaghan, Britton, O'Grady, M'Eachern, Magan, Moloney, Flood, Connor, Anglim, Groarke and Birmingham have entered.

**Advice has been received from D. J. Cussen that he intends travelling from London to compete in the Championships.**

In view of his recent performances across-Channel, we may take it that the 100 yards will be a very exciting event.

#### SCHOOLBOY JUMPER.

An entry has been received from Gutienez, of St. Joseph's College, Clondalkin, for the Hop, Step, and Jump, and it has been decided to accept same in view of his excellent performance in the Schools and Colleges Championships recently held.

#### CUSSEN'S FINE FORM.

For the second time within a short period, D. J. Cussen accomplished the notable feat of beating A. E. Porritt, the famous New Zealand sprinter, in the 100 yards, his time in each case being 10 seconds dead. In the first instance it was at the St. Mary's Hospital sports; on Thursday last he did it at the United Hospitals' sports, and Cussen was also second in the long jump and the 16lb. shot.

It is good news to learn that he is coming over for the Irish championships, for his performances have been better than any seen on Irish tracks this year.

---

Denis Cussen arrived back in Dublin for the National Championships at the end of June 1928. While he hadn't competed in the event for two years, there were some familiar challengers. The defending champion Sean Lavan, Gregan, Gummer, Eustace and Bertie Cussen had all raced against Cussen before.

Bertie was in the first heat. He was up against JB Eustace and JV Connell. Eustace won the heat in 10.2 seconds. He was two yards ahead of Connell in second with Bertie coming another three yards behind.

Denis Cussen was in the second heat. His competitors were TD Phelan, JB Flood and M McAlinden. Cussen blew the field away. He clocked a time of 10 seconds, again equalling the national record. He finished a full five yards ahead of the field.

Gummer won the third heat. Defending champion Sean Lavan had to settle for second place and Gregan third. The winner of each heat plus the fastest loser contested the final. Four men lined up for the final, Denis Cussen, Eustace, Gummer and Phelan.

The quartet got away to a fairly level start but Cussen had pulled out in front after twenty yards and, increasing his lead to the finish, won by four yards. Two yards separated Eustace and Gummer. The winning time was 9.8 seconds which was new Irish national record, equal to the world record for 100-yards on grass at the time and just .2

of a second outside the overall world record. Denis Cussen was Ireland's fastest man and equal fastest man in the world.

**MONDAY, Irish Independent JUNE 25, 1928.**

**ATHLETICS**

## D. CUSSEN'S GREAT "HUNDRED"

### HIGH STANDARD IN N.A.C.A. CHAMPIONSHIP EVENTS

*"In a meeting so productive of first-class performances it would be difficult, as well as invidious, to select any one event as the outstanding feature of the gathering. It is not inappropriate that precedence should be given to Denis Cussen's 'hundred', as it was the only event in which an Irish record was made. The race was notable for other reasons. After having had a lease of the title for a number of years, Lavan was beaten by a visiting Irishman, PA Gummer of London. It was a matter of inches, but the significant fact is that the man who beat Lavan was six yards behind Cussen in the final.*

*In view of Cussen's win and his new record, it would have been nice to have had Lavan in the final of the race; but had he gone in as fastest loser, or for any other reason, I cannot believe he would have had anything to say to the result. He would probably have finished in the same relative position to Gummer.*

*Cussen's 'come-back' was notable. He has been out of Ireland since he qualified at Trinity, and his position on the staff of St Mary's Hospital in London does not give him opportunities for following either athletics or Rugby football as keenly as he did in his student days. His recent beatings – two in succession – of Porritt, the New Zealander (who ran so well at the last Olympic Games), was discounted by many; but that Cussen is by no means a 'has been' was amply demonstrated yesterday. To use a hackneyed phrase, Cussen may be said to have spreadeagled the field.*

*The four runners got away to a beautiful start. Mr Clarke and Capt. Harkness were most painstaking in their efforts to see that no one was beaten on the line. Cussen made those opposed to him appear as second-raters, and with every stride he got further away from them, beating Eustace by four yards and Gummer by half a dozen. It was not a surprise* when the timekeepers announced the time as 9 4/5 seconds, the first occasion that 'evens' has been beaten in Ireland. There were five watches on the race and none of them made the time more than the official return. The ground was measured afterwards and was found to be three inches over the distance".

*Cussen crosses the finish line to set the Irish record in 1928*

*The medal Cussen received for winning the 1928 National Title*

## 1928 Ireland's Fastest Man

Renowned GAA Historian Seamus O'Ceallaigh recorded this eye witness account of that unforgettable day at the National Stadium:

*"I have attended many Irish championships and have seen may athletes from different nations in action but the athlete who stands foremost in my mind is Denis Cussen, of Newcastle West, and the day, when he equalled the world's grass track record at Croke Park in June 1928.*

*The successful athlete must be egotistic and self-centred. Denis Cussen had not a scrap of these in his mental make-up. He was a very finely built man, and ran with an easy grace, yet with that latent power in every stride. I have never seen a sprinter with such broad shoulders and deep chest, and I did not know which to admire most, the swift moving legs or the powerful torso.*

*But that day in June 1928, it was a lovely summer's day, not a breath of wind and the large crowd seemed to sense the keenness that was displayed by the athletes, for the Irish Olympic team was being picked on the results.*

*The heats of the 100-yards were run off early and splendid form was displayed by Eustace, Cussen and Gummer, the two former turning 'evens' while Gummer was only a fifth outside.*

*When the four got on their marks for the final, a hush fell on the crowd and all eyes were on the four white intent figures as the crouched on the line. The pistol report released them as one man and as on man they came together for twenty or thirty yards.*

*Here Eustace and Cussen drew away from the others, side by side up to the half-way mark. An extraordinary change then came over Cussen's style. He seemed to get his head more forward, his arms threshed the air like flails and his stride lengthened until it appeared as if his legs were being driven out of his body by big powerful springs. He shot away from Eustace, who seemed to be running backwards by contrast.*

*His running captured the imagination of the crowd, who started to their feet cheering and shouting while he was yet twenty yards out from the tape.*

*The cheering spurred him on to further effort, and rising his chest, as if with a deep breath, he literally burnt up the last ten yards and flung himself at the tape as if his very life depended on it.*

*He breasted the tape to a regular salvo of cheering which was succeeded by an eerie silence as everyone listened intently for the time. When the world record time of 9.8 seconds was announced, the cheering broke out anew, for everyone felt that they had seen a truly memorable performance.*

*Cussen is the second or third man in the history of world's athletics to have run 100-yards in 9.8 seconds on a grass track, and in my opinion this time will never be beaten on the grass. I am quite confident, from the power, and speed he displayed that afternoon, that if he was running on cinders, he would have returned 9.5 seconds.*

*I never saw Denis Cussen running again, and I often felt since that if he had been an American or even an Englishman, instead of an Irishman, to what heights would he not have attained in athletic spheres. Like many other Irish athlete, he had abundance of natural ability, but he never seemed to develop it to its fullest capacity, except on that wonderful June afternoon in Croke Park."*

After qualifying for the Irish team at the National Championships in Dublin on 23rd and 24th June, Denis Cussen returned to London where he continued to work and train ahead of the Olympic Games.

He took part in the Amateur Athletic Association of England Championships which took place at Stamford Bridge, London on 6th and 7th July. He won his heat in a time of 10.3 seconds but performed poorly by his standards and lost to South African Wilfred (Billie) Legg against whom he would also race at the Olympic Games. In a letter home after the race, he explained his poor performance.

*"I did a lot of work during the week. Standing around giving anaesthetic and assisting at operations. On the morning of the event, I didn't rest from 9 o'clock in the morning and had to give two anaesthetics. I felt like a log. No snap in the muscles at all, just heavy... Still, with rest I hope to do better."*

*Denis Cussen at the 1928 National Championships at Croke Park*

1928 Ireland's Fastest Man

*General Eoin O'Duffy congratulating Denis Cussen after his record-breaking performance at Croke Park in 1928*

After his record-breaking performance, Denis was congratulated and received his medal from General Eoin O'Duffy who was at that time the president of the National Athletic and Cycling Association. O'Duffy had been a member of the Irish Volunteers and was active during the war of independence. He was pro-treaty and worked hard

1928 Ireland's Fastest Man

to prevent the civil war. When the Garda Siochana was established, he became Garda Commissioner. O'Duffy was dismissed from his role as Garda Commissioner in 1933 by Eamon de Valera. Later, O'Duffy's career took a controversial turn when he became leader of the fascist-inspired Army Comrades Association also known as the 'Blueshirts'.

## Denis Cussen's Record

Denis' time for 100-yards of 9.8 seconds would make his 100m time around 10.7 seconds. Today's 100m sprinters regularly break ten seconds and there is no doubt that they are better trained, have a better diet and equipment. Today's sprinters run on synthetic running tracks that are designed to give a degree of bounce. Denis' time was achieved on grass which is naturally a slower surface. Denis ran in a pair of spikes with a goatskin upper, leather insole and wrought iron spikes. Running shoes today are fundamentally different. Sprinters today have starting blocks which are designed to give a firm footing to allow the best possible traction at the start. In the 1920s, sprinters carried a trowel with them and dug small holes in the turf at the start line to give them a footing. With all of the technical advantages that today's sprinters have, a little under a one second advance is not a lot. We can never tell how Cussen would match with today's runners, but he wouldn't have been far off the pace.

The record set by Denis Cussen on 23rd June 1928 technically still stands as the Irish record. It was matched by Fred Moran on 30th August 1937. Coincidentally Moran was also a rugby player who was capped by Ireland on nine occasions in the 1930s. The record was again matched, by Paddy Lowry, on 2nd July 1960. These three shared the record of 9.8 seconds for 100-yards which then fell from favour, with 100 metres becoming the preferred distance. There is no doubt that Irish people have run faster but these have been over 100 metres. In order for Denis Cussen's record to be officially beaten, someone would need to run an official 100-yards race.

In 1968, Limerickman Brendan O'Regan beat the time when he ran 10.5 seconds for 100m. Cussen's 100m time would have been around 10.71 seconds. The current Irish 100m record is held by Israel Olatunde who ran 10.08 seconds in August 2025. Rhasidat Adeleke holds the women's' record at 11.33 seconds.

# International Athletics

## Ireland and the Early Olympic Games

### 1896 Olympic Games, Athens

The modern Olympic Games, inspired by the ancient Greek festival and revived by Baron Pierre de Coubertin, began with the 1896 Athens Games, marking a pivotal moment in global sports history. Held from April 6 to 15, 1896, the Games featured 241 athletes from 14 nations competing in 43 events across nine sports, including athletics, cycling, fencing, gymnastics, shooting, swimming, tennis, weightlifting, and wrestling. Hosted at the Panathenaic Stadium, the event drew significant international attention, with Greece covering substantial costs to restore the historic venue. At the time, Ireland was part of the United Kingdom, and Irish athletes competed under the British flag, their achievements officially credited to Great Britain.

The 1896 Games were notable for their modest scale compared to modern Olympics, yet they laid the foundation for the global sporting tradition. Athletes were predominantly male, as women's events were not introduced until 1900, and most competitors were from Europe, with the United States and Australia among the few non-European participants. The absence of standard rules and the informal nature of some events reflected the fledgeling state of the modern Olympic movement.

James Connolly, arguably and Irishman, was the first modern Olympic champion. Born in Boston to Irish immigrants John Connolly and Ann O'Donnell from the Aran Islands, Connolly competed in the inaugural event, the triple jump (then called the hop, skip, and jump). His winning leap of 13.71 meters outdistanced his nearest rival by over one meter, securing the first gold medal of the modern Olympics. Connolly also claimed a silver in the high jump and a bronze in the long jump, showcasing his versatility. His victory was particularly significant for Irish communities, though his medals were recorded as American due to his U.S. citizenship.

Another standout was John Pius Boland, Ireland's first Olympic medallist. A Dublin native from the prominent Boland's Mills family, Boland was in Athens on holiday when he entered the tennis competition. He won gold in both the singles and doubles events, a remarkable feat for an impromptu participant. Boland later became a prominent Irish nationalist politician, but his Olympic successes were officially attributed to Great Britain due to Ireland's political status.

**1900 Olympic Games, Paris**

The 1900 Olympic Games, held in Paris from May 14 to October 28 as part of the Universal Exposition, marked the second iteration of the modern Olympic movement. Over 1,000 athletes from 24 nations competed in 19 sports, including athletics, swimming, tennis, rugby, and water polo, among others. Unlike the 1896 Games, the 1900 Olympics were less structured, with events spread over months and some competitions lacking clear Olympic designation, reflecting the era's evolving organisational framework. Women participated for the first time, though their involvement was limited to sports like tennis and golf. Ireland, still under British rule, saw its athletes compete under the British or American flags due to political and citizenship circumstances.

Harold Mahony, a Scottish-born Irishman who identified strongly with his Irish heritage, was a standout in the tennis events. Born in Edinburgh but raised primarily in County Kerry, Mahony had previously won Wimbledon in 1896, making him the last Irishman to claim that prestigious title. At the 1900 Olympics, he secured two silver medals in the men's singles and mixed doubles, along with a bronze in the men's doubles, showcasing his prowess on the international stage. His achievements, however, were officially recorded as British victories due to Ireland's status within the United Kingdom.

Another notable figure was John Flanagan, born in Ballinvreena, County Limerick, who competed for the United States after emigrating there. A world record holder in the hammer throw, Flanagan won his first of three Olympic gold medals in the event at the 1900 Games. He repeated this success at the 1904 St. Louis Olympics, where he also earned a silver in the now-obsolete "weight for height" event, and retained his hammer throw title at the 1908 London Olympics. Flanagan's dominance cemented his legacy as one of the era's premier athletes. After his competitive career, he returned to Limerick, where he lived until his death in 1938 at age 70. He is buried in Ballingaddy graveyard near Kilmallock.

Other Irish athletes also excelled in Paris, representing Great Britain due to Ireland's political status. Patrick Leahy won medals in the high jump and long jump, Denis Daly contributed to a medal in water polo, and James Cantlon earned a medal in rugby.

*Olympic Champion John Flanagan from Limerick*

## 1904 Olympic Games, St Louis, Missouri

The 1904 Olympic Games, held in St. Louis, Missouri, from July 1 to November 23 as part of the Louisiana Purchase Exposition, were the third modern Olympic Games and the first hosted outside Europe. Featuring 651 athletes from 12 nations, the Games included 17 sports, though participation was heavily skewed toward North American competitors due to the event's location and limited international travel. The 1904 Olympics were notable for their inclusion of demonstration sports, uniquely featuring Irish sports hurling and Gaelic football alongside American football and basketball. These demonstration events, while not part of the official medal tally, highlighted cultural sports traditions, with hurling marking its only appearance in Olympic history.

The hurling demonstration featured teams composed of Irish immigrants or Irish-American athletes, though exact team names, rosters, and match outcomes were unfortunately poorly documented. Contemporary accounts suggest the event was played at the World's Fair grounds, possibly at Francis Field, the main Olympic venue. The GAA, which had a growing presence in American cities with large Irish communities like Chicago and New York, likely coordinated the event, emphasising cultural pride among the diaspora. The demonstration aimed to showcase hurling's fast-paced, physical nature, though its impact was limited by the Games' low international attendance and the dominance of American and Canadian participants.

John Flanagan and Martin Sheridan of the Irish American Athletic Club, with fellow Irishman James Mitchell of the New York Athletic Club at the 1904 Olympic Games in St. Louis, Missouri

John Flanagan, from Ballinvreena, County Limerick, and competing for the United States, defended his Olympic hammer throw title, securing his second of three consecutive gold medals in the event (1900, 1904, 1908). He also won a silver medal in the weight for height event, a discipline unique to the 1904 Games.

Martin Sheridan, born in Bohola, County Mayo, and also representing the United States, claimed gold in the discus throw, establishing himself as one of the era's dominant athletes. James Mitchel, hailing from Emly, County Tipperary, earned a bronze in the hammer throw, further contributing to the strong Irish presence in American athletics.

The 1904 Games saw numerous American medallists with Irish surnames, including O'Connor, Murphy, Finnegan, Egan, Downing, Hurley, Kehoe, and Brady, many of whom were likely of Irish descent or Irish-born. This reflected the significant wave of Irish immigration to the United States in the late 19th and early 20th centuries. While their achievements bolstered the U.S. medal tally, the prominence of Irish and Irish-American athletes underscored Ireland's indirect but substantial influence on the early Olympic movement, despite the absence of an independent Irish team.

## 1908 Olympic Games, London

The 1908 Olympic Games, held in London from April 27 to October 31, were the fourth modern Olympiad and a significant milestone in the evolution of the Olympic movement. Hosted as part of the British Exhibition, the Games featured 2,008 athletes from 22 nations competing in 22 sports across 110 events. Great Britain, leveraging its host status, fielded 676 competitors and dominated the medal table with 146 medals, including 56 golds. The United States secured second place with 47 medals. Ireland, still under British rule, had no independent team, with Irish athletes competing primarily for Great Britain and the United States.

A defining moment occurred during the opening ceremony when the U.S. team's flag bearer, Ralph Rose, an Irish-American, refused to dip the flag as the team passed the Royal Box, a customary gesture of respect to the British monarch. This act was widely seen as a statement of solidarity with Ireland's struggle for independence. Defending discus champion, Martin Sheridan, reportedly declared, "This flag dips

1928 Amsterdam Olympics

to no earthly king," a sentiment resonating with Irish-American athletes. Sheridan, successfully defended his title at the games and did so again at the 1912 games.

The marathon proved to be the Games' most dramatic event, centred on Italy's Dorando Pietri. Starting conservatively, Pietri surged to the lead after 20 miles but succumbed to dehydration upon entering the Olympic Stadium. Before 75,000 spectators, he took a wrong turn, requiring guidance from umpires, and collapsed five times during the final lap. Umpire Michael Bulger, an Irishman educated at Blackrock College alongside Bob Cussen, assisted Pietri to his feet. Despite crossing the finish line first after a gruelling ten-minute stadium lap, Pietri was disqualified following an American appeal, which argued he received improper assistance. The gold was awarded to John Hayes, an American whose parents hailed from Nenagh, County Tipperary, who finished thirty seconds behind Pietri.

*Bulger (right) assisting Pietri over the line*

In the hammer throw, Irish-born athletes dominated the podium, though representing different nations. John Flanagan, won his third consecutive Olympic gold for the United States. Matt McGrath, born in Ballina, County Tipperary, took silver for the U.S., while Con Walsh, from Carriganimmy, County Cork, secured bronze for Canada. This historic sweep highlighted the remarkable contribution of Irish emigrants to the 1908 Games, despite their medals being credited to other nations due to Ireland's lack of Olympic independence.

**1912 Olympic Games, Stockholm**

The 1912 Olympic Games, the fifth modern Olympiad, took place in Stockholm, Sweden, from May 5 to July 27, amid rising global tensions preceding World War I. A total of 2,408 athletes from 28 nations, including 48 women, competed in 102 events across 14 sports. The United States led the gold medal count with 26, while host nation Sweden topped the overall medal table with 65. The Games were notable for their organisational advancements, including the introduction of electronic timing and a purpose-built stadium, marking a step forward in the professionalisation of the Olympic movement. Ireland, still under British rule, had no independent team, with Irish athletes competing primarily for the United States or Great Britain due to emigration or political status.

A standout performance came from Native American Jim Thorpe, who won gold in both the pentathlon and decathlon, showcasing extraordinary athletic versatility. However, in 1913, Thorpe was stripped of his medals after it was revealed he had previously played professional baseball, violating the era's strict amateurism rules. In 1983, seventy years later, the International Olympic Committee reinstated Thorpe as a double Olympic champion, recognising his historic achievements.

Irish athletes made significant contributions, particularly in athletics for the United States. Matt McGrath, born in Curraghmore near Nenagh, County Tipperary, secured gold in the hammer throw, building on his 1908 silver medal performance. Pat McDonald, from Killard, County Clare, claimed gold in the shot put and silver in the two-handed shot put, a unique event requiring throws with both hands. Both athletes, competing under the U.S. flag, underscored the impact of Irish emigrants on the American team's success.

Several Irish athletes represented Great Britain, reflecting Ireland's status within the United Kingdom. Denis Carey from Limerick competed in the hammer throw but did not medal. Timothy "Timmy" Carroll from Cork participated in the triple jump and high jump, while Thomas O'Donoghue from Kilmihil, County Clare, also competed in the high jump. Patrick Quinn from County Tipperary took part in the discus throw, and Bernard Doyle from Wexford and Michael Walker from Dublin represented Great Britain in cycling. Edward Barrett from Ballyduff, County Kerry, competed in wrestling. Though none of these athletes medalled, their participation highlights the breadth of Irish involvement across diverse events, despite the absence of an independent Irish Olympic team.

**1920 Olympic Games, Antwerp**

The 1920 Olympic Games, held in Antwerp, Belgium, from April 20 to September 12, marked the seventh modern Olympiad and the first Games following the cancellation of the 1916 Berlin Olympics due to World War I. Awarded to Antwerp to honour Belgium's resilience during the war, the Games featured 2,626 athletes from 29 nations competing in 156 events across 22 sports. The United States topped the medal table with 41 golds, while host nation Belgium placed eighth. The 1920 Games introduced enduring Olympic traditions, including the Olympic flag with its five interlocking rings and the Olympic oath. For Ireland, still under British rule, this was the final Olympics where Irish athletes competed as part of the Great Britain team, as the Irish War of Independence (1919–1921) paved the way for Ireland's independent participation starting in 1924.

Rugby union was included as an Olympic sport, with the United States securing gold by defeating France, the only other competitor, in a single match. The U.S. rugby team included players with Irish surnames, Daniel Carroll, James Fitzpatrick, Charles Mehan, and John O'Neil, likely of Irish descent, reflecting the significant Irish-American population. Their victory highlighted the growing influence of the Irish diaspora in American sports.

Irish athletes representing Great Britain included William Hehir from Lisdoonvarna, County Clare, who competed in racewalking but did not medal. Timothy "Timmy" Carroll from Cork, a veteran of the 1912 Olympics, returned to compete in athletics, participating in the triple jump and high jump without securing a medal. Anton Hegarty from Derry earned a silver medal in the individual cross-country run, a notable achievement for the Great Britain team, though officially credited to the United Kingdom.

Irish-born athletes competing for the United States excelled, particularly in athletics and shooting. Patrick "Paddy" Ryan from Newport, County Tipperary, won gold in the hammer throw and silver in the 56-pound weight throw, showcasing his dominance in field events. Pat McDonald, born in Killard, County Clare, successfully defended his 1912 shot put title, claiming gold and solidifying his legacy as one of the era's premier throwers. Denis Fenton from Ventry, County Kerry, achieved remarkable success in shooting, earning three gold medals in team events (military rifle, prone, 300m; military rifle, standing, 300m; and running deer, single shot) and a bronze in the individual running deer, single shot event. Patrick Flynn from Bandon, County Cork, secured silver in the 3,000-meter steeplechase, adding to the U.S. medal tally.

## 1924 Olympic Games, Paris

The 1924 Olympic Games, held in Paris from May 4 to July 27, marked a historic milestone for Ireland, as the newly established Irish Free State competed as an independent nation for the first time following the 1922 Anglo-Irish Treaty. Denis Cussen had aimed to qualify for the Games but was hindered by an ankle injury sustained in 1923. Despite his potential to match the world's elite runners, Ireland's limited budget restricted the size of its Olympic team, and Cussen was unable to participate. Instead, he focused on training and competing in Ireland, preparing for the Tailteann Games which were held a month later.

Ireland sent a modest team to Paris, competing in football, boxing, tennis, water polo, and athletics. While the Irish contingent did not secure any medals in athletic or team events, the nation achieved notable success in the Olympic art competitions, a unique feature of the early modern Games. Jack B. Yeats won a silver medal for his painting "The Liffey Swim", and Oliver St. John Gogarty, a writer and surgeon, earned a bronze for his poem "Ode to the Tailteann Games".

Irish-born athletes representing other nations, particularly the United States, continued to excel. Pat McDonald, born in Killard, County Clare,

## 1928 Amsterdam Olympics

and a two-time Olympic shot-put champion (1912 and 1920), served as the U.S. flag bearer during the opening ceremony. He competed in the shot put but did not medal. Matt McGrath, from Curraghmore, County Tipperary, a hammer throw gold medallist in 1912 and silver medallist in 1908 and 1920, won another silver in the hammer throw for the United States at age the grand age of forty-seven. Patrick "Paddy" Ryan, from Newport, County Tipperary, the defending hammer throw champion from 1920, also competed for the U.S. but did not medal.

Cussen, though absent from Paris, closely followed the sprinting events, particularly the 100m, where he believed he could have been competitive. Harold Abrahams of Great Britain won gold with a time of 10.6 seconds, a mark Cussen was capable of achieving based on his performances. Jackson Scholz of the United States took silver, and Arthur Porritt of New Zealand, whom Cussen later befriended, claimed bronze. The world record at the time, 10.4 seconds, was held by American Charlie Paddock. William "Bill" Lowe, representing Ireland, competed in the 100m but placed fourth in his heat (won by Canada's George Hester in 11.2 seconds) and did not advance.

*The start line for the 100m final in Paris 1924*
*The title was won by Harold Abrahams and the bronze by Arthur Porritt, both were firm friends of Denis Cussen*

Cussen also took interest in the 200m and, though not a competitor at the distance, the 400m, particularly due to the participation of Eric Liddell, a fellow international rugby player. In the 200m, Ireland's Sean Lavan won his heat, and Bill Lowe finished second in his, behind Australia's Slip Carr. Both advanced to the quarterfinals, where Lavan placed fourth behind Liddell and Carr, and Lowe finished fifth behind Porritt and France's André Mourlon. In the final, Scholz won gold, Paddock took silver, and Liddell secured bronze. The 400m, famously depicted in the film "Chariots of Fire", saw Liddell set a world record of 47.6 seconds to win gold. Ireland's Sean Lavan competed but was eliminated in the second round, missing the historic final.

## Sean Lavan (1898-1973)

Sean Lavan was a contemporary of Denis Cussen and a remarkable athlete. Lavan was born in 1898 in Kiltimagh, County Mayo. Growing up he was a Gaelic Football player and played for both Kiltimagh and the Mayo County teams. He won two Connacht senior championships with Mayo and is said to have invented the hand-to-toe solo run which is now a central part of the game.

In 1923 he entered UCD to study medicine. He was a champion boxer, soccer player and played rugby for UCD. He won the Collingwood Cup (Soccer) and the Sigerson Cup (Gaelic Football) with the university teams.

He emerged onto the national athletics scene in 1923. He won six straight national titles at 440-yards from 1923 to 1928. He also won four straight national titles at 220-yards from 1925-1928. In 1926 and 1927 after Cussen had left Ireland, Lavan won the 100-yards national title but relinquished it to Cussen on his return in 1928.

Lavan represented Ireland in the 200m and 400m at the Paris Olympic Games in 1924, though didn't make the final in either event. In 1928 he was appointed the Irish Olympic Team captain and competed alongside Cussen at the 1928 games in Amsterdam.

Like Cussen, Lavan was a doctor and was the doctor to the Irish Olympic team in 1956. After graduating from UCD, Lavan was appointed as a surgeon in Temple Street Hospital, Dublin and worked there until 1972. He lectured in anatomy at UCD, was surgeon to An Garda Siochana and also had a general practice at Terenure.

1928 Amsterdam Olympics

# 1928 Amsterdam Olympics

The 1928 Olympic Games, held in Amsterdam from May 17 to August 12, were the ninth modern Olympiad, with the official opening ceremony on July 28. The Games included preliminary competitions in football, field hockey, and art before the ceremony, reflecting the era's broad interpretation of Olympic events. A total of 2,883 athletes from 46 nations competed in 109 events across 14 sports. The 1928 Games were historic for introducing women's athletics and gymnastics, with Ireland among the nations sending female athletes, building on their participation in the 1924 Tailteann Games.

Ireland's participation in 1928 was a significant achievement, given logistical and financial challenges. The Irish Olympic Council, effectively disbanded after the 1924 Paris Games, was re-established following a critical meeting at Dublin's Shelbourne Hotel in January 1928. The council faced hurdles in securing funding, arranging travel, and determining team composition. A debate over the national flag arose, with Northern Ireland representatives advocating for the traditional Irish flag featuring a golden harp on a blue background. Ultimately, the tri-colour, used in 1924, was retained and has remained Ireland's Olympic flag ever since. Ireland sent a team of 38 athletes to compete in 27 events across athletics, boxing, cycling, swimming, water polo, and art competitions, though no medals were won in sporting events.

In the Olympic art competitions, Ireland submitted notable entries. Oliver Sheppard's sculpture "Death of Cúchulainn" did not win but later gained prominence as the official memorial to the 1916 Easter Rising, unveiled by Éamon de Valera at Dublin's General Post Office on April 21, 1935, where it remains today.

Limerickman Sean Keating's painting "The Tipperary Hurler", also failed to medal. However, the art competition's gold medal in the drawing category, awarded to Luxembourg's Jean Jacoby for his work "Rugby", likely resonated with Denis Cussen who played the game.

## 1928 Amsterdam Olympics

*Left: Death of Cúchulainn by Oliver Sheppard.*

*Above: 'The Tipperary Hurler' by Sean Keating*

*Left 'Rugby' by Jean Jacoby*

The Irish team's journey to Amsterdam began on July 23, departing by train from Westland Row (now Pearse Station) in Dublin. At Dún Laoghaire, they were farewelled by William T. Cosgrave, President of the Executive Council, accompanied by the Garda Band. After a stopover at London's St. Pancras Hotel, where Denis Cussen joined the team, they travelled by train to Harwich, boarded a Dutch steamship to Flushing, Netherlands, and completed a four-hour train journey to Amsterdam. Due to limited accommodation in the city, the Irish team stayed on the ship "Oranje Nassau", moored 25 minutes by bus from the Olympic Stadium, sharing the vessel with the Belgian delegation. Many other nations also used accommodation ships.

*The accommodation ship Oranje Nassau*

On July 26, the Irish team received their uniforms: green blazers with a single-leaf shamrock on a white badge, white trousers, white sweaters, and straw hats with green bands. With the opening ceremony three days away, they participated in a dress rehearsal and visited the Olympic City to view the stadium. However, training was complicated by the incomplete running track at the Olympic Stadium, which remained off-limits. Teams were forced to find alternative training venues, with larger delegations like the United States dominating available spaces. Canadian journalist Bobby Robinson, writing in the "Hamilton Spectator", described the American team's arrival with "huge cars" and "150 track athletes" accompanied by coaches, trainers, and support staff, highlighting the disparity with Ireland's modest £5,000 budget for the Games.

Tensions escalated when it was revealed that American athletes had accessed the unfinished stadium track for training, prompting official complaints from multiple nations. The French team, denied entry the day before the opening ceremony, clashed with a gatekeeper who reportedly struck a French delegate, leading to an apology from the Dutch Olympic Committee. The Irish team, including Denis Cussen, likely had no opportunity to train inside the stadium before the Games began, underscoring the challenges faced by smaller delegations.

# 1928 Amsterdam Olympics

1928 Amsterdam Olympics

**Opening Ceremony**

Drama surrounded the opening ceremony on Saturday 28th July. When the French team arrived at the stadium to take part in the Opening Ceremony, the same gatekeeper who had the previous day refused them entry, was on duty and he again refused them admission. Another argument occurred and the French team withdrew from the ceremony. There was even talk that they might withdraw from the games altogether.

The Irish team had no difficulty getting access to the stadium and took part in the ceremony without hitch. The sprint events were the first to be held the following morning and so most of those taking part in those, didn't take part in the ceremony. Instead, they sat in the stand and enjoyed the spectacle.

*Prince Consort Henry arriving for the Opening Ceremony*

The ceremony began at two o'clock with the arrival of Prince Consort Henry, who would open the Games on behalf of Holland's Queen Wilhelmina. The deeply religious Queen had refused to take part

# 1928 Amsterdam Olympics

because it was a Sunday. The Dutch anthem was played and a fanfare of trumpets played as the prince took his place in the royal box.

The ceremonial parade of the athletes then started. The Irish Independent reported:

*"Ireland played its part with distinction in the great opening ceremony at the Olympic Stadium this afternoon. The team, which came 17th in the assemblage of 43 nations, marched well, and looked smart in their green uniforms.*

*Captain Chisholm headed the party bearing a standard on which was the name of the nation, and he was followed by M Flanagan bearing the Irish flag. Then followed the other members of the team two by two.*

*A curious coincidence was the fact that South Africa, except for their different flag, were dressed exactly the same as the Irishmen.*

*All of the members of the Irish team are fit and in good fettle."*

Another article described some of the broader ceremonial aspects. Under a headline France Absent from Grand March it read:

*"Lowering clouds, through which glimpses of sun were seen, failed the dull the splendour of this afternoon's opening ceremony of the 9th Olympiad. The only regrettable incident was that which resulted in the absence of the French team from the picturesque pageant.*

*The Olympic flag was run up to the central masthead; guns thundered the salute; trumpeters at the summit of the lofty Marathon Tower, on which the Olympic flame had been lit, sounded a fanfare; and thousands of pigeons were released, rising up towards the aeroplanes already roaring in the grey sky above.*

## 1928 Amsterdam Olympics

*A continuous storm of cheering from forty thousand spectators greeted the imposing march of the athletes past the prince.*

*Greece, as home of the Olympic games, headed the parade, and the first British Empire contingent was that from Australia, with Winter, the hop, step and jump champion bearing the standard. India followed soon afterwards, and then came the big Canadian team, both men and girls dressed in white.*

*Headed by two pipers, the British team was accorded a reception, as was also the Irish team, second in enthusiasm only to that given Holland, the home county, who modestly brought up the rear.*

*HM Abrahams, the Olympic 100 metres champion, carried the ensign, and the Union Jack was borne by MC Nokes, the burley hammer thrower.*

*Other striking features of the parade were: -*
- *The Fascist salute given by the Italians, who were dressed in bright blue shirts and grey flannel suits, and led by a Carabinieri cavalryman in full uniform*
- *The saxe blue blazers of the Japanese*
- *A pretty Lithuanian girl in green shorts, white singlet, and red, green and yellow bandana, who carried her country's ensign*
- *Three brawny Luxembourg wrestlers, in purple bathing suits*
- *The tiny boy scouts who led the one-man Monaco contingent*
- *The little coxswain among the formidable American team*
- *The striking bevy of Polish girls*
- *And the Czecho-Slovaks, in their bright red shirts, grey capes and feathered caps.*

*A hush fell over the huge assembly when Harry Denis, the Dutch football captain, with the standard-bearers assembled around him, took the solemn Olympic oath on behalf of all the athletes participating in the games.*

*The magnificent singing of the Dutch choir of 1,200 voices, which took a leading part in the ceremony, won universal admiration."*

# 1928 Amsterdam Olympics

*Athletes taking part in the Opening Ceremony*

*Overhead shot of the Opening Ceremony*

# 1928 Amsterdam Olympics

*The 1928 Olympic Opening Ceremony*

The fanfare of the opening ceremony took four hours to finish. It was after 8pm by the time Denis and the Irish team got back to the Oranje Nassau. It would have been a restless night was Cussen contemplated the competition the following morning.

## The 100m Competitors

The 1928 Olympic Games featured a highly competitive men's 100m race. American sprinters had dominated the event, winning six of the eight previous Olympic 100m titles, with Great Britain claiming the other two. The 1924 Olympic champion and record holder, Harold Abrahams of Great Britain, had retired in 1925 after a leg injury and did not compete in 1928. The world record stood at 10.4 seconds, set by

# 1928 Amsterdam Olympics

American Charlie Paddock in 1921, who had won the 100m in 1920 but opted to compete in the 200m in 1928.

Denis Cussen had a personal best of 9.8 seconds in the 100-yards, equivalent to approximately 10.75 seconds over the Olympic 100m distance (109 yards and 10 inches). While competitive, this time placed him slightly behind the leading favourites.

American Frank Wykoff emerged as a top contender, having equalled the Olympic record of 10.6 seconds at the U.S. Olympic trials in Los Angeles a month prior. Canada's Percy Williams also matched this mark at the Canadian trials, positioning him as another formidable rival. Other notable contenders included Jack London of Great Britain and Georg Lammers of Germany, both seen as potential medallists.

The U.S. sprint team was exceptionally strong, featuring Wykoff, Claude Bracey, Henry Russell, and Bob McAllister, any of whom could challenge for the podium. Canada's team was equally impressive, led by Percy Williams, who won both the 100m and 200m at the Canadian trials. Williams was joined by George Hester, a 1924 Olympian, John Fitzpatrick, and Ralph Adams. Cyril Coaffee, another strong Canadian sprinter who had defeated Cussen at the 1924 Tailteann Games, was sidelined by injury and missed the Olympic trials.

Arthur Porritt of New Zealand, the 1924 100m bronze medallist, was the only returning medallist from the previous Games, making him a seasoned competitor. Germany, readmitted to the Olympics after a 12-year absence due to their role in World War I, fielded a promising sprint team, with Lammers as a potential dark horse.

The 1928 100m race promised intense competition, with established powers like the United States and Canada facing emerging talents and returning nations, setting the stage for a thrilling showdown in Amsterdam. Denis Cussen was up against it.

## 1928 Amsterdam Olympics

*The Irish 1928 Olympic Track and Field Team*
Back row: Tom Maguire (coach), Con O'Callaghan (decathlon), Denis Cussen (100m), Pat O'Callaghan (hammer), Alister Clarke (110m hurdles), Denis Cullen (200m), Theo Phelan (triple jump)
Front row: Pat Anglim (long jump), Norman McEachern (800m), Sean Lavin (200/400m), Albert Donnelly (1km cycling), GM Coughlan (800m)

## Sunday 29th July 1928

**MONDAY, Irish Independent JULY 30, 1928.**

### VIII. OLYMPIAD OPENS

### IRELAND'S REPRESENTATIVES IN ACTION AT AMSTERDAM

#### M'EACHERN QUALIFIES FOR SEMI-FINAL

IRELAND was trebly represented in the first day's Olympic programme at Amsterdam yesterday. Dr. D. J. Cussen ran in the 100 metres, and Lieut. G. N. Coughlan and Norman McEachern in the 800 metres. Only McEachern remains to contest the closing stages of the latter event.

*Newspaper coverage back home*

# 1928 Amsterdam Olympics

The 1928 Olympic track and field events commenced at the Amsterdam Olympic Stadium on the morning following the opening ceremony. The 400m heats opened the day's competitions. Ireland's Sean Lavan ran in the sixth heat and came in second place behind USA's RJ Barbuti. In the second round he only managed to come in fourth place and so was eliminated. Barbuti who had beaten Lavan in the first round, went on to win the gold medal.

Once the 400m preliminary rounds were out of the way, it was time for the 100m. At 2:30 p.m., the eighty-seven athletes from across the globe emerged into the stadium for the highly anticipated event. With an unprecedented number of competitors, the event was organised into 16 heats, scheduled to begin at 2:45 p.m. The large field underscored the global appeal of the sprint and marked it as the marquee Olympic event.

**100m First Round**

Denis Cussen was drawn in the 15th heat and was set to compete near 4:00 p.m. The delayed start allowed him to observe earlier races, gaining insight into the competition's pace and intensity. The first-round heats showcased rapid times, with several athletes approaching or surpassing the 11-second mark, signalling a fiercely competitive field.

**Heat 1:** John Fitzpatrick (Canada) and Hubert Corts (Germany) advanced, recording times of 11.0 seconds.

**Heat 2:** Norman Atkinson (South Africa) and André Mourlon (France) qualified with a time of 11.2 seconds.

**Heat 3:** One of the favourites Frank Wykoff (United States) and René Brochart (Belgium) progressed, matching the 11.0-second mark.

**Heat 4:** István Gerö (Hungary) and Eric Burton-Durham (South Africa) broke the 11-second barrier, qualifying with a time of 10.8 seconds, just 0.4 seconds shy of the world record.

**Heat 5:** Jack London (Great Britain) and George Hester (Canada) also surpassed 11 seconds, advancing with a time of 10.8 seconds.

# 1928 Amsterdam Olympics

**Heats 6–8:** qualifiers included Carlos Pina (Argentina), Ralph Adams (Canada), Charles Legg (South Africa), Walter Gill (Great Britain), Johannes Houben (Germany), and Petrus Viljoen (South Africa), all recording times of approximately 11.0 seconds.

**Heat 9:** Georg Lammers (Germany) and Augustin Thread (Haiti) qualified with a standout time of 10.8 seconds, matching the fastest heats.

**Heats 10–14:** Advancers included Walter Rangeley (Great Britain), Karel van den Berge (Netherlands), Gyula Raggambi (Hungary), William Carlton (Australia), Percy Williams (Canada), František Vykoupil (Czechoslovakia), Jesús Barrientos Schweyer (Cuba), Robert Cerbonney (France), Claude Bracey (United States), and Paul Auvergne (France), all posting times around 11.0 seconds.

*The stadium was crammed for the 100m races*

With multiple athletes approaching the world record pace, Cussen watched on perhaps using the time to stretch, to strategise or perhaps

1928 Amsterdam Olympics

just to try and maintain his focus amidst the intense atmosphere of the Olympic Stadium.

Finally, the 15th heat was called and Denis Cussen was up. There were four runners in his heat and two would progress to the second round. Having watched the earlier heats, Cussen would have been relatively confident of progressing but also conscious that anything could happen in a race.

Henry Argue (Hank) Russell was a narrow favourite. He was a twenty-three-year-old student at Cornell University. He had come third in the US Olympic trials. At the games he competed in the 100m and the 4x100m relay. In the latter he won a gold medal with the US team equalling the world record in the event at 41 seconds flat.

Switzerland's Willy Tschopp also ran in the heat. He was also twenty-three years old. His Olympics would include the 100m, the 200m and the 4x100m in which Switzerland came fifth. He was an outside chance in this first heat as his personal best was over eleven seconds.

The fourth runner was Adolphe Groscol from Belgium. He was the youngest in the race at twenty-two years old. He also ran in the 200m and in the 4x100m relay but was eliminated in the first heat in each event.

As expected, the favourite, Hank Russell won the heat in 11 second flat. Cussen was just behind him in second place and so qualified for the second round. The Irish Independent reported on his Olympic debut:

> *"Cussen got away splendidly and led until about three-quarters way, where the American commenced to draw level, and eventually drew clear to win by one and a half yards in 11 seconds, a similar time to that in ten of the other heats"*

In the final heat McAllister (USA) and Gonzaga (Philippines) qualified in 10.8 seconds.

Fifty-five athletes were now eliminated out of the eighty-seven who started. Safely qualified, Cussen had a short break before the second round in which he had been drawn in the first heat. Retrospectively, it is interesting to note that those drawn in the earlier heats had a longer recovery time. Cussen had the worst possible opportunity to recover.

# 1928 Amsterdam Olympics

Nonetheless, if he could qualify in this race, he would be in the semi-finals which were the following day.

**100m Second Round**

Round two, heat one would be difficult. Cussen was drawn to race against Billie Legg (South Africa), John Fitzpatrick (Canada), Ferenc Gerö (Hungry), Rinus Van den Berge (Holland) and Jaroslav Vykoupil (Czechoslovakia).

The competitors – Round 2 Heat 1 – 100m Amsterdam 1928

| Billie Legg (South Africa) | John Fitzpatrick (Canada) | Ferenc Gerő (Hungry) |
| Rinus van den Berge (Holland) | Jaroslav Vykoupil (Czechoslovakia) | Denis Cussen (Ireland) |

1928 Amsterdam Olympics

*Denis Cussen (far right) competing at the 1928 Olympic Games*

Van den Berge, Vykoupil and Gerö had each competed in the 400m earlier but all three had come third in the opening round and had been eliminated. The effort expended in the longer race didn't seem to have impacted Gerö as he had won his heat in a very strong time of 10.8 seconds.

Fitzpatrick, Legg had also won their heats. John Fitzpatrick, a student from Montreal had a personal best of 10.66 seconds and had won his heat in 11 seconds. South African Billie Legg had beaten Cussen at the AAA Championships just a few weeks beforehand and had won his heat, also in a time of 11 seconds.

Perhaps feeling the strain of having already competed at 400m, twenty-eight-year-old Rinus Van den Berge had come second in his heat with a time just over 11 seconds. He would later also compete in the 4x100m and win a bronze medal for the Dutch.

Jaroslav Vykoupil from Czechoslovakia was the oldest in the race at thirty. He had competed in the previous games in Paris so had experience. He had also been eliminated from the 400m that morning

# 1928 Amsterdam Olympics

but had come second in his 100m heat behind Percy Williams of Canada.

Cussen lined up and, after a false start by one of the other runners, got away well but wasn't able to compete unfortunately.

> "In the second round the Irishman found himself in a very hot heat. Not that all the heats were not hot, but there was Legg, the AAA Champion, and Gerö, a surprise man from Hungary, who had done a fifth better than 'evens' in his heat.
>
> Cussen is always of a very nervous temperament, and it may be that his chances were affected by a false start in which he was left. Be that as it may, he got away quite well at the second attempt, but after holding his own well for the first 30 yards seemed to fade out and finished fifth.
>
> Legg won from the Canadian, Fitzpatrick in two fifths worse than the world record time."

It had been very close finish and it took the judges a few minutes to decide on the placings. Reflecting on his performance he wrote to his brother Bertie and said he *'ran very stiffly'* in the first round and felt he *'ran much better'* in the second round *'but not good enough and came in behind Legg and Fitzpatrick. The time was 10.8. I was about 1 ½ yards behind. The officials here are quite satisfied and say I did quite well and put on a good show, but between ourselves, I was rather disappointed. There were 85 in for the event and I got to the last 32."*

## 100m Semi-Finals and Final

Now out of the games, Cussen could only watch on as the rest of the 100m event unfolded. Legg and Fitzpatrick from his race went through along with the first and second placed athletes from the other second round races.

When the semi-finals were run McAllister (USA), Williams (Canada) and Legg (South Africa) qualified from the first. Jack London (Great Britain), Lammers (Germany) and Wykoff (USA) qualified from the second. The winners of both semi-finals (McAllister and London) recorded times of 10.6 seconds equalling the Olympic record.ms (Canada), Legg (South Africa), Jack London (GB), Lammers (Germany) and Wykoff (USA).

1928 Amsterdam Olympics

*The start of the 100m Final – Amsterdam 1928*
*Wykoff, McAllister, London, Williams, Lammers, Legg*

The 100m Final took place at 4pm on 30th July, two hours after the semi-finals had taken place.

There were two false starts as the athletes settled ahead of the race. The first was by South African Legg who was given a warning by the umpire. Then as the athletes again prepared for the starting gun, Frank Wykoff was responsible for another one. The favourite, Wykoff was rattled by it. He was slow to start once the starting gun fired as a result. He struggled to make an impression and was a yard behind the others all through the race. The other five athletes were neck and neck until close to the finish line when the other American in the race McAllister pulled a muscle in his leg and stumbled.

The Americans' misfortune left Percy Williams of Canada to stoop and touch the tape first in a time of 10.8 seconds. Great Britain's Jack London came in second and the bronze medal went to Lammers of Germany. Legg who had beaten Cussen the previous day came in fourth.

1928 Amsterdam Olympics

*Canada's Percy Williams crosses the line to win the 100m*

## Olympic Champion Percy Williams

Percy Williams was born in Vancouver in May 1908. At the Canadian Olympic trials in 1928, he equalled the then Olympic record of 10.6 seconds. At the Olympics themselves, Williams matched that time in the second round and went on to win both the 100m and the 200m events. He was also part of the Canadian relay team that was disqualified for false starts in the final of the 4x100m.

*Percy Williams became a superstar at home in Canada*

After he won the 200m, Williams returned to his hotel to be greeted by huge crowds. His Olympic double had made Percy Williams a superstar. When he returned to Canada he landed at Quebec to a huge homecoming and that was repeated at each city he passed through on his way west to Vancouver. He turned down a Hollywood career to keep running and two years later he set a new world record covering the 100m in 10.3 seconds. That record stood until Jesse Owens topped it in 1936.

*Percy Williams carried from the field by teammates after winning the 100m*

After he retired, Williams became a pilot in the Canadian air force during World War II and later worked in insurance.

In the mid-1960s, Williams donated his two Olympic gold medals from to the British Colombia Sports Hall of Fame, saying he wanted them to be seen and remembered. In 1980, the medals were stolen and it was suspected they had been melted down and sold as gold.

Williams never married and lived alone. As he got older, he suffered from severe arthritis. In November 1982, Percy Williams committed suicide in the bath of his home, shooting himself with a gun he was given as an award for his triumphs at the Amsterdam Olympic Games in 1928.

## Ireland's First Olympic Gold Medal

On the day following Denis Cussen's Olympic competition, 30th July 1928, Ireland won their first ever Olympic gold medal as a nation. At the 1924 games, Ireland had won a silver (Jack Butler Yeats in painting) and a bronze (Oliver St. John Gogarty).

At the Irish trials, Pat O'Callaghan from Kanturk, County Cork won his second consecutive Irish Hammer throw title. This qualified him for

## 1928 Amsterdam Olympics

the Irish team. On the same day, his brother Con won the national shot put and decathlon titles, meaning the brothers would both compete in Amsterdam.

In Amsterdam, Pat came in sixth place in the preliminary round of the hammer competition which qualified him for the final. His first throw in the final was 47.49m which put him initially in third place. His second throw however was a massive 51.39m, winning him the gold medal ahead of Skold of Sweden by 10cm and Black (USA) by over two metres in third.

Pat's brother Con, only managed sixteenth in the Decathlon.

*Pat O'Callaghan  
Ireland's first Olympic Gold  
Medallist*

At the medal ceremony, the Irish Tri-Colour was raised for the first time at an Olympic Games and Ambrán na bhFiann rang out around the stadium. Denis Cussen was there to witness it. O'Callaghan was Ireland's only successful

Like Denis Cussen, O'Callaghan was a doctor and studied at the Royal College of Surgeons in Dublin. He qualified the same year as Cussen had and the two were firm friends.

O'Callaghan went on to win gold in the Hammer at the 1932 Olympic Games in Los Angeles and may well have won a third had Ireland been allowed to compete in the infamous 1936 Olympic Games in Berlin.

## Denis' Olympic Medal

All competitors at the 1928 Olympic Games were awarded a souvenir medal. The medal was designed by J.C Wienecke, a well-known Dutch medallist, and produced by jewellers Gerritsen and Van Kempen. Five thousand one hundred and thirty-nine were produced. Denis was one of the recipients.

*The souvenir medal presented to all Olympians in Amsterdam 1928*
*Denis Cussen received one of these*

# 1928 Tailteann Games, Dublin

Having competed in the Olympic Games in Amsterdam on 29th July, Denis Cussen returned home to Ireland where he took part in the 1928 Tailteann Games.

The 1928 Tailteann Games were, as they had been four years earlier, an extravaganza of sport and a celebration of Irishness. Many of the athletes who had competed in the Olympic Games stopped in Ireland on their way home. Over seven thousand athletes competed across an array of sports and events with over a thousand medals presented to winners. The 1928 games were more restrictive than the first version. To build interest in 1924, the games were open to invited athletes. In 1928, the games were only open to those of Irish descent though it is debatable how strict they were able to be.

*Opening Ceremony of the 1928 Tailteann Games*

# AONACH TAILTEANN
## INTERNATIONAL ATHLETICS

At CROKE PARK,
**TO-MORROW (WEDNESDAY) and SATURDAY,**
Commencing at 2.30 p.m.
**THURSDAY and FRIDAY at 5.30 p.m.**
NINE NATIONS COMPETING.

Admission—Grounds, 6d.; Stand Enclosure, 1/-
Hogan Stand, 2/- extra; Side Line, 2/- extra

**TO-MORROW (WEDNESDAY) at DEPOT,
PHOENIX PARK,**

## NATIONAL HANDBALL
AT 5 P.M.

## INTERNATIONAL HANDBALL
AT 7 P.M.
Admission—1/- and 2/-.

**TO-MORROW (WEDNESDAY) EVENING,**
At 8 p.m., at the PEACOCK THEATRE (Abbey Theatre Buildings),
**"THE WITNESS FOR THE DEFENCE"** and
**"E. and O.E."** Seats 3/6.

## INTERNATIONAL SWIMMING
At BLACKROCK BATHS. 9 Nations Competing.
On AUGUST 18th, 20th, 21st and 22nd.
Entrance, 1/6; Stand, 3/6. Booking at Mansion House.

## CEILIDHE MOR,
At MANSION HOUSE, AUGUST 18th and 25th,
At 9 p.m.
Tickets—5/- each (including Refreshments).

**SUNDAY NEXT, AUGUST 19th.
INTERNATIONAL FOOTBALL,**

## IRELAND v. AMERICA,
At CROKE PARK, at 3.30 p.m.
**CHEAP EXCURSIONS FROM ALL PARTS.**

# 1928 Tailteann Games, Dublin

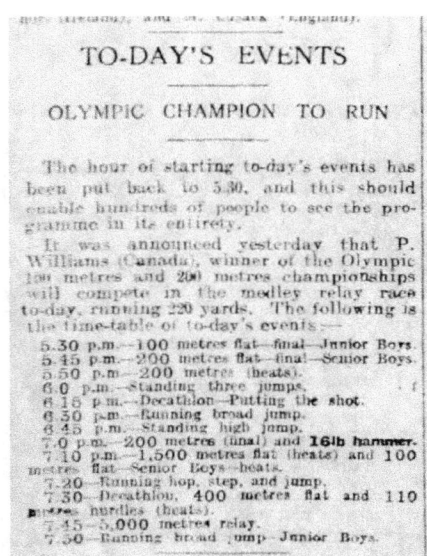

The athletics competition took place at Croke Park between 15th and 18th August. While there was great excitement around Dublin that the games were on, a poor crowd showed up to watch the opening day of athletics. The fact that they were held on a Wednesday, combined with showery and dull weather combined to keep the crowd numbers down and only an estimated 8000 attended.

On the afternoon of the opening day, the 100m event took place. Irishmen from six nations took part; United States, Canada, England, Australia, Wales and Ireland. As Denis Cussen was living in London, he was representing England in the event.

Canada had three men entered in the event, all of whom had been at the Olympic Games. Percy Williams, now a national superstar having won the 100m and 200m double, came to Ireland but only took part in the medley relay event. The chief competition for the Canadians was Denis Cussen. James Carlton, the Australian champion, Denis Manly of Wales and Werner of the United States were expected to make up the numbers.

Cussen took part in the first heat. Also in the heat was Warren Montabone from Canada who had competed in the 110m hurdles in Amsterdam. Another in the heat was Australian James Carlton who, like Cussen, had been eliminated in the second round in Amsterdam.

Cussen and Montabone got away to the best starts and were neck and neck for the first thirty metres. In the second half of the race, Cussen faded. Warren won the heat in a time of 10.8 seconds. Cussen had to settle for third place as he was pipped on the line by Carlton and didn't qualify for the final.

1928 Tailteann Games, Dublin

John Fitzpatrick (Canada) won the second heat in a time of 11 seconds. His compatriot from Canada Ralph Adams won the third heat in 11.2 seconds and Irishman JV Connell won the fourth in 11.6 seconds.

In the 100m final the Canadians won a clean sweep of the medals. The gold was won by Warren Montabone, the silver by Fitzpatrick and the bronze by Adams. In the 200m Canada again swept all before them. J Ball took the gold, Fitzpatrick the silver and Montabone the bronze. Canada also won the medley relay which was run over 1200m. Two runners would run 200m and two others would run 400m legs. The team of Fitzpatrick (200m), Percy Williams (200m), Adams (400m) and Ball (400m) beat the American team. Ireland took the bronze in that event.

The 1928 Tailteann Games were viewed as a success and a third iteration was held in 1932. JJ Walsh, the games instigator and main government sponsor lost his seat in the 1932 general election in which Eamon de Valera took power. He cut funding for the games and, while they went ahead, they were dramatically smaller in scale and lost a lot of their appeal. No further Tailteann Games were held after 1932.

# Post Retirement Athletics

Denis retired from his rugby playing in 1931 and from athletics after the 1928 Tailteann Games by that stage he was in his late twenties and had moved to Harrow where he was working in general practice. He maintained his interest in sport and began to get more and more involved in sports administration and the science of sports medicine. He went on to forge a career in that area that would in itself be the envy of many.

## Roger Bannister – Four-minute mile

Roger Bannister became the first man to run a mile in less than four minutes on 6th May 1954. This event happened at the Iffley Road athletics track in Oxford amid huge media speculation as to when someone would break the once impossible mark. Bannister was a medical student studying at St Mary's Hospital where Cussen had worked. Cussen lived in Surbiton, Surrey which is fifty miles Oxford. Given his proximity, his heavy involvement in British Athletics and the press interest at the time, Cussen was almost certainly on site to witness the occasion.

Bannister had finished fourth in the 1500m at the Helsinki Olympic Games in 1952 and had considered retiring from running. However, he set himself the goal of breaking the four-minute mile and persisted. In an attempt in May 1953, run with a pace setter, he managed 4.03.6. Another attempt two months later brought his time down to 4.02. Other runners were also trying to break the mark; Australian John Landy and American Wes Santee were also close. There was huge interest in the story and athletics became the centre of the sporting world in 1953 and 1954 as the three athletes vied for sporting immortality.

In the lead up to the Empire Games in Vancouver in 1954, an athletics meet between the British AAA and Oxford University was scheduled and it was announced that Bannister was going to run. On the morning of the event, heavy winds meant that conditions weren't ideal and Bannister resigned himself to having to wait for another opportunity. However, as the scheduled start time of 6pm approached,

Professional Life

the winds cleared and the race was on. The race was broadcast live by BBC Radio and commentated by Cussen's old 100-yard adversary Harold Abrahams.

With pace setters Christopher Chataway and Chris Brasher, both of whom had supported his earlier attempts, they set off in a field of six runners. Brasher set the early pace before moving aside to let Chataway keep the pace going. Bannister then kicked for home with a half a lap to go. With 3,000 screaming spectators he ran the last lap in just 59 seconds. As Bannister fell over the line exhausted, the stadium announcer Norris McWhirter announced slowly, *"Ladies and gentlemen, here is the result of event nine, the one mile: first, number forty-one, R. G. Bannister, Amateur Athletic Association and formerly of Exeter and Merton Colleges, Oxford, with a time which is a new meeting and track record, and which, subject to ratification, will be a new English Native, British National, All-Comers, European, British Empire and World Record. The time was three minutes, fifty-nine point four seconds"*. The crowd erupted as soon as they heard the three-minute part of his announcement.

*Roger Bannister crosses the line in 3.59.4*

Six weeks after Bannister achieved the milestone, Australian John Landy became the second man to break four minutes. In doing so he bettered Bannister's World Record of 3m 59.4 seconds by over a second. A month later at the 1954 Empire Games in Vancouver, Landy and Bannister raced each other in what was one of the most anticipated races in history. It is said that over a hundred million people worldwide tuned in to hear radio commentary. In that race, Landy led until the final lap, he looked over his left shoulder to gauge his lead when Bannister overtook him on his right side. Both men beat the four-minute mark and Bannister took gold.

## 1956 Olympics Melbourne

In September 1956 it was announced that Denis Cussen would be the Honorary Chief Medical Officer to the British Olympic Association at the upcoming Olympic Games in Melbourne.

The Melbourne Olympics were held between November 22nd and December 8th of that year. This was to be the first time the Olympics were held in the southern hemisphere.

A week before the start of the games, Cussen had to issue an official statement denying that members of the British team had come down with measles. He pointed at the fact that one of the attendants in the British dining room was suffering from chicken pox as the probable source of the rumours.

A few days later, British cyclist Alan Danson from Wigan, was stung by an insect and Cussen had to treat his leg which had swollen badly.

Those two were the only reported issues that Cussen had to attend to while at the games. He was track-side for the athletics to care for and coach the athletes. This put him in prime position to witness one of Ireland's great Olympic triumphs.

> **DENIS CUSSEN BRITISH OLYMPIC MEDICAL ADVISER**
>
> DR. DENIS CUSSEN, the flying winger, who won fifteen Irish Rugby "caps" between 1921 and 1927 and shares with another Irish Rugby international, Freddie Moran, the Irish native record for 100 yards, at 9.8 secs., is going to Melbourne as honorary medical adviser to the British Olympic team.
>
> A native of Co. Limerick and a former Dublin University player Dr. Cussen is employed in London by the Shell Petroleum Company who, it is understood, are footing the cost of the journey.
>
> A member of several rugby clubs amongst them London-Irish and St. Mary's Hospital, he will leave London next week and return on December 15.

## Professional Life

Denis Cussen was trackside when Ronnie Delany won his gold medal in the 1500m. Immediately after crossing the line, Delany fell to his knees for a moment of prayer. He was pulled to his feet and congratulated by those he had just beaten. He then set off on a victory lap but after just a few paces, Denis Cussen ran up to congratulate his fellow country man. Despite living in the United Kingdom for most of his adult life, Denis was still a proud Irishman.

The British team won seven medals at the games. Cussen was without doubt there for Chris Basher's gold in the 3000m Steeplechase, Derek Johnson's silver in the 800m, Gordon Piries' silver in the 5000m and Thelma Hopkins' silver in the high jump

*Cussen on his way to Melbourne*

*Cussen on his way to Melbourne*

## Empire Games (Commonwealth Games)

The Empire Games, now known as the Commonwealth Games, can be traced back to an article published in the magazine Greater Britain in 1891. The article, titled *Pan-Britannic Festival* and written by Mr J Astley Cooper, proposed a Pan-Britannic Contest and Festival as a means of *"increasing the goodwill and the good understanding of the Empire, also with the hope of drawing closer the family bonds between the United States and the Empire of the Queen"*. The article was met with interest and discussion but there was no immediate follow-up activity at that point. This article was published five years before the first Modern Olympic Games in 1896, though the development of both games in reality coincided.

The coronation of King George V in 1911 was celebrated with a "Festival of the Empire" which was held at Crystal Palace in London. A sports competition called the Inter-Empire Sports Meeting was part of that festival with athletes from various countries invited to take part. Medals for athletics, boxing, swimming and wrestling were all competed for.

In the aftermath of the 1920 Olympic Games, a combined team from the countries of the British Empire took on a United States team in another championship. This one was held at Queen's Club in London. This was repeated after the 1924 Olympic Games, this time at Stamford Bridge. These competitions sowed the seed of public interest in a games dedicated to the countries of the Empire.

In the aftermath of the 1928 Olympic Games, at which Denis had competed, Canada led a move to establish the first British Empire Games. The first Empire Games were held in Hamilton, Canada in August 1930. Four hundred athletes from eleven countries took part; Australia, Bermuda, Canada, England, British Guyana, Newfoundland, New Zealand, Northern Ireland, Scotland, South Africa and Wales. By this time, Ireland was an independent state and no longer part of the Empire so did not compete.

Subsequent games were held in London (1934), Sydney (1938), Auckland (1950) and Vancouver (1954). In 1958 the Empire Games were held in Cardiff, Wales and Denis Cussen was invited to be the Honorary Chief Medical Officer for the English team.

## 1958 Empire Games

1958's Empire Games were the last to be known by that name. The next games, held in Perth, Australia went by the name the Commonwealth Games. By 1958 the games had grown significantly from their inception. In an Empire where the sun never set, thirty-five countries took part; Australia, Bahamas, Barbados, Canada, Ceylon, Dominica, England, Fiji, Ghana, Gibraltar, British Guyana, Hong Kong, India, Isle of Man, Jamaica, Jersey, Kenya, Malaya, Malta, Mauritius, New Zealand, Nigeria, Northern Ireland, Pakistan, Rhodesia, Borneo, Sarawak, Scotland, Sierra Leone, Singapore, South Africa, St Vincent, Tanzania, Trinidad, Uganda and Wales. The 1,238 athletes in 1958 stayed at an athlete's village built at St Athan RAF Station in Barry, seventeen miles from Cardiff.

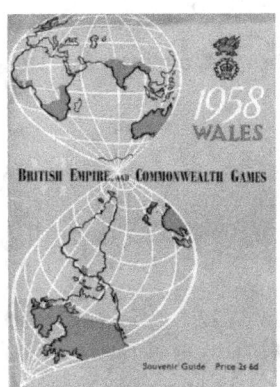

Cussen was called into duty before the games even kicked off. Derek Ibbotson was one of the favourites for the mile event but had lost a bit of form in the lead up to the games. His coach noticed that one of his thighs was smaller than the other and Dr Cussen was called in to investigate as to whether this was a reason for the loss of form.

Cussen drove Ibbotson to the Medical Research Unit base at St Athan RAF Camp near the seaside town of Barry. There he submitted the athlete to a series of tests. The tests proved that the trainer was correct and that one of Ibbotson's legs was a half an inch thinner just above the knee.

*"It all adds up to the fact that he is all right. Derek had power efficiency tests for his legs and back for about 15 minutes by the research unit when it was found that he was above average. So far as his legs are concerned, they were well above average and up with the efficiency found in wrestlers and weight-lifters, people one would expect to have more propelling power. This is unusual for runners. The thinness was due to natural wastage, as found in footballers who use their right leg more often than the left. Derek had no idea that one of his legs was thinner than the other, and when it was first discovered it was thought that this was the result of his loss of form because of some disease."*

Ibbotson, who had won bronze at the Melbourne Olympic Games, had a poor games and finished tenth in his event.

Also ahead of the games, one of the English boxers Stuart Pearson was diagnosed by Cussen with a septic foot. He was quoted in the press as saying *"It is not serious, but we do not want to take chances with any of these boys. Pearson should be out again very quickly"*. Pearson won silver in the Light Heavyweight event.

The games were opened on July 18th by HRH The Prince Phillip, Duke of Edinburgh opened it. The final carrier of the Queen's torch relay which brought the flame into the stadium was, like Denis, an international rugby player and Olympic sprinter. Ken Jones had played forty-four times for Wales, five times for the Barbarians and three times for the British and Irish Lions in 1950. He had won a silver medal in the 4x100m at the 1948 Olympic Games in London.

Over the following eight days, athletics, bowls, boxing, cycling, fencing, rowing, swimming, diving, weight lifting and wrestling were all competed in.

In Denis' beloved 100-yards, Jamaican Keith Gardner won in 9.5 seconds. Thirty years on from his own record, the times had improved but just a fraction of a second. Gardner also won the 120-yard hurdles and came second in the 220-yards. The 220-yards was won by Tom Robinson from Bahamas in 21.0 seconds. Jamaican Paul Foreman won the long jump with a leap of 24 feet 5 inches. In 1922 Denis managed 21 feet 8.7 inches. The long jump had moved on from his time.

This was the golden age of men's long-distance running. Dr Roger Bannister had won the mile in 1954 in 3 minutes 58.8 seconds. There is no doubt that Denis was watching on as Australian Herb Elliot won it in 1958 in 3 minutes 59.9 seconds. Elliott famously never lost a competitive race over one mile. He retired with a perfect thirty-six wins out of thirty-six. Seventeen of those were completed within the mythical four minutes.

England won the 4 x 100 relay in 40.72 seconds. They won silver in the 4x 440 yards. Arthur Rowe won the pole vault competition, Mike Elliott the hammer throw and Colin Smith the javelin. In the women's events, England won the 4x 110-yard relay, Sheila Hoskin and Mary Bignal scored a first and second place in the long jump and Suzanne Allday won the discus.

Other than the incident before the games started, there were no reports of any medical issues that Denis had to be involved with during the games.

## 1960 Olympics Rome

The 1960 Summer Olympics were held in Rome. By this time Denis Cussen was working for Shell International as their Deputy Principal Medical Officer. Again, he was appointed Honorary Chief Medical Advisor to the British Olympic team. By coincidence, the Irish Olympic doctor in Rome was also an ex Irish rugby international. Dr Kevin Flanagan played three times for Ireland in the 1940s. Flanagan also played soccer at the highest level. He played for Arsenal and Brentford and was capped by the Irish football team on ten occasions.

### Strong team

Fielding one of the strongest teams in the coming Rome Olympics is the Shell company.

At least nine Shellmen will be at Rome, headed by Australia's world record miler **Herb Elliot**, who works for Shell Australia.

One of the oldest competitors is a Shellman — **Marcel Lafortune** — who has appeared at every Olympics since 1928.

He works for the Belgium company and will represent his country in the pistol shooting events.

But a key man for Britain will be **Dr. D. J. Cussen**, a top Shell "medico." He is medical officer to the British team.

An indication of why Cussen was so important to the British team was the preparation work that he did with the team that year. Ahead of the games, Denis took the athletes to the National Institute of Medical Research in Hampstead where he worked with Professor Otto Edholm on an innovative preparation. Edholm was an expert in human physiology and had spent years researching how the body responds to changes in climate. While the bulk of that work was regarding cold climates (in fact, Edholm Point in Antarctica is named after him), Cussen and Edholm worked on conditioning the athletes for the heat of Rome in the summer.

Professional Life

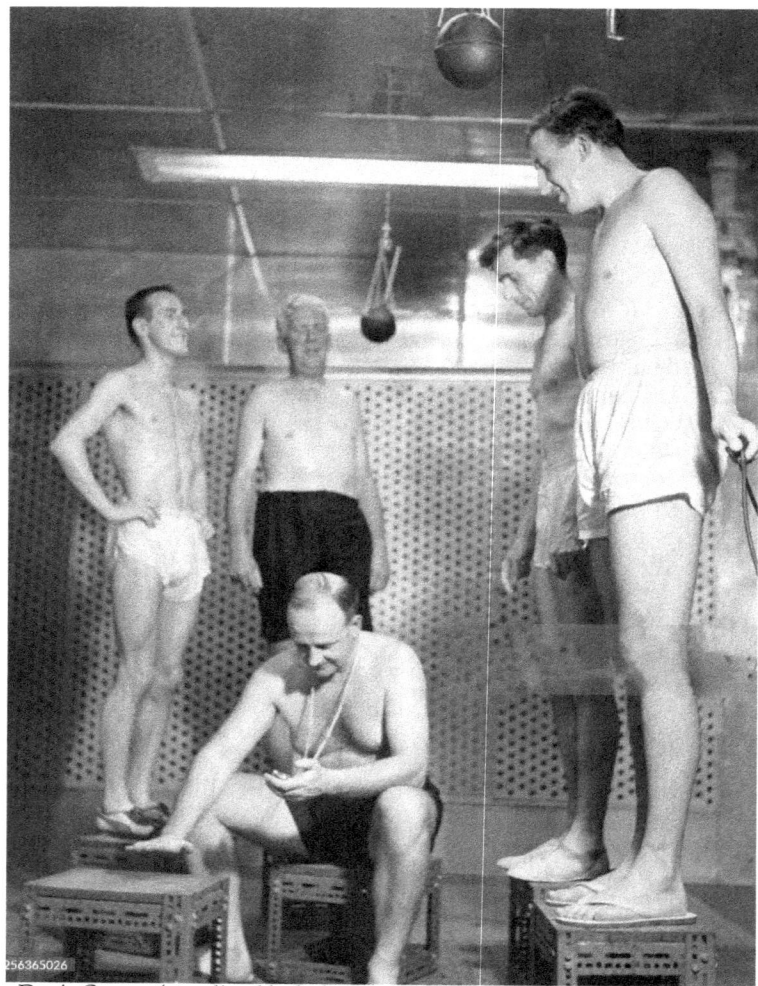

*Denis Cussen (standing black shorts) and Major JN Adam RAMC (seated) conditioning athletes Frank Salvat, Jim Hinds and John Hovell in 1960*

Through the month of July, athletes were invited to take part in the preparation. The first three to volunteer were Frank Salvat a three-mile runner, cyclist Jim Hinds and 1500m runner John Hovell. The three athletes, along with Cussen himself, sweated through four-hour sessions in a 'sweat box' while heated air and steam were pumped into the room. The athletes alternated between having thirty minutes in the heat (104 degrees Fahrenheit and 70% humidity), followed by having thirty minutes of rest. This was revolutionary for the time and showed Cussen's grasp of advances in sports medicine. In an interview Cussen commented, *"now what we want is something to acclimatise our chaps for heights, the thin air our soccer teams have to breathe in Bogota. I was talking to some Columbian doctors there and they said that barrel-chested men manage best at those heights. Can you see us picking a barrel-chested soccer team?"*.

Salvat famously had a pre-race ritual where two hours before every race, he would drink a pint of beer and eat a pie. Neither that ritual, nor the acclimatisation did him any good. He failed to advance from his heat in the Olympic Games 5000m event. Hinds and Hovell also failed to make an impression at the games.

## Olympic diver Brian Phelps 'much better'

Brian Phelps, Britain's main Olympic diving hope, was today examined by the team's doctor, Dr. Denis Cussen, and found to be much better.

Ten days before the games, British Olympic diving medal prospect injured his shoulder while diving off of a high board. There was concern about his ability to recover in time for the games. Denis was prominent in the press re-assuring the British public that he would recover in time.

Cussen also treated Olympic Dragon boater, Jonathan Janson. A strained back was diagnosed as an attack of lumbago and was treated with simple massage.

The most unusual action Cussen had in Rome in 1960 was when a complaint was made against the British team that one of their athletes, competing in the women's events, was in fact male. The unnamed athlete was competing in the athletics events and two European teams made official complaints.

## Professional Life

An official statement was released by the British Team saying, *"The entry forms for all our girl athletes were, under International Amateur Athletics Federation and International Olympic Committee rules, accompanied by a certificate signed by a doctor certifying their sex. This allegation is not calculated to help our team in the fierce competitions ahead."*

The leader of the British team called it a *"slur on the British team"* and Cussen was interviewed by the press on the subject. The issue died down after a few days.

Throughout the games, there were few other requirements for medical intervention amongst the British athletes.

> **CHANGED-SEX ALLEGATION DENIED**
>
> MR. K. S. "SANDY" DUNCAN, who is in charge of the British Olympic team, said yesterday in Rome that he regarded allegations that one of the women competitors was a man as "a slur on the British team."
>
> He read an official statement: "The entry forms for all our girl athletes were, under International Amateur Athletic Federation and International Olympic Committee rules, accompanied by a certificate signed by a doctor certifying their sex. This allegation is not calculated to help our team in the fierce competitions ahead."
>
> He had been asked to comment on British newspaper reports that two European nations had reported one of Britain's women athletes to their Olympic committees, as they believed that she had developed male characteristics and could not be classified as a woman.
>
> **MEDICAL CERTIFICATE**
>
> The competitor is understood to be a member of the track-and-field team. (Only members of the track-and-field teams are compelled to provide a signed medical certificate as to their sex before taking part in the games).
>
> The official doctor to the British team, Dr. Denis Cussen, said that he had not been asked to sign any certificate by any member of the British team.
>
> There has never in any previous Olympic Games been any suggestion that a British woman competitor might have changed her sex, but several instances have occurred of women being banned from taking part in international athletic competitions because of a sex change.
>
> 22/8/60

> pion, Christian Dorola (France).
>
> **OLYMPIC JEALOUSY**
>
> Team managers of the various British contingents in Rome are delighted—and very much relieved—by the way their competitors are standing up to the extreme heat and change of conditions.
>
> All have reported a clean bill of health to the British headquarters in the Olympic Village.
>
> "The medical precautions we have taken are paying handsome dividends," said Dr. Cussen.
>
> He said that many other countries were jealous of the clean bill of health of the British team, which had no cases of dysentery or sunburn.

The Rome Olympic Games were held from 25th August to 11th September 1960. Rome had previously been awarded the honour to host the games in 1906 however the eruption of Mount Vesuvius in

## Professional Life

1906 left them unable to host and the games were instead moved to London.

Two hundred and fifty-three British competitors (206 men and 47 women), took part in one hundred and thirty events across seventeen sports at the games. Despite the size of the team, Britain only won two gold medals (down from six in 1956). Overall, they won twenty medals and finished twelfth in the medal table.

In the track events where Denis had a particular interest, he was there to witness former polio patient, Wilma Rudolph, win three gold medals. She had been part of the bronze medal winning USA relay team in 1956. In 1960 she won the 100m, 200m and was on the 4x100m winning team.

In the men's sprint race a photo finish was required to split German Admin Hary and American Dave Sime. Both finished in Olympic record time of 10.2 seconds. Peter Radford from the British team won bronze.

Cussen, a champion boxer during his university years, would also have paid a keen interest in the boxing events where Cassius Clay, aged just eighteen, won the light heavyweight gold medal.

*Cassius Clay wins gold at the 1960 Rome Olympics*

Ireland also competed at the 1960 Summer Olympics. A team of forty-nine competitors took part in thirty-nine events. After the success of Ronnie Delaney in Melbourne, he only made the quarter final in 1960 and Ireland won no medals.

Despite the preparation that Cussen and the athletes did in conditioning ahead of the games, Britain's poor performance overall led to an enquiry after the games. There was also an inquiry into rumours that some of the British women competitors had male characteristics. A report was issued the following year which stated that two, including an unnamed 100m sprinter, were intersex.

## BRITAIN TO HOLD ENQUIRY INTO ROME 'FAILURES'

**OLYMPIC REPORT**

A FULL-SCALE enquiry into the effect of the Rome climate on Britain's Olympic team is to be held. It will be aimed at finding out to what extent the failure of some of our track stars can be blamed on the weather, and a questionnaire compiled by doctors and athletic officials will be sent to all team managers.

It will be compiled by Mr. Sandy Duncan, head of the British Olympic delegation, and Dr. D. J. Cussen, the team's medical adviser.

an enquiry may throw new light on the problem.

"Team mangares are in touch with their athletes and will be able to tell us individual reactions.

"We shall also ask managers

**DON'T RETIRE**

# Professional Life

## St Marys (1926-1930)

Denis Cussen graduated from Trinity College in December 1925. He briefly considered working in Ireland as a GP and applied for a role at a medical practice in Taghmon, Co. Wicklow. It was a very political time in Ireland and while the Cussen family were catholic, they didn't hold strong republican views. That, plus the fact that Trinity was viewed as both protestant and the establishment, meant that Denis' application for the role wasn't received welcomingly. Instead, Denis applied for and accepted the role of Casualty House Surgeon at St Mary's Hospital in Paddington, London. As outlined earlier, Denis moved to London in January 1926. In his first few months he played for nine different rugby teams, criss-crossing the Irish Sea to play in Five Nations and Bateman Cup games.

As Casualty House Surgeon, Denis' role was to deal with any patients presenting at the casualty department in this busy London hospital and perform any surgery required. A large volume of the patients would have been people requiring minor surgeries or stitches to deal with minor cuts. There were, however, he attended to some more significant cases. On a number of occasions, he was called to testify in coroners' inquiries into deaths. His own father Bob Cussen was the coroner for East Limerick so he was well familiar with what was involved.

On August 1st 1926, Denis testified in the coroner's enquiry into the death of Elsie May Weller. Elsie May was parlour maid in a house in Epsom. The house was owned by Baron Bonde from Sweden. The Bonde family were away for the weekend and Weller and the caretaker were the only ones in the house. A fire broke out and by the time the fire brigade arrived, the house was engulfed. Weller was on the fourth floor, at the back of the building. The firemen were close to rescuing her when she couldn't take the heat anymore and jumped to her death. She was removed to St Marys Hospital but was dead on arrival. Cussen testified that her arms were badly burned but it was a broken spine and haemorrhaging that was the cause of her death. Recording a verdict of accidental death, the coroner remarked that it was not surprising that the deceased lost her head. If she could have waited a minute or two more, the fire brigade would have rescued her.

Another sad case that Denis was involved with came to a coroner's inquiry on 27th September 1926. A bridegroom, Eric Chappell, fell to his death just two hours before his wedding ceremony. Builder Eric Chappell was getting married but just a few hours beforehand, he fell from a window, dropped thirty feet and impaled himself on a railing outside the building. He died instantly. Cussen testified that on the body he found an entrance wound three inches long in the left side near the back and there was an exit would in the right chest. Six ribs were broken and the heart was torn, while the left lung was also punctured. The coroner ruled it a sheer accident.

In December 1928, Denis gave evidence into the death of Mrs Eleanor Bassett (55) who was knocked down by a car and was removed unconscious to St Mary's. Denis was unable to revive her and she passed away. The coroner said the deceased appeared to have acted with gross carelessness and ruled it an accidental death.

Later that same month, he was called to give evidence into the death of Elizabeth Roy. She was working as a cook in the home of Mrs Douglas. While Roy was attending to the kitchen fire, her apron caught alight and she was quickly engulfed in flames. She was rushed to St Marys where she died shortly afterwards. Cussen gave evidence that she was conscious when she was admitted but lost conscious shortly after and died the following morning. He said her death was from shock associated from her extensive burns.

**COOK BURNED TO DEATH.**

**Coroner Commends West Chelsea Woman.**

The story of the efforts of a Chelsea woman in extinguishing the flaming clothing of a servant whose apron caught fire at a house in Gloucester-place, Marylebone, was told at the Marylebone Coroner's Court on Saturday. An inquest was held on Elizabeth Roy, 24, a cook, employed at 7 Gloucester-place, who died in St. Mary's Hospital from the effect of burns.

Mrs. Rose Havstaff, wife of a boiler

While working at St Mary's Hospital, Denis held the roles of Casualty House Surgeon (1926) and House Surgeon, Out Patient House Surgeon and House Physician. He worked at the hospital until the end of 1930 when he moved to Harrow.

While Denis was working at St Mary's Hospital in 1928, the Daily Mirror published an article announcing he was to marry a colleague, Dr Dorothy Dale Forster.

## Professional Life

### SURGEONS TO WED

#### Romance of Rugby International and Woman Doctor

Two surgeons at St. Mary's Hospital, Paddington, have become engaged to be married. They are Dr. D. J. Cussen, the Irish international Rugby player and Irish 100 yards champion, and Dr. Dorothy Forster. Miss Forster is casualty officer at the hospital.

Dr. D. J Cussen, Irish international Rugby player, is engaged to Miss D. Forster. Both are surgeons at a Paddington hospital.

*Daily Mirror report of engagement Oct 1928*

The story was reported in a number of newspapers however, the following day the Daily Mirror published a second article reporting that Cussen had corrected them and that he was not, in fact, engaged.

**Erroneous Report.**—Dr. D. J. Cussen, the Irish international Rugby player, a surgeon at St. Mary's Hospital, Paddington, asks us to state that the report of his engagement to be married to Dr. Dorothy Forster, of the same hospital, is incorrect.

*Daily Mirror correction published 1st November 1928*

Dorothy was from Hartlepool and came through the St Mary's Hospital training school and qualified in 1926. She was House Surgeon and Casualty House Surgeon at St Mary's in 1927. In 1928, when the story was reported, she was Resident Anaesthetist.

Following an investigation by the hospital, it turned out that the announcement was in fact a practical joke, played on Cussen by a colleague Dr Sadler.

Denis went on to marry Lilian Pickford in 1936. Dorothy went on to be Deputy Medical Superintendent at Heatherwood Hospital in Ascot.

> **HOSPITAL HOAX.**
>
> **ENGAGEMENT ANNOUNCEMENT AS JOKE.**
>
> A remarkable practical joke has been played on two of the doctors at St. Mary's Hospital, Paddington, by another doctor of the hospital staff.
>
> On Monday last a notice appeared in a number of London papers to the effect that Dr. Cussen, of St. Mary's Hospital, was engaged to be married to Dr. Dorothy Dale Forster, of the same hospital.
>
> Friends, surprised by the romantic announcement, hastened to congratulate the supposedly happy couple.
>
> Their good wishes were greeted with surprise by Dr. Cussen and Dr. Dorothy Forster. They were not engaged.
>
> The medical staff of the hospital were extremely indignant at the practical joke played on two of their members. They demanded a full inquiry into the matter, and the staff were called together.
>
> The investigators had not far to look. Dr. C. G. A. Sadler, a member of the staff, admitted his guilt. As a sequel the following statement was made public by Dr. Sadler:—
>
> "With regard to the announcement in the press of the engagement of Dr. Cussen and Dr. Forster, I wish to say that this erroneous information was merely intended as a practical joke on my part. I have apologised to Dr. Cussen and Dr. Forster for any inconvenience it may have caused them.—
> DR. C. G. A. SADLER, "St. Mary's Hospital."
>
> "The matter is closed as far as I am concerned," said Dr. Sadler to a newspaper representative.
>
> "For the sake of all the parties it is better not to say any more about it."

She never married and died at a relatively young age in December 1944 at Paddington Hospital

It isn't the only rumoured engagement that Denis Cussen had. Noted Irish historian and writer, Ulick O'Connor, once claimed that Cussen had been engaged to his mother. There is no way to know for sure. O'Connor's mother, Eileen Murphy, was from Booterstown in South Dublin. She married Matthew O'Connor in January 1928. Matthew, like Cussen, was a doctor. The timelines fit so perhaps it's true.

*The hoax unveiled in the Western Mail in November 1928*

## Harrow (1931-1936)

As the game of football was developing, before formal structures and rules were put in place, it was common for each school to play a different variant of the game. This was the case at Harrow School where 'Harrow Football' was the game played by the students over the winter months.

Denis Cussen's Irish and Blackheath colleague, Ian Stuart took up a teaching job at Harrow in early 1927. He arranged for an exhibition game of rugby to be played at the school. He coached and played on a 'whites' team; Denis coached and played on a 'colours' team. The game was played at Harrow School on 7th October 1927.

*The Whites v Colours game played at Harrow School 7th October 1927
Denis is back row, 2nd from the left*

*The Whites v Colours game played at Harrow School 7th October 1927*

Both teams were packed with international players and even some of the British and Irish Lions who had just returned from a tour of Argentina. Lining up on Denis' team were BS Chantrill (England), Rev Fulljames (Barbarians), JC Gibbs (England), RS Sprong (British and Irish Lions), RRF MacLennan (England) and R Cove-Smith (British and Irish Lions). On the Whites team were Guy Morgan (Wales), Rowe Harding (Wales), Windsor Lewis (Wales), WC Powell (Wales), David MacMyn (Scotland) and GB Coghlan (British and Irish Lions).

No one knows for sure who won the game but an article in the Harrovian raved about this sport and gave tips to budding players. That game was historic as it was the point at which the game of rugby replaced Harrow Football as the winter sport played at the school.

Harrow School's rugby history has gone on to be very successful. As well as winning multiple competitions over the years, the school has produced players like Maro Itoje, Billy Vunipola and Henry Arundell. Denis' intervention with Ian Stuart in 1927 had this possible.

On 15th November 1930 there was an interesting gathering of former Irish players at a game played on the Sixth Form ground at Harrow School. Harrow School were playing the Harrow County School. Ian Stuart was coach of the Harrow School team. The game was referred by Cussen's fellow Limerickman Dr William Roche who played for both Ireland and the British and Irish Lions, and Denis Cussen himself was on the sidelines to watch.

> On Saturday afternoon there were at least three International Rugby players on the Sixth Form ground, on the next pitch to which the Harrow County School were putting up an excellent display against Harrow School Colts. There was Mr. I. M. B. Stuart, who has played for Ireland, dodging about on the line; Dr. Roche, the old Welsh International, was refereeing; and close at hand was Dr. D. J. Cussen, of St. John's-road, who was in the Irish fifteen a season or so ago. Dr. Cussen is the successor to Dr. C. F. Mayne, also a great Rugby enthusiast.

Denis' friendship with Stuart and no doubt the time he spent there in rugby circles led to him being invited to move to Harrow. In 1930, Denis was invited by a fellow rugby enthusiast to take up general practice in Harrow. Dr Frederick A Maybe MBE had a practice, Lambert, Pennefather & Mayne, and recruited Denis to replace himself.

Mayne was awarded his MBE after WW1. At its outbreak he was serving as house surgeon at St George's Hospital, Hyde Park. He left that role to join the Naval Brigade. He served on HMS Kildonan Castle in the Gallipoli Expedition and was evacuated to join the British Expeditionary Force on the Western Front in 1916, in time for the Battle of the Somme.

> **DIED FROM A SCRATCH.**
>
> **HARROW LADY'S SAD DEATH.**
>
> An inquest was held at the Wesleyan Schoolroom, Bessborough-road, Harrow, on Friday afternoon on the body of Emma Anderton, a spinster, aged 79 years, of 9, Whitmore-road, Harrow. Stanley Anderton Haywood, a professional cricketer, of 9, Whitmore-road, Harrow, said the deceased was his aunt. On July 23 she complained to him that her first finger and thumb were very painful. She told him that she might have scratched it, but she could not find any signs of injury. He sent for a doctor, who ordered her removal to the Harrow Hospital the following day. In spite of all possible medical treatment she died on Thursday.
> The Coroner, Dr. G. Cohen, said the medical evidence of Dr. D. J. Cussen stated that deceased died from septicæmia resulting from a poisoned hand. He could not, however, ascertain the nature of the injury.
> A verdict in accordance with the medical evidence was returned.

Denis continued to testify in coroners' enquiries in his new role. In August 1930, he testified at the inquest into the death of Emma Anderton (79). Unmarried, she was the aunt of international cricketer Stanley Anderton Haywood. She complained to him that she had a pain, first in her finger, then in her thumb. Stanley sent her to the doctor (Cussen) who referred her immediately to Harrow Hospital where she died. The coroner ruled that she died from septicaemia probably from a scratch to her finger.

On 30th September 1930 he testified in a coroner's inquiry. They were inquiring into the death of Mrs Martha Louis Hill (84). Mrs Hill had been knocked down by a motorbike the previous Saturday. Dr Cussen was called to the scene and found the deceased lying on the pavement. He had her removed to Harrow Hospital where she later died of multiple fractures. The perpetrator was only identified because of a mysterious note left by an anonymous person on the stretcher as Mrs Hill was being removed to the hospital.

> **KILLED AT EIGHTY-FOUR**
>
> **A NOTE ON A STRETCHER.**
>
> How the action of an unknown woman who placed a note on a stretcher in Station-road, Harrow, after an accident led to the police tracing the driver of a car, the only witness of the fatality, was revealed at an inquest held at the Wesleyan Church Schoolroom, Bessborough-road, Harrow, on Tuesday. The Coroner, Dr. G. A. Cohen, sat with a jury to inquire into the death of Mrs. Martha Louise Hill, aged 84, of 1, Angel-road, Harrow, who died on Sunday in the Harrow Hospital from injuries received through being knocked down by a motor-cycle in Station-road on Saturday morning. P.c. C. Hedges was coroner's officer.

Denis worked in Harrow and lived at 9 St Johns Road, Harrow on Hill until 1936 when he decided to get married and go into general practice.

## Marriage and General Practice in Surbiton

Denis married Lilian Pickford at St Raphael's Roman Catholic Church in Kingston-on-Thames on 15th April 1936.

Lilian who was eight years younger than Denis, was the daughter of Walter Pickford, a farmer and his wife Ethel Cary. The family were from the town of Christian Malford in Wiltshire, near Bath.

The wedding was a small affair with just a dozen guests. Afterwards the couple went on honeymoon in Paris. On their return from honeymoon, the couple settled at a home at 86 Chiltern Drive, Surbiton Hill in Surrey, not far from Wimbledon. Denis opened a medical general practice and the couple settled into family life.

On 25th February 1940, the couple welcomed their first child, a daughter named Catherine Cussen aka Gillian.

### Murder Suicide

On Wednesday 7th January 1942 he was summoned to the home of a near neighbour and was witness to a tragic scene. The Strutt family lived at 271 Raeburn Avenue which was one street away from the Cussen residence. Leslie Strutt lived at the address with his wife, Gladys and young daughter, Gillian Strutt.

Leslie Strutt was the youngest son of George and Ellen Strutt and, like his father, was a master tailor. Leslie had married Gladys Crofton in 1938 and they had Gillian, their daughter in 1940. Gladys had had a difficult childhood. Her mother died when she was just a few years old and she was adopted by Henry Grubb, a plumber, and his wife Emily.

When Denis arrived at the home, he found Mrs Strutt dead and her daughter also dead. He tried to revive them but it was too late.

*271 Raeburn Ave*

An inquest was held a few days later at which it was ruled that Mrs Gladys Strutt, aged 28, had murdered her fourteen-month-old baby Gillian Strutt by gas and that she had then committed suicide in the same manner. Their pet dog was also killed in the incident. She was ruled to be of unsound mind at the time.

Mrs Strutt's husband Leslie testified that *"his wife had no worries of any kind, except that she may have worried over the crying of the baby, who was teething. His wife and child were quite all right when he left home at 9.15am that morning. On returning at 1.25pm, he found his wife lying on the floor in the kitchen, and the child on a small mattress. The gas taps wee full on"*.

A copy of a note which Mr Strutt said he found on the kitchen table, was handed to the jury and the coroner, but it was not read aloud.

Mrs Agnes West, a neighbour, said that *"Mr Strutt told her of the tragedy, and she called Dr Cussen, who arrived almost immediately. Witness added that Mrs Strutt had spoken to her of the baby's teething and crying out at night as worrying, but witness had not regarded that statement as more than a manner of speech."*

Gladys and Gillian were laid to rest at the nearby Surbiton Cemetery. Leslie Strutt understandably moved away from the tragic home. He settled in Twickenham where he re-married to Josephine Pateman. They didn't have any children. Leslie Strutt died in Plymouth in 1978.

Professional Life

## World War Two

World War Two broke out on 1st September 1939. As it progressed in 1940 and there was a risk of the Germans invading Britain, the Home Guard was established. Made famous by the television show Dad's Army, the Home Guard was an unpaid armed citizen militia. Over one and a half civilians signed up to help the war effort. At the same time, the Ministry of Health, conscious that there would be a need to manage medical care closely both on the battlefield and at home where civilians might be injured in air-raids, set up the Emergency Hospital Service.

In February 1941 Denis enlisted in the Home Guard. He was given the role of Platoon Commander and he served for the next two years as part of the signals corp.

He resigned from the Home Guard at the end of December 1942 when he was commissioned into the army.

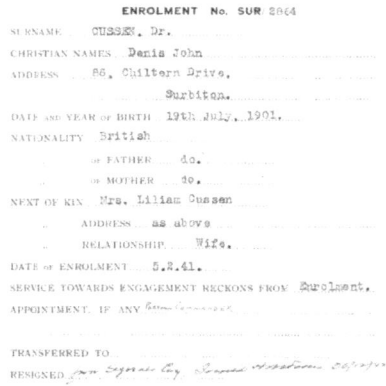

*Denis' Home Guard Enrolment Form*

On 2nd January 1943, Denis Cussen received an Emergency Army Commission and became a Lieutenant in the Royal Army Medical Corp. His army records are still sealed so it is difficult to know what exactly his activities were but it is almost certain that he served as a surgeon at one of the emergency hospitals around London.

With London under regular nightly air-raids, underground operating theatres were established that operated around the clock treating people injured during the attacks. They also catered for normal medical care as life went on. The below photo shows an underground operating theatre at Guys Hospital in 1941. Four surgeries taking place simultaneously.

*Denis in his Home Guard helmet*

Professional Life

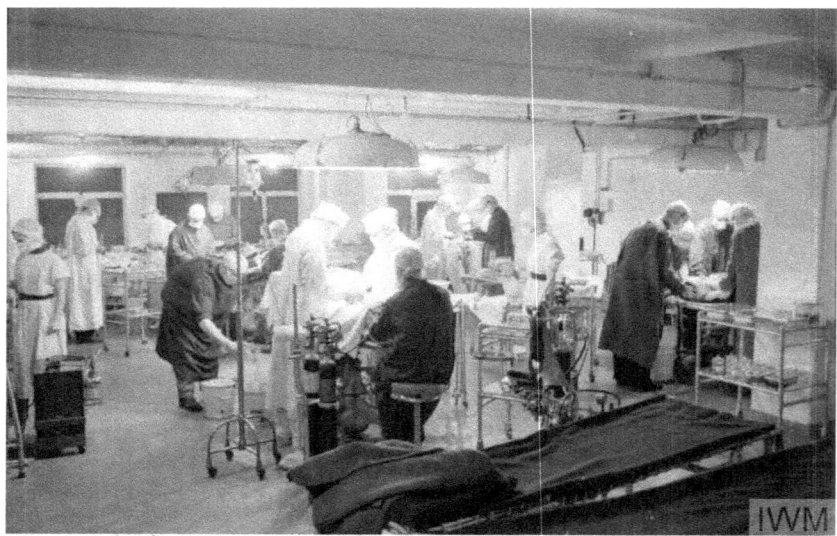
*An example of an Emergency Hospital during WW2 – Guys Hospital, London 1941*

A year after he was commissioned, Cussen was made War Substantive Captain, meaning he was given the rank of captain for the duration of the war, after which he would fall back to Lieutenant.

*Captain Denis Cussen listed in the Army List in 1943*

316

Professional Life

Denis was awarded two medals for his service during WW2. The Defence Medal was a campaign medal that was instituted in May 1945 and awarded to subjects of the British Commonwealth for both non-operational military and certain types of civilian service during the Second World War. Denis earned this for his service in the Home Guard.

The War Medal 1939–1945 is a British campaign medal instituted in August 1945. The medal was awarded to subjects of the British Commonwealth who had served full-time in the Armed Forces for at least 28 days during the war years. Denis earned this having been commissioned into the army.

## British Association of Sports Medicine (Now BASEM)

When Roger Bannister completed his historic four-minute mile in 1954, he attributed a lot of his success to Sir Adolphe Abrahams. Abrahams was the brother of Harold Abrahams, the 100m sprinter who won gold in the 1924 Olympic Games and against whom Denis had competed.

Abrahams was a thought-leading doctor who was focused on using science and medicine to increase elite athletic performance. He was the Chief Medical Officer with the British Olympic Team from 1924 until 1954 after which that role moved to Denis Cussen.

In 1952, Abrahams and Arthur Porritt founded the British Association of Sports Medicine (BASM). Porritt was, like Cussen, a sprinter in his youth. He competed in and came third in the 1924 Olympic Games behind Adolphe's brother Harold Abrahams. When Cussen joined St Mary's Hospital in 1926 as Casualty House Surgeon, Porritt was House Surgeon and later that year was appointed as the surgeon to the King. Cussen and Porritt were work colleagues, but they were also competitors. Cussen had beaten Porritt on two occasions in the lead up to the 1928 Olympic Games. Porritt was later made Sir Arthur Porritt and returned to his native New Zealand in 1967 where he was Governor-General until 1972.

Professional Life

The British Association of Sports Medicine (BASM), now known as the British Association of Sport and Exercise Medicine (BASEM) was founded as a representative body for physiotherapists, doctors and other medical specialists who focused on sports medicine.

Porritt's recollection of how BASM came about was published in the British Medical Journal on the jubilee of its founding.

> *'If I remember rightly, it was a chance conversation between Dr Tegner and myself which sowed the first seed; we later enlisted the help and advice of Sir Adolphe Abrahams, collected a few personal friends – including the secretary of the British Olympic Association, and, in the early part of 1952 held a number of informal "unofficial" meetings leading up to the first "Executive" in June"*

The line 'collected a few personal friends' includes Denis Cussen. His friendship with Porritt and no doubt Abrahams, saw him as an early member of BASM. Denis was involved in BASM from its founding. He was appointed as secretary and treasurer of BASM in 1955 and served in the latter role until 1964. In 1967 he was elected Vice President.

BASM provided a community of interest for sports medicine. Its first meetings were in effect lectures given by experts in various aspects of sports. They provided clinics for athletes to advise both the athlete and their coaches on best practice in training and nutrition. As the organisation grew, they broadened to include things like providing guidance on doping in sport to the sports bodies. BASM also lobbied educational organisations to provide sports medicine university courses. From 1968, BASM published the British Journal of Sports Medicine and Denis was a regular contributor.

Denis would also arrange interesting events that show his broad view of how athletic performance could be impacted. A great example of this is a 'symposium on the relationship between sport and ballet'. Another example of Denis' work in BASM was the 'symposium on the future of sports medicine in Britain. Answering sports needs' which he led in 1975.

As a voluntary body, BASM often struggled with funding shortages. When he stepped down as treasurer, Denis turned down honorary life membership, saying that he would prefer to continue to support the organisation through his annual subscription.

Professional Life

Denis Cussen's central role in BASM is also visible by the fact that he led and was a founder of the British Institute of Sport in 1963.

## British Institute of Sports Medicine

The British Institute of Sports Medicine was founded in 1963 by BASM, British Olympic Association (BOA) and British Physical Education Association (PEA).

After Britain's poor performance at the 1960 Olympic Games, BASM felt that there was a need to set up an institute, closely aligned with the medical profession and the universities, to study athletic performance. BASM's constitution as a representative body prevented them from creating it on their own and so they partnered with the BOA and PEA to set it up.

On 19th October 1963, Denis was one of five contributors to a paper circulated discussing the concept of founding the Institute of Sports Medicine.

> 6. A paper was circulated on the aims and objects of an "Institute of Sports Medicine". The Chairman remarked that the aims of such an Institute in no way differed and in fact were identical with those of B.A.S.M. However, further study was necessary. Accordingly a working party was proposed to go into the practical aspects of such a project. The following were nominated.
>
> Dr. D. J. Cussen
> Mr. K. S. Duncan
> Mr. P. Sebastian
> Mr. W. G. Tucker
> Dr. J. V. Williams
>
> Sir Arthur Porritt agreed to become nominal Chairman.
>
> 7. The next meeting 19th October, 1963.

*Cussen's name listed on the founders list of the Institute of Sports Medicine*

It took two years but on 29th July 1965, a memorandum of association of the Institute was signed by Sir Arthur Porritt, William Tucker, Denis Cussen, John Pascoe Williams, Alexander Ross, Kenneth Duncan and Peter Sebastian. The Certificate of Incorporation was granted a week later. Prince Phillip became the first President of the institute in November 1967.

The British Institute of Sports Medicine has contributed to the development of sport in Britain in numerous ways since it was founded. As early as 1965 they were engaged to do random drug testing for the Tour of Britain. From 1976, they were contributing to the syllabus of various third level courses and they have been involved in an array of academic studies on sports performance.

An example of the work that Denis Cussen did with the Institute of Sports Medicine was a study done on sleep deprivation in aviators. In 1966 British aviator Sheila Scott planned a record-breaking solo trip around the world in a Piper Aztec twin-engine aircraft. During the flight which covered 31,000 miles in thirty-four days. She was the first Briton to solo fly around the world and only the third woman ever to do so. As she prepared for the flight, Denis was one of three doctors who studied her sleep patterns and how they impacted her fatigue and ability to focus. The intent was to help her understand her physiology and optimise her capacity to fly for long periods. The study was later published as 'Sleep patterns in a lone global pilot'.

## Retirement

Denis Cussen left general practice in 1965 and moved from Surbiton to Ham Farm. He worked for a few years with the Shell Oil Company before retiring.

Lillian was a member of the Conservative Party and became the vice-chairperson of the Women's Committee of the Ham and Petersham Conservative Association. Both she and Denis spent a lot of time raising funds for local charities including Forbes and Craig House which was an old folk's home. Denis also volunteered as a clinical assistant with the Samaritans.

Denis and Lillian's daughter, Gillian, grew up in Richmond with her parents. She was passionate about the arts, sang with the BBC choir and acted on stage. In 1965 she moved to Fife in Scotland where she joined a nunnery at the Convent of Marie Reparatrice. After two years she decided against a religious life and returned to London.

Denis Cussen died on 15th December 1980. He was seventy-nine years old. He is buried at Richmond and East Sheen Cemetery, near

Twickenham, in London. His modest grave marker leaves no indication of his incredible talent and achievements.

*The final resting place of Denis Cussen at Richmond Cemetery*

Denis' wife, Lillian, died on 5th July 1987 in Chippenham, Wiltshire. She was buried with him. Their daughter Gillian Cussen never married and passed away in a London nursing home in May 2018.

Professional Life

# The Cussen Family

The surname Cussen (often pronounced "Cushen" locally) commonly found in Limerick and Cork, is likely of Norman derivation. Certainly, the Cussens were supporters of the Norman Fitzgeralds (Earls of Desmond).

A Robert Og Cussen was killed in the Desmond Rebellion in the late 16th century and likely lost his lands as tenants of the Desmond Estate which would have been their only wealth at that time.

The Cussens held on, however, in some fashion, and gradually gained back their lands as tenants of the Elizabethan landlords, the Courtenays of Powderham Castle in Devon.

Joseph Cussen became wealthy in the 19th century, probably through moneylending and he assisted his nephews to obtain land as tenants. One of those nephews was John Cussen of Newcastle West. He became a butter merchant and built up a large landholding in Limerick. One of his seventeen children was Robert (Bob) Cussen.

## Robert (Bob) Cussen (1865-1940)
## Mary Moylan Cussen (1879-1969)

The patriarch of the Cussen family, Bob Cussen returned to Limerick after his time at Blackrock College and the Four Courts in Dublin. Once home he established a successful legal practice in Newcastle West, Co. Limerick not far from his native Rathkeale. That practice is still running today. In addition, Bob served as the coroner for West Limerick.

In 1899 Bob married a local girl from Newcastle West, Mary Moylan whose scrapbooks made this book possible. The couple had six children. John, Denis, Robert, Catherine, Margaret and Michael.

Mary, as well as rearing her six children, worked in the local post office where her father, John Moylan, had been the postmaster until his death in 1908.

As can be gleaned from this book, Bob's love of rugby was passed on to his children. Having been the captain of the first Blackrock College team in 1882, he was a passionate rugby man and was one of the key men behind the establishment of a rugby club in Newcastle West in 1925.

In the same year that Newcastle West Rugby Club was established, 1925, Garryowen Football Club presented a cup, known as the Garryowen Cup, to be competed for by North Munster Junior Provincial clubs. In its first season, Newcastle West competed but did not win.

The following year (1926/27), Bob Cussen was elected club president and was as the helm during a very successful period for the Newcastle West club. With his son Bertie as captain and another son Mick also on the team, Newcastle West won the Garryowen Cup in April 1928 by beating Ennis 11-0 at The Markets Field in Limerick.

Bob Cussen (standing on right) with the Newcastle West team that won the
Garryowen Cup in 1927/28
Bertie Cussen is captain and is sitting in the centre holding the ball
Mick Cussen is sitting on the extreme left

Bob Cussen passed away aged seventy-five in September 1940. His wife Mary passed away in 1969. They are buried together at Grange cemetery in Co. Limerick

## John (Jack) Cussen (1900-1974)

John, known as Jack, was the eldest son of Bob and Mary Cussen. He was born on 7th July 1900. He was educated at Blackrock College in Dublin from 1914 until 1918. While at school he, along with his brother Denis, was on the Leinster Schools Senior Cup winning team of 1917/18.

*Blackrock College 1917/18*
Back row: Kelly, McCormick, Sullivan, Glynn, Gilleece, Brodrick, Walsh
Middle row: Browne, McVickar, O'Mahoy, Denis Cussen, Jack Cussen, Carew, Coghlan
Front: Healy, Kelly

Having graduated from Blackrock and progressing to Trinity, Jack played for the Blackrock Castle XV in 1919. The 'Castle' team was a team for students who had graduated from Blackrock College.

## The Cussen Family

Jack went to Trinity College Dublin where he studied medicine. After graduating he enlisted in the Royal Navy and rose through the ranks to become the Surgeon Commander onboard HMS Exeter.

While onboard HMS Exeter in 1939, Jack took part in the Battle of River Plate. The Exeter encountered German warship Admiral Graf Spee off the coast of Argentina and a fierce battle ensued during which the Exeter took severe damage. Over sixty sailors were killed onboard and many more were injured during the battle. As Surgeon Commander, Cussen was responsible for the medical response to the Exeter and the other two British ships involved in the battle (HMS Ajax and HMS Achilles). Cussen was distinguished when he was *'mentioned in dispatches'* after the battle. The Exeter limped into port at Port Stanley in the Falkland Islands where she underwent a year of repair work. It remained there for almost a year before returning to Britain where it was received by a distinguished party which included Winston Churchill who went aboard to meet the crew and acknowledge their sacrifice.

*The damage inflicted on HMS Exeter in 1939*

Jack Cussen was awarded the 1939-1945 Star and the 1939-1945 War Medal for his service during WW2. He later served on HMS Greenwich and retired from the Navy in 1967.

In 1956 Jack was consultant on the British war film The Battle of the River Plate. Directed by Michael Powell and Emeric Pressburger, and staring John Gregson, Anthony Quayle, Bernard Lee and Peter Finch, the film tells the story of the battle that defined Jack Cussen's career in the navy. The grand premiere of the movie was held at the Empire Theatre, Leicester Square in October 1956 in the presence of Queen Elizabeth II, Princess Margaret and Marilyn Monroe.

*Jack Cussen*

In October 1940, Jack married Dorothy McElligott from Listowel, County Kerry. The wedding took place in Kent, England. His holiness the Pope sent the couple of special blessing to mark the occasion. Jack and Dorothy lived in Esher on the outskirts of London and had one daughter, Elizabeth, who lives in Listowel.

Jack died in Walton-on-Thames on 2nd April 1974. He was 73.

## Robert (Bertie) Cussen (1903-1992)

Robert Cussen, known as Bertie, was born two years after Denis and would follow very closely in many of his older brothers' footsteps. Not as naturally athletic as Denis, Bertie was very successful in sports more through hard work and perseverance.

Following his schooling at Courteney School, Bertie joined his older brothers Jack and Denis at Blackrock College. He joined the ranks of the Blackrock borders in 1917.

While at Blackrock, Bertie showed his sporting talents. At the National Schools Athletics Championships in 1918, he won the National Junior High Jump with a jump of 1.37m.

He was on the Blackrock senior cup team in 1919 and in 1920. The 1919 team, captained by Denis, won the Leinster Schools Senior Cup. The following year, Bertie made a remarkable sporting statement by winning six competitions in the Blackrock sports carnival. He took gold in the 100-yards, 220-yards, 440 yards, Long Jump, High Jump and High Hurdles.

In 1921 Bertie followed his brother to Trinity where he studied law, ultimately earning a Doctorate of Law. He continued his sporting achievements while he studied.

In 1923/24 Bertie played for Trinity's 2nd XV team but in 1925/26 he was promoted to the first XV that won the Leinster Senior Cup and the Bateman Cup. That year he also played on the Trinity team that played in the first ever Rugby Sevens competition played in Ireland. The Evening Mail Cup was won on that occasion by the Trinity team. He went on to captain the Trinity first XV in the 1927/28 season.

During his university years, Bertie also continued his athletics. In the 1924 Trinity Sports Carnival he won the 100-yards and the Long Jump competitions. He went on to become the Varsity Long Jump Champion that year. The following year, he retained all of those achievements.

# The Cussen Family

**Trinity First XV 1926/27**
Back row: Lyburn, Odbert, Stuart, Paul, McGuire, Dixon, Hewitt, McIntosh
Front row: Wallace, Pike, Millin, Bertie Cussen (Capt), Cherry, Buchannan, Flood

**Bertie Cussen winning a 100y sprint at College Park**
*This photo is often mistakenly labelled as Denis*

At the 1926 National Championships he came third in the 100-yards behind Sean Lavan and JB Eustace. He won the National Long Jump title by jumping 6.94m. He went on to win a silver medal at the Tri-Nations International athletic meeting at Hamden Park in Glasgow.

He retained the National title the following year (1927) but then retired from athletics. He continued to be involved in the sport. He was vice-president of the Limerick County Athletics Board for many years.

Having graduated from Trinity, Bertie returned to Newcastle West and joined his father's legal practice. This practice is still in operation today and run by his granddaughter, son and nephew.

Having returned to Limerick, Bertie played for two seasons with Bohemians. In November 1927, Bertie was selected for the Munster Provincial team. He earned one cap in a game against Ulster played in Cork. Unfortunately, the game wasn't his best and Munster were beaten 17-3. He was dropped for the following game in December.

**MUNSTER.**
Full-back—J. W. Stokes (Bohemians).
Three-quarters—M. Murphy (Constitution), M. O'Connor (Garryowen), R. J. Cussen (Bohemians), M. McMahon (Garryowen).
Half-backs—T. Murphy (Constitution), J. O'Neill (Dolphin).
Forwards—C. J. Hanrahan (Dolphin), J. J. Casey (Young Munsters), T. Neville (U.C.C.), V. Murphy (Constitution), J. Mullane (Bohemians), A. Nellan (Young Munsetrs), T. Hanley (Garryowen), T. K. White (U.C.C.).
**ULSTER.**

*26th Nov 1927 Munster v Ulster in Cork*

Bertie moved to play his rugby with the Newcastle West team in 1928. With his brother Mick also on the team, Newcastle West won the Garryowen Cup in 1928.

Bertie was a successful solicitor in Limerick and was assistant coroner for a number of years. In 1929 he married Kathleen McCartan. Kathleen was from Newcastle, County Down and was the daughter of Daniel

McCartan, Clerk of the Crown of Peace. His brother Denis was his best man.

The **Wedding** took place at Newcastle, Co. Down, of Mr. Robert Cussen, solicitor, Newcastle West, to Miss Kathleen M'Cartan, daughter of Mr. Daniel M'Cartan, Clerk of the Crown and Peace, Eastern Villa, Newcastle, Co. Down. Miss Alice M'Cartan, sister of the bride, was bridesmaid, and the best man was Dr. Dennis Cussen, brother of the bridegroom and well-known Rugby international.
—Lafayette.

Bertie and Kathleen had seven children including John Cussen (co-author), and Clíodna Cussen. Clíodna, a renowned artist and sculptor married Pádraig Ó Snodaigh. Her son Aengus Ó Snodaigh became a Sinn Fein TD. Three of Clíodna's children, Rónán, Rossa and Colm, are members of the Irish folk band Kíla.

Bertie Cussen died on 24th January 1992. He was 88 years old.

# The Cussen Family

*Ronan O'Snodaigh*     *Colm O'Snodaigh*     *Rossa O'Snodaigh*
*Bertie Cussen's Grandsons in the band Kíla*

Athletics
- 1918 National Junior Boys High jump Champion
- 1920 Blackrock sports. 100y, 200y, 440y, Long jump, High jump, High hurdles Champion
- 1924 Trinity sports – 100y and Long jump Champion
- 1924 – Inter-University Long jump Champion
- 1926 National Championships
    - Long Jump National Champion
    - 100-yards – Bronze
- 1926 Tri-Nations International Athletics
    - Long Jump Silver
- 1927 National Championships
    - Long Jump National Champion
- 1927 Tri-Nations International Athletics
    - Long Jump Silver

Rugby
- Leinster Schools Senior Cup winner 1919 (Blackrock)
- Leinster Senior Cup winner 1926 (Trinity)
- Bateman Cup winner 1926 (Trinity)
- Captained Trinity 1927/28
- Played in the first Irish Rugby Sevens competition in 1921
- 1 x Munster Cap – Nov 1927

- Garryowen Cup Winner 1928 (Captain) (Newcastle West)

## Catherine Cussen (1904-1978)

Catherine (known as Kitty) Cussen was born in 1904.

In February 1936 she married Dublin solicitor Clifford O'Farrell. Clifford was the son of another solicitor Michael O'Farrell and was an acquaintance of Catherine's younger brother Michael who studied law in Dublin.

Clifford's legal practice ran into difficulty with the Law Society and a long running legal case that went all the way to the supreme court prevented them from practice.

The couple had two children, Patrick and Mary but the couple sadly broke up. Catherine returned to the family home in Limerick and later moved to Cambridge in England where she died in March 1978. She was 73. Clifford died in April 1984.

## Margaret Cussen (1907-1965)

Margaret (Maura) was born in 1907. Maura never married. She lived in Dublin, ironically on Lansdowne Road. She worked for the National Sweepstakes. She died on 8th January 1965 at her home at 26 Lansdowne Road. She was 58.

## Michael Cussen (1909-1988)

Michael was the youngest of the four Cussen brothers. Like the others, Michael went to Blackrock College where he studied from 1923 to 1927. While there, he too, won the Leinster Schools Senior Cup in 1926. It is remarkable that the Cussen brothers hold six Leinster Senior Schools Cup medals between them. Denis with three and Jack, Bertie and Michael each with one.

At the 1926 National Schools Championships, Michael was on the Blackrock College 4 x 440 yards relay team that won gold.

Michael went on to study law at Trinity. While there he played on the Trinity first XV that won the Leinster Senior Cup in 1928. He then fell back to Trinity's second XV in 1929, 30 and 31.

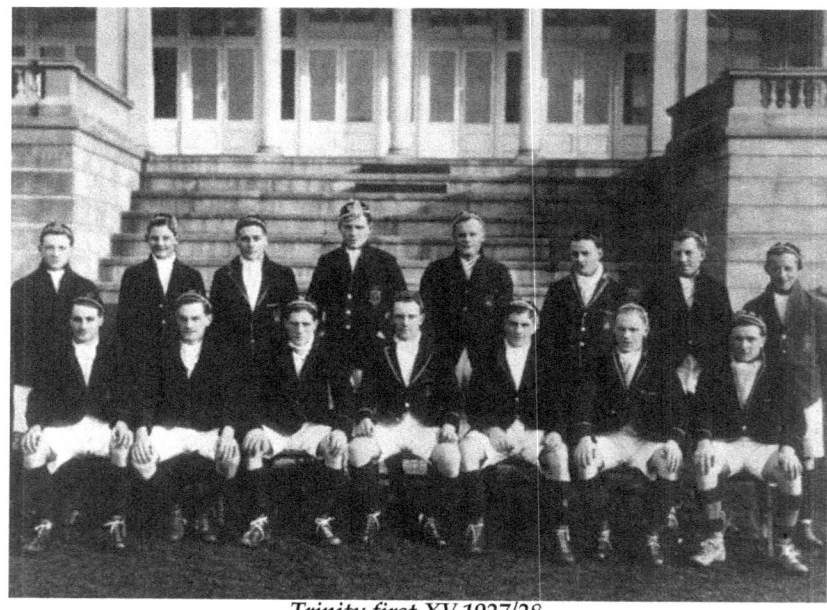

*Trinity first XV 1927/28*
Back row: Michael Cussen, Grealy, McNeilly, Tighe, McDowel, Knott, Pike, Lyburn
Front row: Hewitt, McGuire, Nunns, Buchannan, Pike, Cherry, Dixon

While still studying, he played rugby for Newcastle West and, with his brother Bertie, was on the team that won the Garryowen Cup in 1928. He also played with Bohemians in Limerick.

After completing his education at Trinity, Michael returned to Newcastle West where he worked alongside his brother Bertie in the family legal practice in Rathkeale.

Michael married Lucy Nash in Limerick on 21st September 1943. Lucy was from the family of Nash's Lemonade fame. They had three children. Sadly, one of their children, a son named Denis, was killed in a car accident in June 1928.

Michael died on 6th February 1988. He was 78. His wife Lucy had died in October 1978.

Athletics
- National Schools 4x440 yard relay champion

Rugby
- Leinster Schools Senior Cup winner 1926 (Blackrock)
- Leinster Senior Cup winner 1928 (Trinity)
- Garryowen Cup Winner with Newcastle West in 1927/28

The Cussen Family

www.ingramcontent.com/pod-product-compliance
Lightning Source LLC
Chambersburg PA
CBHW071148070526
44584CB00019B/2701